CW01095993

AN OLD ULSTER HOUSE

Springhill

AN OLD ULSTER HOUSE

Springhill

and the people who lived in it

MINA LENOX-CONYNGHAM

ULSTER HISTORICAL FOUNDATION

Ulster Historical Foundation is pleased to acknowledge support for this publication from the Belfast Natural History and Philosophical Society, the Drapers' Company, The Honourable The Irish Society, The Esme Mitchell Trust and Ulster Garden Villages Ltd. All contributions are gratefully acknowledged.

First published in 2005
by the Ulster Historical Foundation
12 College Square East, Belfast, BT1 6DD
www.ancestryireland.com

Except as otherwise permitted under the Copyright, Designs and Patents Act 1988, this publication may only be reproduced, stored or transmitted in any form or by any means with the prior permission in writing of the publisher or, in the case of reprographic reproduction, in accordance with the terms of a licence issued by The Copyright Licensing Agency. Enquiries concerning reproduction outside those terms should be sent to the publisher.

© **Mina Lenox-Conyngham**, 2005

Printed by **Bath Press**
Design and production, Dunbar Design

ISBN 1-903688-**38-8**

PREVIOUS PAGES: The front of Springhill in early spring with the Dutch Barn on the left of the sweep showing the dormer window in the night nursery, since removed

ABOVE: View of the rear of the house from the Watchtower looking down the replanted Beech Walk.

Contents

Springhill, 2004

Mina, William and their daughter Diana, *c.*1920

Introduction

SPRINGHILL, PAINTED WHITE against a background of ancient, dark trees, is a unique survival of an intact Irish seventeenth-century house in west Ulster. The story of this house and the family who lived here up till the 1960s is told by its last mistress, Mina Lenox-Conyngham, in an opulent narrative drawn from family papers and family traditions. She wrote *An Old Ulster House* in the 1940s, a grand old lady in her 70s by then. The book was published by William Tempest at Dundalgan Press in 1946 when she was 79. It is a wonderful testament to her towering energy and devotion to the family, and provides the modern reader with a detailed portrait of a house and family, resident nearly three centuries in Ulster, but also with a period view of such a family and place.

The house was built by 'Good Will' Conyngham (d. 1721) who had married Anne Upton in 1680 and had undertaken to provide her with 'a convenient house of lime and stone' under the terms of their marriage settlement. It appeals by its almost vernacular charm and its enchanting setting on the western side of Lough Neagh, on a long ridge above Moneymore. As Mark Bence-Jones has commented it is the influence of Scotland that may mark it out from other Irish houses, no doubt because of the Scottish origins of the plantation family who were to live there. Ten generations of Conynghams and Lenox-Conynghams were to call Springhill their home. The Conynghams, later the Lenox-Conynghams, exemplify very well the Ulster Scottish gentry family whose role in developing the locality and in building, maintaining and adding to this house and its collections was so important.

The founder of the family in Ulster, an earlier William Conyngham (d.1666), was one of Oliver Cromwell's Commissioners in county Armagh during and immediately after the rebellion of 1641. He actually bought the 'town, village, hamlet, place, baliboe or parcel of land called Ballydrum (Springhill) in the parish of Ardtra (Ardtrea)', an area of 350 acres, for the sum of £200 in 1653. The house was built by his son, and added to by succeeding generations but never totally demolished or extensively rebuilt. Hence the rare charm of being able to trace the activities of all the different members of the family in the house and its collections. It was another William Lenox-Conyngham (1903–1957) who transferred Springhill to the National Trust in 1957 shortly before his death.

Through the generations, the family provided soldiers to support the establishment of the Crown in Ireland, many served in local volunteer or militia regiments, and others served abroad protecting the interests of the British Empire overseas. As well, many of the sons were merchants who generated wealth for themselves and their dependants, providing for their style of life as leaders of local society in west Ulster. There was a particularly interesting connection with the Belfast merchant networks of the 18 century, especially with the McCartney family, one of whom, Lord McCartney the ambassador, gave Springhill the famous China rose which still grows in the Dutch garden.

Like many Ulster gentry families, the Lenox-Conynghams lived at Springhill, their main seat, with visits to Derry, Belfast and Dublin for provisions, business and for social life. Except for those soldiering and merchant sons, they moved about locally to see their friends and neighbours in Antrim, Donegal, Londonderry and Tyrone. They made appropriate marriages with neighbouring gentry families, very often with cousins. They lived active lives, and despite occasional 'characters' among the generations, there were no real horrors, scandals or lawsuits. According to the present mythology of Springhill, there are a few ghosts, but this is only to be expected!

As the nineteenth century advanced, the family became more adventurous in their movements, spending time in Brussels and Cheltenham to widen their social circle and to introduce their daughters to a broader range of marriage partners. A most advantageous marriage made by William Fitzwilliam Lenox-

Conyngham (1824–1906), in 1856, with Laura Arbuthnot of Elderslie in Surrey, gave rise to the most accomplished Lenox-Conyngham generation. This William was later knighted. All his children were educated in Edinburgh. He had seven sons, four who were colonels who fought in the first World War. One was John Staples Molesworth or 'Jack' (1861–1916), who commanded the 6th Battalion Connaught Rangers and was killed leading his troops over the top at Guillemont during the battle of the Somme in September 1916. Gerald Ponsonby (1866–1956) was a Royal Engineer in charge of the Trigonometrical Survey of India (1912–21), Reader in Geodesy at Cambridge University (1922–47) and a pioneering expert on the earth's crust. These were the generation known to the author Mina in the flesh and they are more authentically portrayed than some of the earlier generations whom she interpreted through the stories and letters that came down to her.

The family accumulated some interesting possessions which remain in the house. Among them are the guns including the blunderbusses, the duelling pistols and a long gun presented to James Lenox after the siege of Derry in 1689. Although Mina did not know it, the gun room also contained another treasure, the rare handprinted wallpaper made in England c. 1760 and installed by 'extravagant' William (1723–84) who redecorated Springhill in 1765. This was later hidden by panelling and only rediscovered in the 1960s when the National Trust was repairing the wood panels. In the hall, the brass bound jewel boxes from Sumatra, brought back by one of the earlier Derry merchant members of the family, also impress the visitor.

The Library bears testament to the intellectual and spiritual life of the family,

Sir William in bathchair, Lady Lenox-Conyngham standing behind him, Frank Bushe (Mina's half-brother), Alice L-C, William Arbuthnot L-C with Diana. Charlotte L-C, Mina (seated) with William her son, Fanny Bushe (Mina's half-sister), Mrs Arthur L-C (Emmeline), and Mrs MacGregor Greer (Mina's sister Dorinda).

with its intact collection of the different generations' reading matter: religious and theological works, travel literature and novels of the 18th century to divert the family in their comparatively remote country house, and as well, some interesting 19th-century works including two copies of *Ordnance Survey Memoir for Londonderry: Parish of Templemore, 1837* by Colonel Thomas Colby. A particularly detailed analysis of the town of Coagh, its population and economy is recorded in 1840 in Ordnance Survey Memoir for Tamlaght (the parish in which Coagh lies). The modern town was built by George Butle Conyngham (d. 1765), of whom more anon, after he succeeded his uncle William in 1721.

As well as books, the family preserved all their papers, letters and formal documents, which are now in the Public Record Office of Northern Ireland. These papers form the backbone of Mina Lenox-Conyngham's account of the family. Among the collection is a fascinating survival of an unique archive of Irish Catholic historical documents. These papers are known as the Fottrell papers from the name of the Dominican Provincial Prior who was arrested with these at Toome Bridge in 6 June 1739 by George Butle Conyngham, in his capacity as local magistrate. With Father John Fottrell on that fateful day, was Dr Michael MacDonough, Bishop of Kilmore, and between them they were carrying a most significant and interesting set of documents. This was partly because Father John

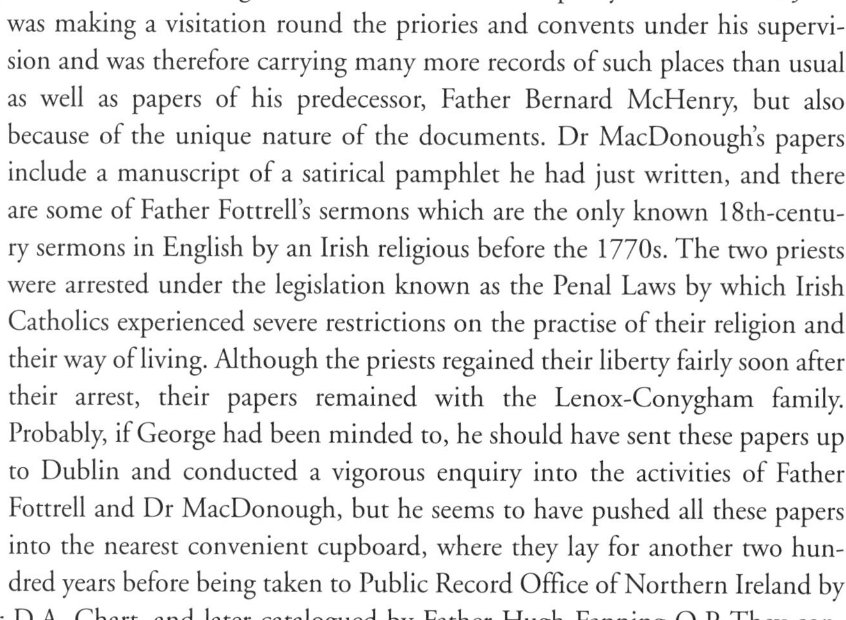

Mina in old age

was making a visitation round the priories and convents under his supervision and was therefore carrying many more records of such places than usual as well as papers of his predecessor, Father Bernard McHenry, but also because of the unique nature of the documents. Dr MacDonough's papers include a manuscript of a satirical pamphlet he had just written, and there are some of Father Fottrell's sermons which are the only known 18th-century sermons in English by an Irish religious before the 1770s. The two priests were arrested under the legislation known as the Penal Laws by which Irish Catholics experienced severe restrictions on the practise of their religion and their way of living. Although the priests regained their liberty fairly soon after their arrest, their papers remained with the Lenox-Conygham family. Probably, if George had been minded to, he should have sent these papers up to Dublin and conducted a vigorous enquiry into the activities of Father Fottrell and Dr MacDonough, but he seems to have pushed all these papers into the nearest convenient cupboard, where they lay for another two hundred years before being taken to Public Record Office of Northern Ireland by Dr D.A. Chart, and later catalogued by Father Hugh Fanning O.P. They constitute a very valuable and fascinating, not to mention wholely unexpected, aspect of the Lenox-Conynghams and their collections.

And now to Mina, the author of the present narrative. She was born in 1867, the younger daughter of James Corry Jones Lowry, J.P., D.L. Co. Tyrone, formerly in the Royal Artillery whose home was Rockdale near Sandholes, Dungannon Co. Tyrone. Her mother was Elizabeth Jackson Greer from nearby Tullylagan, close to the ancient O'Neill inauguration site of Tullyhogue,

Co. Tyrone. Her father was a Conservative and Unionist of the old school, with a strong sense of public duty and she seems to have accepted these attitudes and outlooks without question. Her elder sister, Dorinda, married another Greer cousin and went to live in Seapark, on the shores of Belfast Lough, and was a great influence on Mina. Dorinda was active in public politics, speaking on behalf of the Unionist party on occasions, while Mina limited her efforts to supporting her husband and sister in the cause.

Mina was described as 'intelligent, strong willed and beautiful' by her grand-daughter Kate Clements, now Mrs Okuno. Mina grew up in west Ulster gentry circles, educated by governesses and imbued with a strong sense of family feeling. Her father died in 1897 and then, in 1899, she married William Arbuthnot Lenox-Conyngham (1857–1938) whom she had first met while acting in Richard Brinsley Sheridan's *The Rivals*, in amateur theatricals at Springhill, which were a frequent feature of winter life amongst the county set in the country. Indeed she mentions dressing up in Springhill costumes for these dramas, perhaps in those very costumes which remain in the Springhill collection.

This love of drama and theatre was engrained deep in her character. Her grand-daughter Kate writes:

'I remember her as an old lady with snow-white hair, wide brimmed 'Gainsborough' hats and layered black velvet garments. Her fingers were decorated with diamond and emerald rings, she wore a long string of pearls round her neck and had a bunch of keys hanging from her waist on a ribbon. She entertained us with poems, recited from memory, endless stories about our ancestors and ghost stories in which she herself featured'. She was also energetic. A reflection on her character may be found in one of her letters to her husband William, who had left very soon after their wedding in 1899 to fight in the Boer War. She asks: 'What do you mean? I am "rapid". I know I am not conventional and have rather high spirits but don't want to be rapid because my notion is that fastness is the last resource of dull girls who are not nice looking specially'.

Mina, in 'wide brimmed Gainsborough hat', with her grandson Marcus Clements, at the rear of Springhill beside the smoking room which is now demolished. 1937.

Mina's story tells something of her reign at Springhill. Between 1912–14, the Ulster Volunteer Force era, she organised a Nursing Corps and eleven hospital centres in south Derry while her husband enrolled the South Derry regiment. There is a marvellous description of a dinner party given for Sir Edward Carson, the great orator and Unionist politician, in April 1914. Sixteen cartloads of sand had been carried from the shores of Lough Neagh to make the roads approaching the house appropriately fine for such a guest. Many of the family circle were in attendance, including Mina's sister Dorinda whose inspiring eloquence was noted proudly.

Mina's energy did not diminish with advancing years and she was able to maintain her place at Springhill because no suitable bride appeared for her eldest son, Captain William Lowry Lenox-Conyngham, who eventually gave Springhill to the National Trust. Dorinda Percival, now Lady Dunleath, her great-niece, tells how at a great age she went to America and visited the Guggenheims. This New World dynasty had come into Mina's life through her neighbours the Stuarts of Stewartstown, Co. Tyrone. The 7th Earl of Castle Stewart had married Eleanor Guggenheim of Long Island, New York, and despite their regrettable decision to live in Sussex most of the time, Mina continued to call on their Tyrone seat, leaving her card at Stuart Hall, reminding them of her presence. Dorinda adds that on the American trip Mina tipped the driver leaving her to the airport in New York with a dime and a majestic gesture!

William Lowry L-C, who gave Springhill to the National Trust in 1957, with his mother Mina.

Mina's narrative style is very idiosyncratic and owes much to the oral traditions of her class. In the telling of her tale, she employs all the tricks of a woman brought up to communicate strikingly in her social circles: the thrilling tones, the exaggerated descriptions, the *bons mots* often repeated, the oblique opinion. Very rarely does she permit herself to criticise a character in the family outright though she shows her disapproval of several down the years. The text carries the mark of the *conversazione* of the Ulster gentry society of her day.

She was also interested in only one side of the Irish story, but despite that she had the sense to provide full quotations from the family papers and other sources which make this work both valuable and illuminating. *An Old Ulster House* is a fascinating work because it documents a family and a wonderful house through the redoubtable character of Mina Lenox-Conyngham. She may not have had a scholar's approach to history but she certainly knew how to tell a story in her own inimitable way. The Ulster Historical Foundation believe that this narrative can tell us much about Springhill, a beautiful house, and the Lenox-Conynghams and their ilk but also about the Unionist mindset of that era in the 1940s and that this will contribute to our understanding of the complex historical processes at play in modern Ulster.

Mina died in Springhill, in her ninety-fourth year. Her son William had transferred it to the National Trust just before his death in 1957. It is one of their most delightful properties in Northern Ireland.

I would like to thank Kate Okuno and Dorinda Dunleath for information and family anecdotes, as well as Anthony Malcomson for his help and for his useful summary of the Lenox-Conyngham papers available on the Public Record Office of Northern Ireland's website (www.proni.gov.uk).

ANGÉLIQUE DAY,
TRUSTEE, ULSTER HISTORICAL FOUNDATION

AN OLD ULSTER HOUSE

MINA LENOX-CONYNGHAM

Foreword

Here is a book to rejoice anyone who desires to see light thrown on Irish history, none the less revealing because it traces through nine generations the fortunes of a leading Ulster family and of a great Ulster house.

The Conynghams, who became later Lenox-Conynghams, acquired land in Co. Derry and managed to hold it.

As the years went by they were linked up with almost every prominent family in the province and had their part in all the outstanding events. One of them was among the defenders of Derry in the famous siege. More than one of them was among the Volunteers to whom Grattan owed his victory. When the Union was carried, by means which the author does not fail to stigmatise, the Lenox-Conyngham of that time is said to have declined the bribe of a title offered by Castlereagh; and the legend is the more credible because Major Lenox-Conyngham served in the Regiment of which Stewart (not yet Castlereagh) was then Lieut-Colonel.

Belong yea or nay the family were always devoted supporters of the British power, and generation after generation sent its sons to the Service. But however it happened, the family became associated with the Connaught Rangers, and in the War of 1914–18 John Lenox-Conyngham commanded the battalion of that famous corps in the Irish Division. Under his leadership they had so shaped as to be chosen to lead the advance on Guillemont – and gloriously they and the whole division justified themselves. But John Lenox-Conyngham fell that day at their head. I had the honour to know how he was worshipped by a thousand or so of Irishmen – Catholics almost to a man.

The writer of this book accepts unreservedly the Ulster tradition as the Conynghams understood it, but she has the feeling for all Irish, Catholic or Protestant, which inspired the man who fell at Guillemont and those who followed him.

The book of course is not only, or mainly, concerned with wars or politics. The family at Springhill seem to have had the instinct for keeping papers, and a great deal of old and interesting correspondence is here: for instance from Colonel Napier, father of the famous brothers- Sir Charles, Sir William and Sir George – one of whom said; 'We were men of some account, but none of us was our father's equal.'

Or again, we have a full inventory of the plenishing indoor and out, which furnished out Springhill in George III's day.

In short here is a whole mine of information which tells us above all what sort of lives a representative Ulster family lived since Ulster became what we mean by Ulster and also lets us know what kind of men, and women, it bred.

STEPHEN GWYNN

Preface

This book is of varied content – a hotch-potch of history, biography, adventure, ghost stories and gossip, which may interest many types of reader. But it is above all the history of an old family home.

To write the biography of a valued friend must always be a delight, and this has been felt in penning the story of a place which possesses the friendly charm of Springhill. This charm must be largely due to the lingering personality of those who have lived here during the past three hundred years, and whose lives I have tried to depict. I feel grateful to them for having left behind in the old house such a large store of MS. records, both historic and personal. These have never yet been made public, and I can give assurance that all the documents, lists and letters herein quoted are still at Springhill, except for the very few which are clearly mentioned as having been obtained from other sources.

Gratitude is also due to kind friends – Mr. Stephen Gwynn, Dr. D.A. Chart, Mr. T.G.F. Paterson, Viscount Charlemont and Mr. H.G. Tempest who by their interest and wise advice have helped the inexperienced writer of a first book – and to them I give my sincere thanks.

MINA LENOX-CONYNGHAM

LENOX CONYNGHAM

1st and 4th. Argent, a fesse chequy azure and gules, over all a shake fork sable, and in chieef a lion rampant of the third (gules). 2nd and 3rd. Argent, a saltire indented vert, between four roses gules.

Crests—1. A unicorn's head argent, armed sable. 2. A demi-lion rampant purpure, armed and langued argent.

FAMILY MOTTO

Over Fork Over

Its origin is told in a legend which relates that when King Malcolm Canmore of Scotland was being pursued by his enemy, Macbeth, he took refuge in Conyngham's hayfield. Conyngham saved his life by hiding him in the hay, calling to his men

'Over, fork over.'

Introduction

The English are a gregarious race. Visitors to their island find it studded with large towns and seamed with roads which display an almost unbroken succession of motor cars. These roads unite villages which are rapidly producing shoals of villas and bungalows of mushroom growth and are fast expanding into towns. The aloofness of the stately homes of bygone days has become distasteful to their occupants, who prefer to be surrounded by the 'madding crowd,' feasting no longer in baronial banqueting halls, but in hotels and restaurants, and evidently sharing the sentimcntal expressed in Browning's poem:

'With souls should souls have place.'

The Englishman who desires solitude might expect to find it in the many deserted demesnes: but that is often a vain hope, for he is apt to find that the mansion has been converted into a Public School or perhaps a Lunatic Asylum and the park into a golf-course, or that it is thronged with noisy excursionists. Even in the hoped for seclusion of the New Forest we wander into ferny glades, hitherto the supposed haunt of fairies, to find traces of their present day successors in orange peel, broken glass and the fluttering scraps of newspaper.

It is in Ireland – the sister island – that the charm of stillness and solitude may more easily be found. There it is possible to drives for leagues along lonely roads where a stray donkey-cart may be the only vehicle to be encountered in the course of eight or nine miles. And though many of the larger mansions have perished in revolutionary flames, there are still parts of the country where these can be found in the possession of the families which have owned them for centuries, and who wish for nothing better than to dwell year by year in the old homestead, giving leadership and help to less fortunate neighbours, as an inherited sense of responsibility prompts them.

It is one of these homes which I am about to describe, and if my reader professes to be bored by the tale of a place which he may regard as a backwater, and prefers to centre his interest in up-to-date 'desirable residences,' I beg him to cry off and to refuse to accompany me to the remote and old-fashioned seclusion of Springhill.

1946

LENOX CONYNGHAM

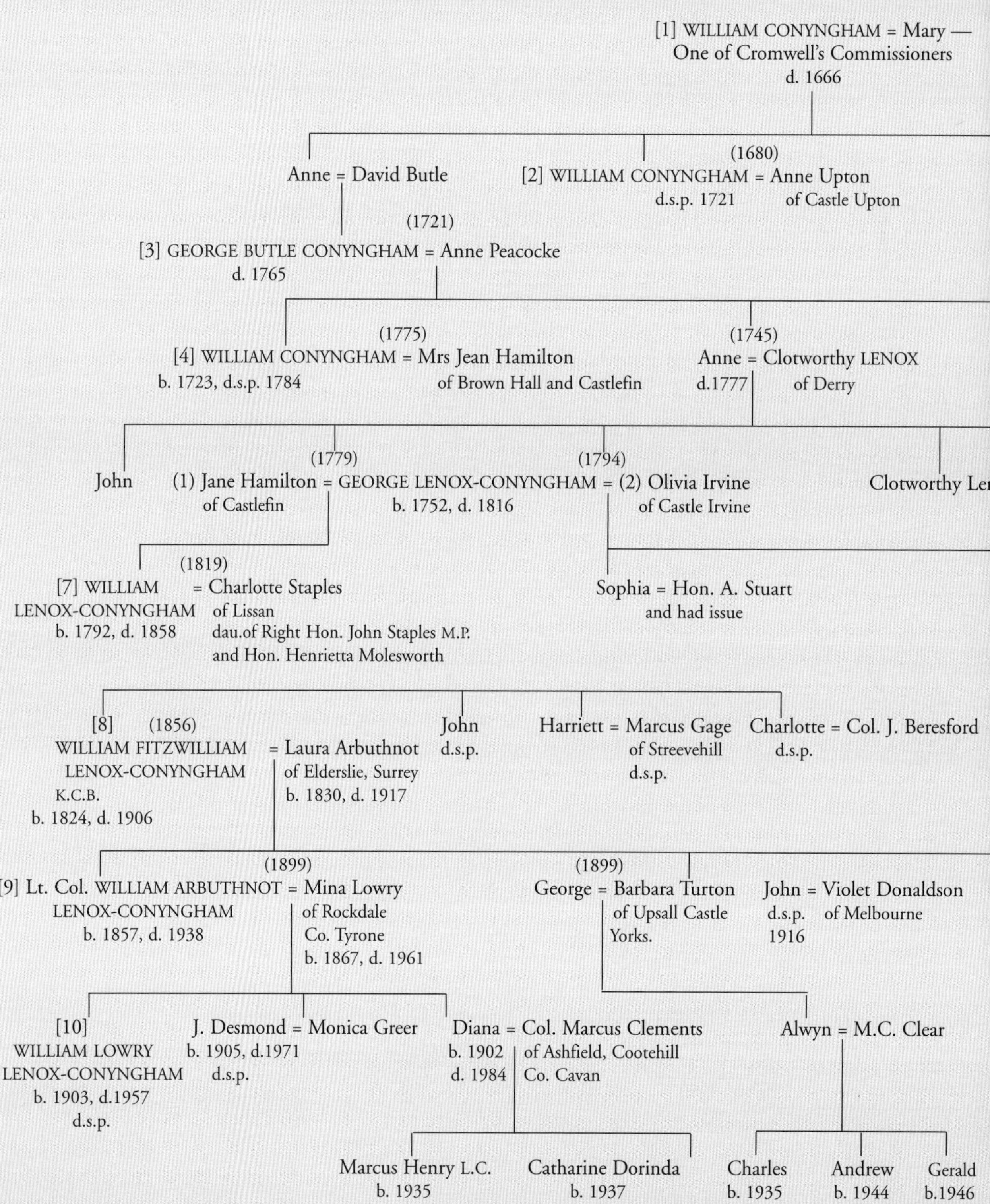

OF SPRINGHILL

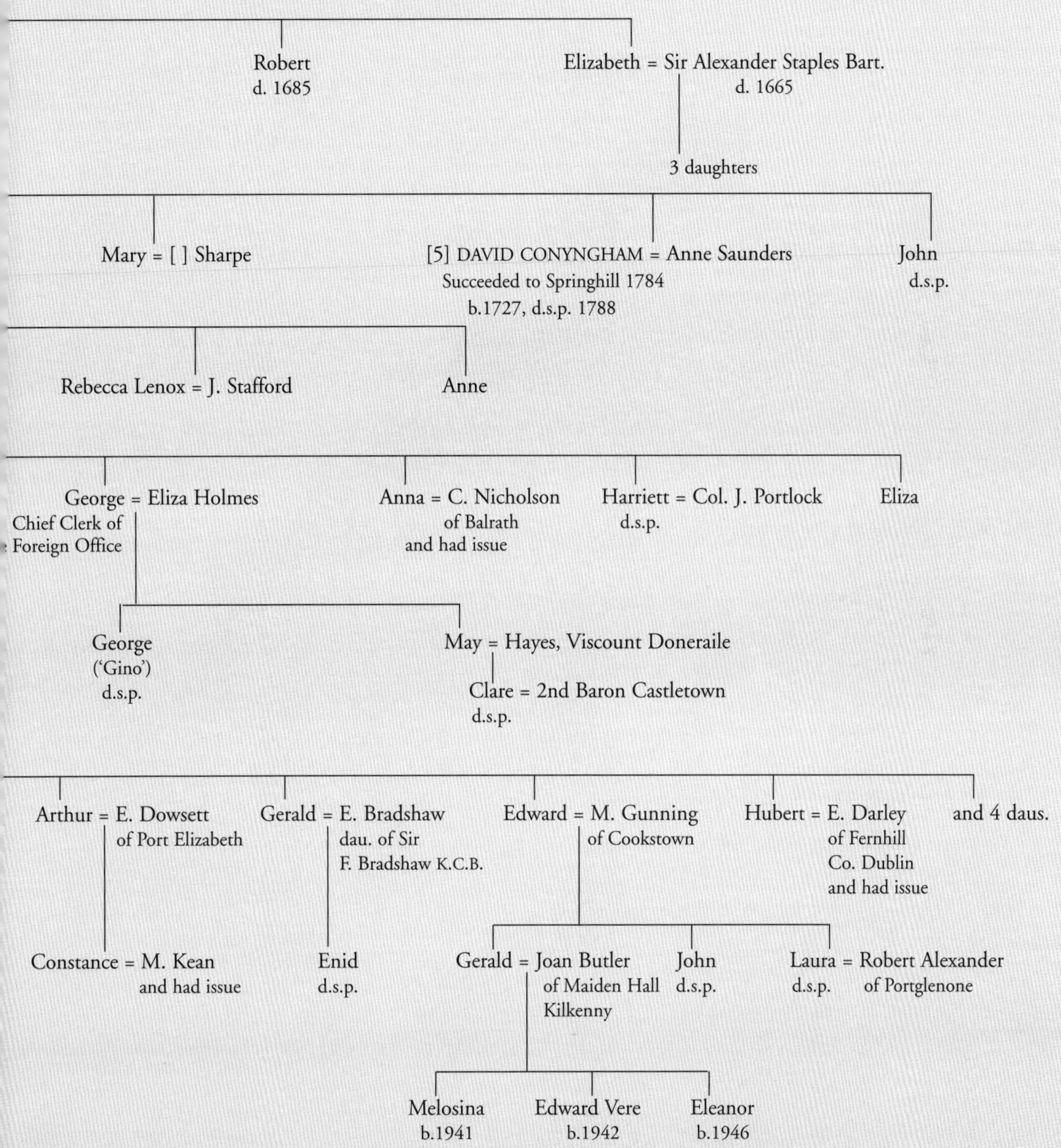

I

Springhill

IN ONE OF THE NORTHERN COUNTIES there is a high hill, its sides clothed with woods which are visible from most of the surrounding country. And on the summit of that hill stands the ancient house amid its purple beeches, yews and oaks, which must have been planted to shelter an exposed position from the stormy blasts of Winter. A straight avenue leads to the long whitewashed building that faces the newcomer, spreading its wings like arms stretched out in welcome. There are few Jacobean houses in Ireland, and at first sight the building gives the impression of having more resemblance to a French Chateau than to the square Georgian pile which is so common in the Emerald Isle.

Above:
The slated side wall at the rear of Springhill

Opposite:
Springhill from the rear with the Sperrin Mountains in the background.

The house is built round three sides of a wide, open courtyard, though the side buildings – with graceful curved gables surmounted by stone urns – are not joined to the main part of the dwelling. To the left, beyond an arched doorway, the old Brew-house, Turf shed, Slaughter-house and Laundry surround a square grass-plot, beyond which a walled alley leads up hill to the ancient and once fortified barn and onwards to the Kitchen-garden. If a door in the wall to the left of this alley is opened, you have the surprise of finding yourself in a sequestered and old-world Dutch garden, ivy-walled and gay with box-edged flower-beds sloping to the South West. Bygone hands have planted sweetbriar, honeysuckle, jessamine and old-fashioned roses in this garden and have filled beds with auriculas, blue anemones and dog-tooth violets; and on the north wall still blossoms the Macartney rose, the first to be brought to Ireland, towards the end of the eighteenth century, by the then Ambassador in China – Lord Macartney.

But to return to the Court and pass to the far side of the house, where the side walls are slated from roof to ground, and where formerly a second Court – or 'Bawn' – existed, we find an avenue of gigantic beeches leading up to a ruined Watch tower. On turning to face the back of the house, it can be seen that its irregular pile has not the symmetry of the front, each successive generation having added a bit here and there at their own sweet will.

But Spring is here, and her enchantment bids us stay outside yet awhile. She has transformed this haunt into a veritable fairyland, for the lawns which slope away from the 'Beech walk' to the lower woods are shimmering with bluebells which scent the air with sweetness, while a hundred birds warble in the pale green of woven branches. If the fabled dryads still inhabit these trees, they could tell many a tale of the nine generations of the family who have walked beneath their shade and have talked together of interests and projects, fears and misgivings for the dear old home, whose spell must have twined itself around their hearts. In Cromwell's day it may have been the two Williams – father and son – planning a place for the new 'Bog-orchard,' or, in James II's reign, 'Good Will' (the younger) pacing to and fro while scanning the fateful anonymous letter which told of coming massacre. Or later it may have been old George hastening to find Captain Ashe robbing his armoury, or his daughter, Mistress Anne, clinging to the arm of her gallant young brother who was about to sail with his regiment to take part in the Seven Years' War.

All have walked this way engrossed in their joys and sorrows, and have gone to return no more; though the great Cedar behind the house, which fell eighty-eight years ago, has layered itself and sprung up into new vigour, and every year Springtime has renewed its foliage and painted the lawns with flowery delights. If those who have left these precincts and passed through death to another world are given as shining a renewal as Spring confers on this weary earth, what a transfiguration must be theirs! and it may be that Spring's magical transformation is sent to us year by year to show how wonderful that change will be.

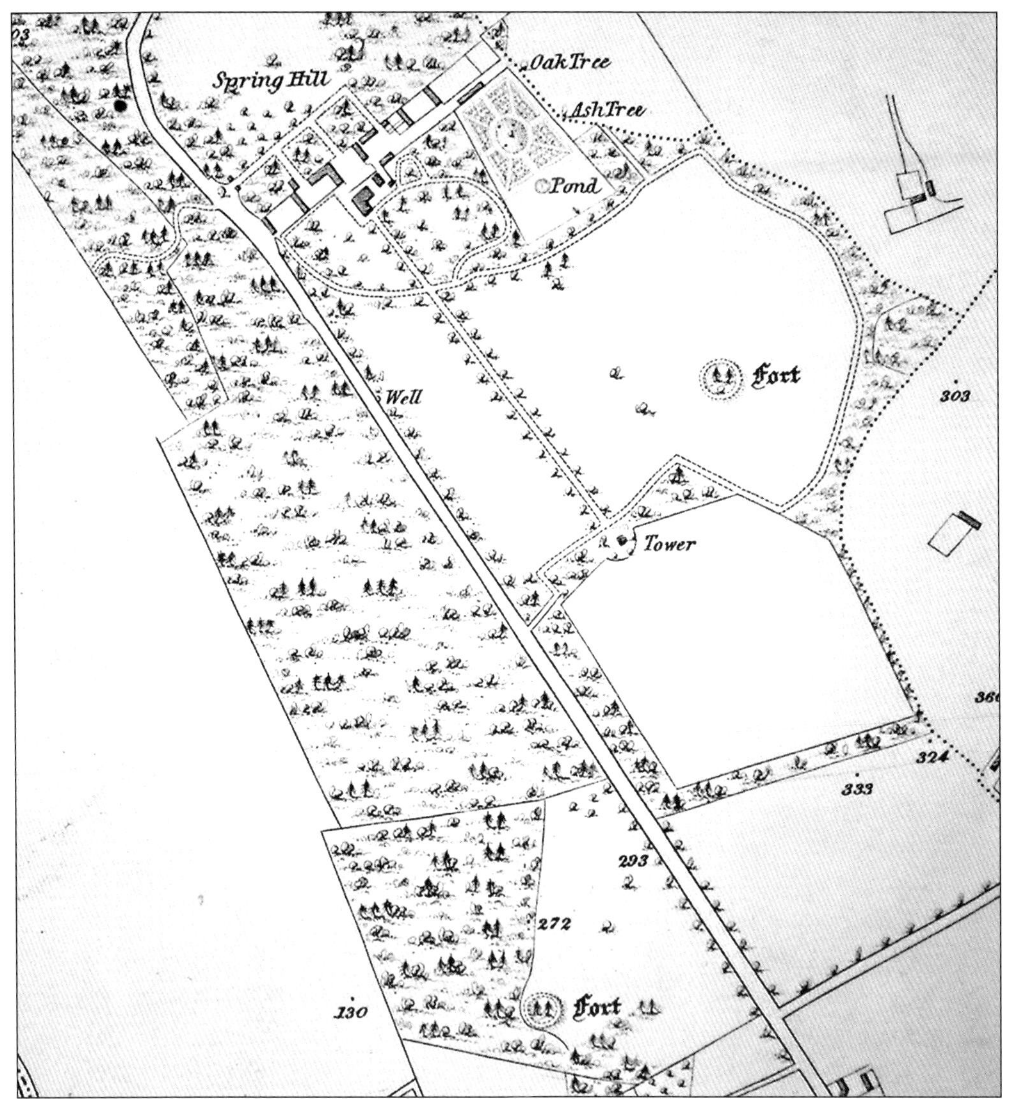

Springhill from the 1st edition Ordnance Survey map of 1834

II

The Settlers

BEFORE THE DAYS of Queen Elizabeth the North of Ireland was a wild, half civilized region largely covered with forest and overrun by septs, whose chiefs led them to frequent wars with neighbouring tribes, and who in times of peace pastured their flocks on the hill-sides and sowed corn in the valleys. The countryside was divided, as now, into small tracts called 'Townlands,' the names of which date from the dim past and still cling to these areas. The townland of Ballindrum – or Ballindroma – in which Springhill is situated, covers several hundred acres and bears the old name which signifies 'the township of the hill's ridge.' Here at one time was the ancient forest of

Killetragh, and a grove of large yew-trees near the house may well have belonged to that bygone forest. Of this territory the O'Cahans were lords, and a little further South the famous O'Neills held sway, having as their stronghold the fort of Tullaghogue, or 'hill of the youths.'

It is not surprising that great wrath seized the original owners when King James the First brought from Scotland and England the Settlers who formed the Plantation of Ulster. This undertaking was ostensibly to bring peace to a turbulent province, but the wily James had his own selfish reasons for the transaction. He owed much money to the Scottish lairds and to the great London Companies, and having claimed Northern Ireland as Crown property after the O'Neill rebellion, he thought to pay his debtors with Irish land. It was said; 'He was munificent in his gifts at the expense of his hapless Irish subjects.'

Accordingly, the former lords of the soil were forced to yield their lands to the newcomers, and though a few Irish 'of good note' were granted some land, the bulk of the people were driven to the barren mountain tracts and to the shores of Lough Neagh, while the 'undertakers' apportioned the forfeited properties among the strangers. These consisted of a hundred thousand Scotch and twenty thousand English, most of whom faced dangerous hostility for the sake of the coveted acres. They must have had a hard struggle to guard their homes and cattle from pillage. Nearly four million acres had been confiscated, and perhaps the most disputed region was that of the 'fastnesses between Tyrone and Coleraine'[1] where many 'wood kerne' refuged in the woods and lived by levying blackmail on all who lived within reach. Springhill, then called Ballydrum, being in this region must have undergone many a panic. The great Barn still shows in its walls the loopholes for guns, and the Court was once the bawn into which the cattle were driven every night for safety.

These Irish rebel subjects of King James the First were by no means simpletons. There is an amusing description of them in the Record Tower of Dublin Castle, given in a report written in 1605 to Sir Arthur Chichester by Sir Toby Caulfeild[2] afterwards first Lord Charlemont:

> After travel in many countries I have found nothing like them for cunning and duplicity. Full of sorrowful grievances they do address the unwary in garments so unseemly as to give weight to their pleadings of poverty. Yet I have known many who, when tested, be more well to do than ye bettermost common folk in England. It can truly be said of them greater liars cannot be found than in this province, and in craftiness they do compare well with ye best diplomatists! Withal there be much to like in them. Few be more ready to do kindness without hope of reward. They can bear much hardship and are yet not sombre, but in scanty clothing go merry to their work, which they can well do when the eye is on them, but when off, God wot they trouble themselves not.

As the first forty years of the Seventeenth Century rolled by, the dispossessed people, styled 'the mere[3] Irish,' brooded over their wrongs. The Chiefs were especially bitter, the rank and file having less cause for complaint, for whereas these had owned no land at all when ruled by their Irish masters, each could now boast of a few acres of his own, even if those acres were of an inferior quality.

The Settlers, being short of retainers, employed many of the Irish in helping to build the stone houses which they were pledged to erect. But though there may have been an outward show of friendliness, bitter animosity was seething in the minds of the dispossessed, and in 1641, on Oct. 23rd, the pent up torrent burst. The people arose and laid waste the homes of the settlers, slaughtering and wreaking dire vengeance on all who had ousted them from their lands. The accounts of that terrible time are bloodcurdling indeed. In one morning nine hundred and fifty-four persons were killed in the County Antrim. Over a thousand were drowned in the River Bann. In Lord Clarendon's account we read of 'six hundred murthered at Garvagh by Sir Phelim O'Neill, eighteen Scotch infants hanged on clothiers' tenter-hooks.' One woman at Loughgall 'murthered five and forty with her own hands,' and there were many other atrocities too terrible to describe, the reprisals being equally abominable. Many of the victims were women and children, put to death with the most revolting cruelty. Even nowadays, mutilated bodies in seventeenth century dress are sometimes found in turf bogs, preserved by the antiseptic peat.

As almost every house belonging to the settlers was burnt, we cannot suppose that Springhill escaped. Indeed an old existing document tells that the title deeds had been destroyed in the rebellion. The tradition is that the Conyngham owner was saved from perishing with his house because of absence at an estate which he owned in Tipperary. But others were not so fortunate. A neighbour of the Conynghams – Lady Charity Staples – was seized at her home of Lissane by an arch rebel, Neil Ogue O'Quin, and imprisoned in the Castle of Moneymore, which had been built by the London Companies. Her deposition can be seen in the library of Trinity College, Dublin, and she describes seeing from her window a number of wretched Scottish folk being led away to be murdered. She named the Widow Russell and poor Archy Lagan, with one ear half severed from his head. The rebel Cormac O'Hagan was commanding the insurgents in Moneymore and had seized the Castle.

In this village lived James Clotworthy, brother of the famous Sir John[4]; and it was James' young servant, Owen O'Conolly – a convert to Protestantism – who rode from Moneymore to Dublin to warn the Government of the impending rising, his evidence being at first disbelieved, as he was thought to be drunk. Yet the warning was only too well founded, and the appalling state of Ireland which followed lasted for some years, the furious animosity engendered by cruelties on both sides being quite enough to account for the party feeling which still persists among the inhabitants.

A historian has told of a curious apparition which was seen shortly after the Rebellion:

> The sea ringed the green island round, the white cold winter descended upon it, and while the wretched remnant of the Protestant inhabitants were gathered in all parts in stalls and outhouses about Dublin or in other parts of its Eastern fringe whence they could gaze across towards the mother lands and call to them for help, the spectres of the murdered, it was said, haunted the interior desolation.

Take this fragment from the Deposition afterwards made by Elizabeth, the wife of Captain Rice:

> She and other women whose husbands were murdered, hearing of divers apparitions and visions which were seen near Portadown Bridge since the drowning of the children and the rest of the Protestants there, went unto the bridge aforesaid about twilight in the evening, and then and there on a sudden there appeared unto them a vision, or spirit, assuming the shape of a woman, naked, with elevated and closed hands, her hair hanging down, very white, her eyes seeming to twinkle and her skin white as snow, whose spirit seemed to stand straight upright in the water, often repeating the words: 'Revenge! Revenge! Revenge!' whereat the deponent and the rest being put into a strong amazement and affright, walked from the place.

It is but the disordered fancy of a poor bereaved woman, but the historian might labour long before he could devise a more exact image of the state of Ireland in the Winter of 1641–42 as it appeared to the Protestants of Britain, than this ghastly one of the naked woman emerging each nightfall from the pool of an inland Irish river, stretching clutched hands in the solitude and calling ere she sank; 'Revenge! Revenge! Revenge!'

III

William Conyngham

OF THE SIEGE

d.1721

BY 1649 THE STORM had passed, and with stolid fortitude the settlers remained on their lands, building up what had been destroyed, tilling, fencing and felling. Lord Strafford, under Charles the First, had persecuted the Scottish Ulster Presbyterians, to which body the Conynghams belonged, but under Cromwell's rule their state was easier, until the oppression was fiercely renewed in Charles the Second's time. It was Cromwell who granted new title deeds to the Conynghams in 1652, 'the old ones having been

William Conyngham

destroyed in the recent Wars.' Indeed 'William Conyngham the elder'[5] added new estates, which he bought in the neighbouring County of Tyrone in 1663, three years before his death in 1666, in which year he had been High Sheriff of Co. Derry at the Assizes, which in those days were held in the little town of Desertmartin. The only known relics of this owner, which remain at Springhill, are his Bible and an old Law book in which he had written his name.

Springhill stands about five miles from the great lake, Lough Neagh: and recently an old letter was discovered, written from Belturbet by Francis Nevil Esq. to the Lord Bishop of Clogher and dated Feb. 2nd, 1712–13, which runs thus:

> There is some healing quality in this Lough (Neagh). There is a certain bay in it called the Fishing Bay, which is about half a mile broad, it is bounded by the school lands of Dungannon, hath a fine sandy bottom, not a pebble in it. … I have been in it several times when multitudes have been there, and I have observed that, as I walked, the bottom has changed from cold to warm and from warm to cold. … Several have made the same observation. The first occasion of taking notice of this Bay for cure happened to be no longer ago than in the reign of King Charles the Second, and was thus:
>
> There was a Mr. Cunningham, who lived within a few miles of this place, who had an only son, grown to man's estate. This young man had the evil to that degree that it run upon him in eight or ten places. He hath been touched by the King, and all means imaginable used for his recovery, but all did no good, and his body was so wasted that he could not walk. When all hopes of his recovery were passed, he was carried to the Lough, where he was wash'd and bath'd, and in eight days time, bathing each day, all the sores were dried up, and he became cured, grew very healthy, married, begot children and lived nine or ten years after. This account I got from Captain Morris and his brother, who were eye witnesses and at whose home the young man lay while he continued to bath there. After so remarkable a cure many came there who had running sores upon them, and were cur'd after a little time. The natives thought it could not do well but upon some particular time appropriated for that service, but now great crowds come there on Midsummer Eve, of all sorts of sick and sick cattle; and people do believe they receive benefit. I know it dries up running sores and cures the rheumatism, but not with one bathing, and drinking the water will, I am told, stop the flux. I look upon it as one of the greatest wonders.[6]

The earlier history of the family, just after the Plantation of Ulster, is not very clear. The first settler of the name came from Ayrshire in Scotland, it is thought from a place called Glengarnock, and he was said to be a son of the Earl of Glencairn, a peerage now extinct. Alexander Conyngham, Dean of Raphoe, who had twenty children, was probably a near relative, as he was the father of Sir Albert Conyngham, whose portrait has for over two hundred years hung at Springhill and not at Slane Castle, where some of the Dean's certain descendants live. At the time of the Plantation[7] a number of Lord Glencairn's family came over to Northern Ireland – brothers, uncles and nephews, and it has often been said that in the Dublin Record Office – destroyed by rebels in 1916 [sic – actually 1922] – a document had existed which stated that 'William Conyngham, a Scottish Protestant, settled in the townland of Ballydrum in the year 1609.' Alas, this document perished in 1916 when the precious contents of the Record Office were scattered to the winds by explosion, their charred fragments floating down into the Dublin streets.

The earliest member of the Springhill family had connections with the City of Derry ('Conyngham's Corner' was remembered in Shipquay Street) and, as already stated, we know that he owned house property in Armagh.[8] But it is not known at which place the first settler dwelt, nor the surname of 'Mary – the lady who married his son, William Conyngham the elder.' The latter was succeeded by a son, whose name is joined to his in early documents and described as 'William Conyngham the Younger,' and to whom he bequeathed estates in the Counties of Derry, Tyrone, Armagh and Antrim, as given in the Marriage Settlement dated May 1680.

This younger William was known as 'Good Will', and must have been an able and spirited man. Before King William the Third had landed in Ireland, Conyngham had become Captain in a regiment of Dragoons commanded by Colonel Clotworthy Skeffington, and was prepared to fight for 'Guillielmo Henrico, Prince of Orange,' by whom his commission was signed in February,

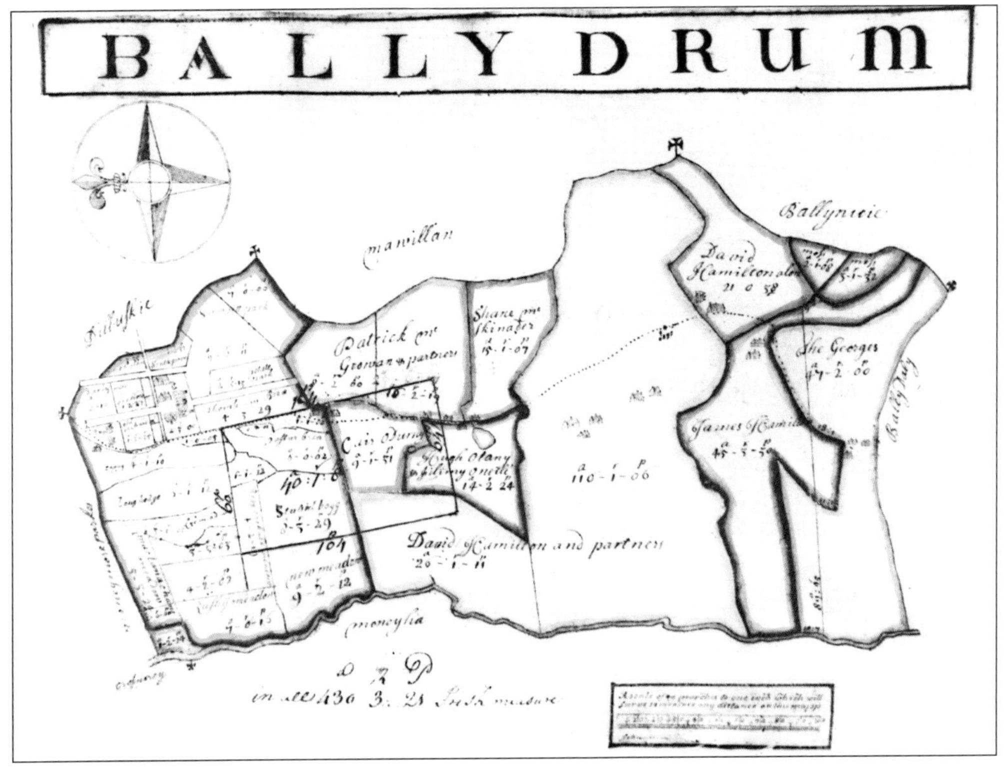

The townland of Ballydrum from a volume of maps of the estate, 1722.
PRONI

1688, old style. It is still at Springhill. He had married a maiden of sixteen – Ann – one of the twenty children of Arthur Upton of Castle Norton – (afterwards Castle Upton) in the County of Antrim, by Dorothy Beresford, daughter of Colonel Michael Beresford of Coleraine. The Beresfords had come to Ulster from Squerries, at Westerham in Kent, and were in the service of the Irish Society, which was composed of the agents of the great London Companies in Ireland, with headquarters in Londonderry.

The marriage of William and Ann was solemnized in May, 1680. It is clear that some rebuilding was done at this time, and new gardens and orchards were made.

We can picture the first few years of the married life of this young couple, the country at that time enjoying a comparatively rare interval of peace. William, who loved trees, engaged in planting his 'new cherry orchard' near the North Grove, Mistress Ann busy with household matters, or riding pillion to visit her parents at Castle Upton, or the Stewarts at Killymoon or the Lindesays at Loughry and her intimate friends the Houstons at Castle Stewart. Perhaps of an evening she listened to her studious young husband reading aloud from some of the serious books which still bear his curly-tailed signature and marginal notes. Thus passed eight happy years, and then came a cloud of trouble.

We can imagine the gusty winter morning on which Ann's husband may have come to her with a letter clenched in his hand and a face of consternation, crying; 'Dearest Wife, there are ill tidings! Danger threatens, and I must send you at once to Derry City for safety. The horses are being saddled' – and Ann's petition that he would accompany her. We can almost hear the words; 'Not so, my Ann. I have much to see to here, and 'twould be grievous to me to expose you to jeopardy. Thank God now that we have no little ones to share the danger. Have no fear! there shall no evil befall me: your father is coming to me from Castle Upton where your brother Clotworthy is raising a regiment, and ere a se'nnight has passed I may be with you in Derry, where our good friend Alderman James Lenox will bid you welcome at his house in the Diamond.'

And then when Ann had departed with her escort, we can picture 'Good Will' pacing up and down the Beech-Walk, reading the missive which he had been careful to conceal from his wife. It was addressed to Lord Mount Alexander and enclosed in a letter from William's father-in-law. It ran thus:

> Good my Lord
>
> I have written to you to let you know that all our Irishmen through Ireland is sworn that on the 9th day of this month they are all to fall on to kill and murder man, wife and child and I desire your Lordship to take care of yourself and all others that are judged by our men to be heads, for whosoever of them that can kill any of you, they are to have a Captain's place. So my desire to Your Honour is to look to yourself, and give other noblemen warning and go not out either night or day without a good guard with you, and let no Irishman come near you whosoever he be. So this is all from him who was your father's friend

> and is your friend, and will be, though I dare not be known as yet for fear of my life.

Mackenzie's *History of the Siege of Derry* states that

> The next day after this letter was dropped, Arthur Upton Esq. William Conyngham Esq. and Mr. Thomas Knox sent an express to Dublin with copies of it, not only to alarm the Protestants in that city, but to give them the opportunity of communicating the notice of it to all other parts of the kingdom. This letter was sent by William Conyngham Esq. from Belfast, enclosed in a letter of his own to George Canning Esq., desiring him to send this to Derry with all expedition.

Later in the campaign we learn that Colonel Canning's Regiment of Foot was 'under the command of Colonel William Conyngham' and that 'it was resolved that they should march towards Derry.' And when Lord Antrim's force came to Derry City demanding admission, there were eleven persons of the City and County appointed to treat with him, one of whom was William Conyngham and another his friend James Lenox. It is also recorded that William Conyngham 'of Ballydrum'[9] was one of the six members of King William's Supreme Council, and that he was attainted by James the Second's Parliament in Dublin. There is no doubt that the owner of Springhill used all his position of influence and authority to support the cause of William of Orange, to whom the Protestants of Ireland looked to save them from their hereditary foes. King James the Second had warmly supported the Irish Catholics, and his Lord Deputy – the hated Tyrconnel – was resolved to trample on Protestantism, and raised four regiments for its destruction. To combat this danger, many Ulster gentlemen raised regiments at their own expense. The air was full of rumours and forebodings, and it was plain that a rising of the Irish was imminent, which struck terror into the hearts of those who remembered the atrocities of 1641. Indeed some of the gentlemen, especially those in Co. Down, fled for safety to England, while the more valiant remained to guard their homes and dependants.

Thus was the brief era of peace ended, and rival factions again moved through the country, once more divided on the subject of religion, 'hating each other for the love of God,' in contradiction to the behests of the founder of Christianity.

And all the time, far away on the throne of France sat the arch instigator of the turmoil – Louis the Fourteenth of France! His design was to keep his most formidable foe – William of Orange – busy in the British Isles, lest he should bring his Dutch regiments to attack France on her North West frontier. It was from no disinterested motive that he supported James the Second and fostered the strife between him and his Dutch son-in-law. At Springhill there is a rare book of which only one or two copies exist; *Les négociations du Comte D'avaux en Irlande*, which reveals France's plots to prolong the Irish unrest and throws many interesting sidelights on the situation. D'Avaux was French Ambassador at the Court of King James the Second, and wrote from Ireland to his royal master giving detailed accounts of the engagements between the rival armies and of the shaping of events. For instance, in June, 1689, when the town of Derry was under siege he wrote:

> Il eust été fort avantageux de pouvoir prendre Londonderry, mais si, comme les apparences le veulent on ne peut réduire cette place, il est bien important de ne pas achever d'y faire périr les troupes dont le Roy d'Angleterre aura besoin pour résister à celles du Prince d'Orange, et de perdre toute idée de passer en Ecosse ni en Angleterre qu' après s'estre bien étably en Irlande ... Les apparences veulent que l'armée du Prince d'Orange descendent plutôt du coté du Nord d'Irlande que du midy, ce qui me feroit croire que le Roy d'Angleterre devroit près de la moitié de ses troupes; Dery pris, Eniskilen tomberoit.

Every movement, every suggestive incident, was thus watched by the lynx eyes of this vigilant Ambassador and secretly conveyed to Paris. And he was not slow to criticize the vacillating character of King James and to make severe comments on his merciful disposition towards 'les rébelles Protestants.'

When severe measures against these were proposed by his French allies James was wont to declare that these people, though Protestants, were *his* subjects and that he would not permit them to be cruelly treated; 'Il a un coeur trop Anglais pour se déterminer à rien qui puisse chagriner les Anglais!'

IV

The Siege
AND AFTER

A view of Derry by Gossett
DERRY CITY COUNCIL

THE SIEGE OF DERRY was one of the most heroic and romantic incidents in the history of warfare. The little hillside city overlooking the river Foyle was defended by men of dauntless resolution: and their fighting force was small, though the place was overcrowded with Protestant fugitives from all parts of Northern Ireland, who had fled there for safety.

When Tyrconnel sent Lord Antrim's regiment to garrison the town, the inhabitants knew that this force was composed of sons of those who had perpetrated the atrocities of 1641. And yet the leaders in Derry at first felt bound to admit them rather than disobey the order of King James' deputy.

It was just as Lord Antrim's troops were approaching the Ferry Gate that a bevy of young men – apprentices in the town – took the law into their own hands, and rushing to the gates, closed and barred them in the very faces of the oncoming soldiers. Two of these spirited lads were members of the Conyngham family – Alexander and John Conyngham, and we may be sure that they lent their shoulders with a will to help in closing the massive gates. This bold step having been taken, the older and more responsible townsmen – Cairns, Lenox, Crookshank and others – decided after some consultation to approve of it. Arms and ammunition were collected, and for more than three months the brave men of Derry withstood the enemy's bombardment outside and starvation and pestilence inside their walls. Gaunt with hunger, the heroes gathered to pray daily in the Cathedral, which stands at the town's highest eminence, and then staggered back to their guns, weak in body, but strengthened in soul by trust in the God on whom they relied for succour.

As the weeks passed the situation of the besieged became desperate. Fifteen officers died of pestilence in one day. The garrison, which had consisted of about 7,500 men, was reduced by shot, famine and sickness to about 4,000, and 7,000 of the unarmed had perished. Provisions were exhausted, and life could only be sustained by eating the flesh of dogs, rats and mice. James Conyngham, who was a merchant in the city, invented a pancake composed of starch and tallow, which was pronounced 'good for food and also for physic.'

Yet in spite of hunger and fatigue, the cry of the beleaguered was always, 'No Surrender!' though the enemy frequently called upon them to capitulate. The women of the town assisted the menfolk in every possible way, and we can surmise that Mistress Ann of Springhill, Elizabeth, the wife of James Lenox, and others did their part in nursing the wounded and soothing the dying.

An account of particulars belonging to James Lenox which were consumed by the garrison at Derry
PRONI

During those hungry, sultry days of early Summer how the gentle Ann must have pined for the leafy glades of Springhill and have called to mind its pleasant fruits and plenteous fare – the river trout and the fat pullets with which tenants in the neighbouring lands of Ballygruby were wont to pay part of their rent to the Conynghams. And above all, what anxiety and sorrow must have been felt for the friends who had not fled to Derry City, and for the many old people and children who had perished in the constant skirmishes, burnings and dangers of the distracted countryside.

But relief came at last to the heroes of Derry. After a hundred and five days, when they were at the last extremity, three ships laden with provisions sailed up the Foyle river and broke the wooden boom with which the enemy had barred the stream. Seeing that help had come to the city, General de Rosen and the other officers of King James realised that it was a vain hope to subdue men of such grit and resolution, so they withdrew their troops and marched southwards.

The Siege was ended! Derry was saved! and joy-bells rang from the Cathedral tower. The Reverend Christophilus Jenny preached an eloquent sermon at the Service of Thanksgiving to Almighty God for His deliverance, and even the Pope of that day, being an opponent of Louis of France and consequently a supporter of King William, sent the victor a message of congratulation on the raising of the Siege! Little do the Orangemen of Ulster now realise this fact!

The Battle of the Boyne, which followed the Siege of Derry, decided Ireland's destiny: and when William the Third had conquered his foes, the Protestant inhabitants were freed from interference and had happier days in store.

Is the dogged perseverance of the present day Ulstermen due to heredity because the blood of heroic forbears flows in their veins, or is it derived from the constant contemplation of an ideal enshrined in memory and perpetuated by the watchwords 'Derry Walls!' and 'No Surrender?' Certain it is that the old spirit had not died in 1912–16. The Volunteer days of these years bear witness to that, and still more so the astounding valour of the Irish and Ulster Divisions in what was then called the 'Great War.' When on July 1st, 1916, the Ulster Division stormed the German trenches at Thiepval, these North Irish lads rushed onwards as far as the fourth line of German trenches. They had remembered that it was the first of July – anniversary of the Battle of the Boyne – and as they went forward to certain death, their cry rang out; 'No Surrender!'

A recently published account of the Siege of Derry honours the name of William Conyngham as

> One of the most noted of the gallant defenders of Derry. He played a conspicuous part, not only in the defence but in the Siege itself. His name is among the attainders in the Dublin Parliament summoned by James IInd. This family is almost unique in the number and directness of its Siege descent.[10]

Conyngham's friend, James Lenox, is also honourably mentioned in every history of this famous Siege:

One of the most conspicuous of the defenders of Derry. He was burgess and alderman at the time of the Revolution in 1688 and took a prominent part among his fellow citizens in the organization for the defence. After the shutting of the gates – Dec. 7th, 1688 – and during the chaotic weeks that followed, it was James Lennox, Norman, Jemmett and Thomas Moncrieff who wrote from the Guard House to the gentry of the neighbouring counties, apprising them of the position and asking for succour and support. James Lennox was one of the Commissioners appointed by the City to treat with Lord Mountjoy. So great was the City's confidence in him that he and Capt. A. Lecky were sent on a mission to Scotland for arms and assistance.

James Lenox 1652–1723

Lenox and Lecky who were Aldermen
For speedy succour into Scotland went.[11]

James Lenox was one of those who signed the Declaration of Union between the Officers of the garrison and those of the County contingents, pledging each and all to stand together for mutual defence (March, 1689). He served throughout the Siege, and after the relief he was one of those who signed the Document appointing Commissioners to repair to London with full powers to settle the City's claim for losses incurred. He was Mayor of Derry 1693 and 1697, Sheriff 1697, and M.P. for the County 1696–1703. He died in 1723, aged seventy-one, and was buried in St. Columb's Cathedral.

James Lenox's portrait hangs at Springhill.

Mention must also be made of a kinsman of the Springhill family, highly distinguished in the Civil War. Sir Albert Conyngham raised a regiment to fight for King William. This was the Inniskilling Dragoons, which fought at the Battle of the Boyne, its Commander being afterwards killed by the Rapparees at Colooney in Co. Sligo, where his monument bears the following curious inscription:

SACRED TO THE MEMORY

of Albert Conyngham an illustrious Knight of the Royal army under the Command of Lord Mount Alexander. Throughout life he was distinguished for extreme ability and active diligence, for perfect probity and the greatest urbanity. Among those of noble birth as well as among those of humble rank he was noted for culture and learning greater than ordinary. Grieved for his persecuted Religion and for the Cause of liberty, he levied a Regiment of Dragoons at his own expense in the glorious Revolution under the invincible Prince of Orange. How many Dangers he encountered, how by an untimely death he fell for his country, lamented by all good men cannot be unknown to thee, O

> Wayfarer, or to posterity. He fell for his country in the vicinity of this town Sept. 5. A.D. 1691.

The portrait by Kneller of Sir Albert Conyngham hangs in the dining-room at Springhill between those of King William the Third and Queen Mary, also by Kneller, and it is said that these portraits were presented to Sir Albert by the King in recognition of his services.

Portrait of Sir Albert Conyngham by Kneller. d. 1691

AFTERMATH OF THE SIEGE

After the raising of the Siege of Derry the state of the town and garrison was in many ways deplorable. Buildings had been wrecked and much property destroyed by gun-fire. Those of the leaders who survived had been impoverished by the expense of raising and equipping troops; and it is sad to realise how little was done by England to compensate those heroes for their sacrifices on behalf of King William.

Great indignation was felt against General Kirke, who had been sent to take charge of the forces in Derry, because he tore many of the soldiers from the command of their beloved Captains and transferred them to other regiments, while hundreds of the invalided men were suffered to roam sick and weak through the country as beggars and to die of want.

Another regrettable circumstance was the jealousy between the Episcopalian and Nonconformist defenders and their disputes as to which had been foremost in the fray.

Some years had to elapse before the many claims were settled and Derry and the surrounding country resumed even a shadow of prosperity. A bundle of old letters – about thirty in number – which were written at this time of transition, are still at Springhill and show something of the state of affairs then existing. Most of them were written by the well-known William Conolly, who was the Derry Corporation's legal agent in Dublin, and at that time evidently lived at a place called New Hall. Born in humble circumstances in Ballyshannon soon after the Restoration, this man acquired great wealth, property and position. In 1691 he bought the Manor of Limavady from George Philips, having inherited a fortune from two maiden ladies to whom he was agent.

Conolly was M.P. for Co, Donegal in King William's first Parliament, 1692, and married Catherine, daughter of Sir Albert Conyngham, in 1694. Six years before his death in 1729 he had built in Co. Kildare the enormous mansion of Castletown, of which Bishop Berkeley wrote:

> Mr. Conolly is building a stone house at Castletown 142 feet by 60 feet and 70 feet high.

On behalf of the Corporation of the City of Derry, between 1680 and 1700, Conolly was busy conducting law suits before the Dublin Courts and the Privy Council: and the letters in his handwriting, which still lie at Springhill, were written in 1691 to some of the leading Derry Aldermen of that day. In one of these, dated in May, he referred to the prospects of a Case which the Corporation of the City had laid before the Commissioners of Revenue, requesting monetary assistance for this purpose.

In June the Lords Commissioners of Treasury wrote to the Commissioners of Revenue in Ireland, transmitting for their consideration the petition of Rose, Marchioness of Antrim, to be restored to the enjoyment of certain quit and other rents issuing out of the lands in the Baronies of Dunluce (Co. Londonderry) Glenarm and Cary (Co. Antrim) and Rathlin Island, which had been seized by the Commissioners of Revenue and granted in Custodiam to the Mayor and Corporation of Londonderry. A copy of the petition of the Marchioness lies with these letters and it is interesting to notice that Dunluce Castle is mentioned as being in Co. Derry instead of, as now, in Co. Antrim, showing that the boundary must have been altered.

'Good Will's' watch given to him by the Irish Society, 1697.

The following copy of one of Mr. Conolly's letters to the Corporation is dated 25 July 1691;

> Mr. David Butle assures mee that the tenants uterly refuse to pay any rent till the Commrs ascertain what the abatement they conceive reasonable for the time of the warr, wc[h] the Commr[s] refuse to intermeddle with. I fear our Comiçon, soe much noised and talked of, is for some time at an end, for last night came in an Express with the accompt that Gallway had capitulated and had the Articles with him to the Queen; in short they have imbraced the King's Declaraçon wch is Life and Estate both real and personall. Its feared the Lord of Antrim is there, if not hee is in Limerick, to wch place the Genl wrote to Tyrconnell offering the same terms, wch is thought hee and many others will accept of. Gallway is to be surrendered the morrow.

Other letters refer to the case of Lord Antrim (who had, it may be remembered, led King James' forces against Derry) and in a letter to Mr. Crookshank are the words;

> I find this night notice from the Secretary's Office to show cause on Monday, on my Caveat why the L[d] of Antrim should not bee restoured. I design to give all ye oposicion I can, though I feare to little purpose.

In another letter Mr. Conolly remarks:

> I feare hee will be restoured, for wee have no evidence agst him. Therefore manage accordingly and get all you can into yr hands and tak Bonds and Securitys for the rest, tho' if hee be restoured wee must continue this yeare's tenants as it is sett to us.

Dec. 20. 1692 (Same to Same)

> Ye Councill Board are so busey and taken up in perparaçon agst the Intended Invasion and other publick affaires that nothing of private buisness has been done these 8 dayes.

The writer, Mr. Conolly, held much land in the neighbourhood of Derry, which has long since passed from his family, though others mentioned in these letters still remain in occupation of their ancestral acres. To one of these – John Harvey,[12] Chamberlain of Londonderry – Conolly wrote on Jan. 28, 1698:

> Now that our Parlmt is up ye may very soon expect to heare from ye Lds. in Engld abt ye Bpp of Derry's affaire. I am allways att Coll Conyngham's with ye Lds Justices.

'Aqua Vitae' bowl with 'Good Will's' initials, 1685

In another letter Mr. Conolly observes:

> Our Citty is yet poore . . . every good man ought to stand up for its defence & import as well as it did for ye preservacion of ye Protestant interest.

With what thankful hearts must William and Ann Conyngham have returned to their country home to live in peace! Ann's joy at the home-coming must, however, have been shadowed by the loss of one of her brothers – Captain Arthur Upton – who fell at the battle of Aughrim fighting for the Protestant Cause.

In succeeding years William held the post of 'Overseer of the woods and forests of Ulster' under the 'Irish Society,' who in 1697 presented him with a gold watch by the famous maker, Quare, as a mark of their appreciation.

His portrait is said to be by Sir Peter Lely, and shows a calm, benevolent face – rather broad and pale – surmounted by a large wig; and he was called 'Good Will,' which betokens his amiable character.

Several other relics of 'Good Will' and his times exist to this day at Springhill. There is a curious bell-shaped metal 'Aqua Vitae' bowl with his initials W.C. 1685, a Syriac Testament, bearing on its last leaf the signature of George Walker, one of the most noted defenders of Derry: and a long gun, its barrel inlaid with silver,[13] which had been used in the Siege and was given by Governor Mitchelbourne to Alderman James Lenox, whose family afterwards united with the Conynghams. Another interesting relic is a very old crumbling paper on which is written in faded ink:

The siege gun

ABSTRACT OF HALF PAY OFFICERS

	PER DIEM	PR. ANNUM
Brigr. Wolseleys	2. 8. 6	885. 2. 6
Brig Echlin's Dragoons	10. 0	182.10. 0
Brigr. Conyngham's Dragoons	14. 0	255.10. 0
Earl Drogheda's Foot	3. 0	54.15. 0
Coll Mitchelbourne's	1.10	547.10. 0
Coll St. John's	1. 8	511.15. 0
Coll Creichton's		
Earl Donegalls	5. 6	100. 0. 0
Lord Mountjoys	2. 0	36. 0. 0
St. Geo. St. Georges	8. 0	146. 0. 0
Capt. Villers	8. 0	146. 0. 0
Lord Charlemonts	11. 0	388. 5. 0
Coll Stanhopes	2. 0	36. 10. 0
Sir Matthew Bridges	16. 0	146. 0. 0
Coll Fred. Hamiltons	4. 0	36.10. 0
Coll Brewers	1. 6. 0	27. 7. 6
Sir Henry Bellasys		
Major General Ingoldsbys		
Coll Seymours		
Brig. Tiffens		

There are others still extant of his documents and books. A paper marked 'Mr. Conyngham's bond for building Coagh bridge' runs thus:

1st June, 1715

> Know all men by these presents that I William Coningham of Springhill in the County of Londonderry am holden & firmly bound unto His Grace Thomas Lord Archbishop of Armach, Primate … in the just and full sum of five hundred pounds good and lawful money of Great Britain to be paid to the said Lord Primate & his Successor to which payment well and truely to be made I do comd. my heirs Exors. and Admrs. firmly by the sd. presents. Seald. in my Bd and dated the eleventh day of June 1715.
>
> The condition of the above obligaceon is such that if the above-bound William Coningham shall not nor will not build or caus to be built the Stone Bridge, already begun at Coagh in the County of Tyrone, nor shall not ... be aiding or assisting in building of same directly or indirectly during the Terme of twenty-one years yet to come, that then and in that case the above obligation to be voyd and of no effect or shod. remain in ful force & virtue in Law.
>
> Signd. Sealed & Delivd.
> W. Conyngham.

William Conyngham of the Siege had certainly two sisters, the mother of his nephew and heir, George Butle – or Buthall (Buttolph?)[14] and another sister, Elizabeth, who had married Sir Alexander Staples, 3rd Baronet, of Lissan, son of Sir Thomas Staples and the aforementioned Lady Charity, who had been imprisoned in Moneymore Castle by the rebels of 1641.

Sir Alexander Staples, Bart., of Lissan and Faughanvale, was High Sheriff for Tyrone 1661 and M.P. for Strabane 1661–5. He died in 1672 and left three daughters Elizabeth, Charity and Jane.

This husband of Elizabeth Conyngham must have been an odd, rebellious character, for the *Irish House of Commons Journal* of 1665 records that he and several others were expelled from the House of Commons because they had formed a plot to kill the Lord Lieutenant and burn Dublin Castle.

One of his daughters married a son of the Revd. George Walker, who had at one time been Rector of Lissan and Desertlyn, the parish in which Springhill is situated.

As well as the two sisters, 'Good Will' seems to have had a brother, Robert, for a small Prayer book exists with these words on the fly leaf:

> Ann Conyngham her book
> left to her by her brother
> Robert Conyngham who dyed
> between 4 and 5 o'clock on
> Monday morning ye 7th Day of Sept. 1685.

We can picture the farewell scene, the dying youth giving his treasured book to his sister who was tending him in the grey dawn of an autumn morning – and we long to know in which chamber of the ancient house this scene was enacted.

It was thirty-two years after the Siege of Derry that 'Good Will' Conyngham bade a last adieu to the wife who had been his faithful companion for forty-one years. He died in 1721 and was laid by his own wish in the family burying-ground in Lissan Churchyard – a lonely tree-clad spot on a hill-top near Slieve Gallion Mountain.

Perhaps the truest glimpse of this man's character and surroundings is given by his Will, made on Dec. 20th, 1720. A portion of it is copied here:

> I leave to my wife Ann a jointure of £80 and if she continues to live at Springhill I leave her for her life the back avenue and park above the Highway, called 'Thompson's Brow' with the Sawpit park and little park within it, as also the land of Dolusky now in my possession … together with my Dwelling house, Barn, stable, brew house, Turf house, Cow house with the sheds thereunto belonging, as also my old orchard, new orchard, cherry-garden, Washing green, Pond garden, Stackyard and Green Garden,[15] except which is hereafter reserved to my heir (provided she keep it all in sufficient repair and maintain a gardner out of the profits of the said gardens orchards and farm to keep up the improvements). I also bequeath to my said dear wife the grass of the North

> Grove together with the grass and little meadow of the South Grove, as also the use of the furniture of the said dwelling-house and office houses, as also the use of my Plaite, jewels, rings, watches and books during the time of her life and residence at Springhill as aforesaid … and if my Heire shall marie and incline to enter into possession of the half of all the houses and furniture thereof and also the half of my gardens, he paying the half of the gardner's wages, provided always that my Dre wife have her choyce of which half she pleases … and I also bequeath six of my best cows and two of my best horses to my said deare Wife, together with what Corn, Hay, Barley, malt and other family provisions may be in my dwelling house, barn, haggard and Kiln at the day of my deceas, except what will be spent thereof at my funeral, as allso what goold or monie is in her possession at the day of my deceas, as also what Moss[16] she shall need out of Ballygrubie, with all the duties of day's worke and pullets due and payable by the tenants of Ballygrubie quarter.

The will bequeaths all lands and possessions (which were very extensive) to five separate heirs – to each in succession, in case of his predecessor's death without issue. These were George Butle, Arthur Butle, his nephew, George Campbell, son of his cousin Colonel Josias Campbell of Dublin, to Patrick Orr of Clogh in the County of Antrim, and to the Revd. Mr. William Boyd, dissenting minister at Macasquin in the Co. of Londonderry.

This very lengthy and detailed Testament throughout shows thought and care for her to whom he always alludes as 'My deare Wife.'

Part of the Springhill estate

V

George Butle Conyngham

A STERN PARENT

d.1765

FOR FORTY-FOUR YEARS of the eighteenth century Springhill was in possession of George Butle Conyngham, and his uncle's widow seems to have lived with him in perfect amity.

George Butle Conyngham

It has not been recorded which part of the house and grounds she chose for her own share, but it is known that she occasionally spent the winter in Derry City with her sister Rebecca, wife of John, the son of James Lenox of Siege fame.

Rebecca, *née* Upton, was mother to the Clotworthy Lenox (who in after years married George Butle Conyngham's daughter Anne), and she was one of the many daughters of Arthur Upton of Castle Upton and Dorothy Beresford, his wife. In 1707 she had married John Lenox, and two little love-letters still exist which were written by the newly married husband to his Rebecca. One of these runs as follows:

Sunday night. Londonderry Ye 11th 1707

Since I left my Dr Beckse[17] I hev not had one minute of pleasant weather, but has gott hither in as good order as if I had been carried in a Chair. If every day's absence from my Dear Life appears soe long to me as this has done, I must bring my fortnight to four nights – (but every day is not Sunday). I din'd at Coolrain on Friday, where I saw yt all frends were well, as I find them also hear. Dr Beckse, take care of Haunce in Kelder or else its Dada will whip Mama when he returns home. I hope to hear from you by tuesday's post yt my Dear is as well as any maid in Cristendom. Please give my Dutty to my Mother and affect. Service to Upton, Hecke & Tom and Carey. I am my Dr Dearest Beckse

Your own
John Lennox

To Mrs. Rebecca Lennox
at Castle Upton, near Antrim.

The recipient of this letter was younger than Mrs. Ann Conyngham of Springhill – who had married William Conyngham in 1680, when only sixteen years of age. It was however, her niece – a younger Anne – who was now mistress of Springhill, for in the first year of his succession to the property, George had married Anne Peacocke, a friend of Dean Swift and the beautiful daughter of Mary, another of the many Upton sisters. Mary's first husband having died, she espoused secondly John Kennedy of Cultra in Co. Down, and it was at his house that his step-daughter's wedding took place on August 3rd, 1721. The trustees of the settlement were Clotworthy Upton of Co. Antrim, John Kennedy of Cultra, Upton Peacocke, Doctor of Physicke of the City of Dublin, and Hercules Upton of Castle Upton Esqre, and Patrick Orr of Clogh in the Co. of Antrim, Gentleman. Anne's Uncle, Clotworthy Upton, paid her a sum of £600 sterling, value of Great Britain, and £80 was settled on the bride out of her husband's estate.

Mrs Anne Conyngham, *née* Peacocke

Tradition tells us that Anne Peacocke's beauty was vaunted in the *Spectator* of that day under the name of 'Corinna.' Her portrait by Lely certainly shows a comely lady, dark-browed and with the double chin so fashionable at that time – indeed so much so that it had to be depicted by every popular artist, even if his model did not possess that enviable appendage. Rich silken draperies festoon the sloping shoulders, and one wonders how the encircling garment was kept from slipping off their deep declivities. Whether this fair lady was happy in her marriage we shall never know, but it seems unlikely, the former chatelaine of Springhill being still in residence, and Anne's husband, though clever and forceful, and probably virtuous and correct, cannot have been amiable. The probabilities are that the marriage was *de convenance*, arranged by the families, and that even Anne's dealings with her children were interfered with by their too stern father and too doting grand-aunt. There were three sons; William, born on April 29, 1723, David, and John – and three daughters; Mary, Anne, and little Dorothy, who died in childhood, possibly in a child's miniature four-post bed which still exists. Not long ago in the space above the Springhill attics the tattered canvas was found of a small girl's portrait, which may have been a likeness of poor little Dorothy.

Of Mary little is known. Some volumes of the *Spectator* bear her signature on the fly leaves – 'Mary Conyngham,' and she married a Mr. Sharpe and died at Springhill at the age of thirty-four. This marriage may have been thought a *mésalliance*, as it is not mentioned in the Family Bible, but she is remembered in her kind old grand-aunt's Will.

If George Conyngham's wife had a difficult and thwarted life, her children must have been her chief solace, and surely her sons, especially the generous, lovable but thoughtless William, must have been the light of her eyes! She had the handsome young John's portrait painted as a Cupid, with little wings, sandalled feet and a pink jerkin. In after years this picture hung outside the nurseries, and several generations of children used to fire at poor little Cupid with his own weapons, piercing the canvas with many a toy arrow.

The two younger boys seem to have been more sedate than William, David docile and, I think, rather commonplace, and John clever and inventive, his deft hands fashioning a silver watch and carving a tiny spinning-wheel which is still preserved in the old house. He and his elder brother, William, joined the Army, while David, through influence, obtained a post at the harbour of Belfast. Judging by their letters, the young people were very fond of each other, and we can picture their games in the Beech-walk and gallops on horseback along 'Thompson's brow' and the 'Saw pit Hill.' Some very old fencing masks witness to their education in that accomplishment.

Meanwhile their father was occupying a prominent position and taking an active part in the affairs of the Province. He has left many papers and documents which prove this. One of these, dated May 6th, 1747 and entitled *Engagement to support rights agst. the Corporation of Derry* gives an idea as to which gentlemen were prominent in the County at that time. It runs thus:

> Forasmuch as it appears to us that severall attempts have of late been made by the Corporation of Londonderry to Invade and Infringe the just rights and privileges of the Inhabitants of the county of Londonderry, we whose names are hereunto subscribed doe hereby mutually promise and engage to each other and to as many as shall adhere to us that we will to the utmost of our power maintain and defend our rights, liberties and priviledges against all attempts to destroy them and will contribute to any Expence that may be necessary to that purpose.

Dated the sixth day of May 1727
To

Tyrone
Fred Hamilton
Geo. Conyngham
Ro. McCausland
Edward Cary
Will Jackson
Henry Cary
Strat. Canning
Thos. Skipton

Five years after George Conyngham succeeded to the Springhill property his name appears in an old list of the Londonderry Militia dated 8th July, 1726 signed by Tho. Ash, Major, and now at Springhill. (See opposite).

The Corps seems to have been one of those belonging to the Militia raised in the Counties of Tyrone and Londonderry in 1715.

In 1744 George Conyngham received his Commission as 'Captain of an independent Company of Foot to consist of a hundred men raised or to be raised for His Majesty's Service in the Militia of the County of Tyrone.' This was signed by the Primate John Armagh[18] (John Hoadley, died 1746) and by Newport and Hen. Boyle. Conyngham soon after this became Colonel of the Regiment.

Other papers issued in the next year are as follows and show that compulsory Service was practised at that time. The Militia raised in 1715 was restricted to Protestants between the ages of sixteen and sixty, who were bound to appear or to provide substitutes.

> By the Lord Lieutenant General and General Governor of Ireland
> Chesterfield
>
> We judging it expedient that the Militia of the Several Counties of this Kingdom should be drawn out trained and exercised do hereby authorise Direct and Require you to cause the Militia of the City and County of Londonderry and town of Coleraine to be drawn out trained and exercised forthwith.
>
> Given at His Majesty's Castle of Dublin the 28th of September 1745. To the Governor of the County and City or in his absence to the Deputy Governor or any of them.

Two months later, George Conyngham took steps to obey this summons and issued the following order:

> By George Conyngham Esq. Deputy Governor of the said County of Londonderry:
> 1. John Woods. 2. Andrew Grier. 3. Joseph Grier. 4. Matthew George. 5. Henry George. 6. Adam Swinson. 7. Robert Johnston. 8. James Wilson all of Ballindrum. 9. John Snipe of Ballydawley. 10. John Alexander of Ballygillon.

A list of Field Officers & Captains who had Commissions formerly granted to them.	A list of those who are to suckseed by new Commissions as Field Officers	Lieuts	Ensigns
Dead Col^{l} Joshua Dawson	Geo. Conyngham Esq.	Wm. Ash Capt. Lieut	Francis Tracy
Dead Lieut. Col^{l} Tho. Blair	Thos. Ash Esq.	John Jackson	Wm. Rainey
Maj^{r} Tho. Ash	Danl Carmichael		
		Matthew Lorinan	
Capt Jon. Rainey of Grenadiers	John Lawson of Grenadiers	James Hamm-ersley &c Hugh Ash	
Capt. Wm. Jackson			
			John Morgan
Capt. Thos. Hammersley	A Comiçon already	Jackson Clark	Comiçon already
Capt. Richard Forliss	A Comiçon already	Hugh Sharp	Clark Jackson
		Jn Tompson	John Stewart
Capt. William Batty liveing now in Co. Tyrone	Thos. Neve	Richd Taylor	Wm Tracy
Capt. Henry Downing now Capt in Col: Conolly's Regt.	George Downing	Jackson Downing Daniel Downing	Windsor Brown Bernard Mulholand
Dead Capt. Thos. Lorinan	Wm. Gauge	Edward Serson	George Shaw
Capt. Wm. Mushett liveing now in Dublin.	James Boyd		
Capt. Hugh Lorinan living in Connaught	Stratford Canning	James York	Saml Graves
	Lieuts.	Ensigns.	
There were 40 firelocks delivered to the late Col^{l} Dawson & 22 firelocks delivered to each Captain when they got their Comiçons & 20 halberts & 6 drums, Some of the arms were lost & a great many more out of order.	All this column have new Comiçons by reason of the alternative of Field Officers & Captains	All this column have new Comiçons except Morgan & Jackson	

11. John Thompson. 12. David Thompson. 13. David Ruddagh. 14. Robert Bryson son of James. 16. John Bryson. 17. James Junk of Maghadowan.

You are hereby commanded in His Majesty's name to summon all the above persons to appear before me at Springhill on Tuesday, the fifth day of this inst November at the hour of nine of the clock in the forenoon to be inlisted according to Law in His Majesty's Service in the Regiment and Company under my Command in the Militia of the Barony of Loughinsholin and County of Londonderry, whereof they are not to fail at their peril of the penalty inflicted by the Statute for making the Militia of this Kingdom more usefull, and you are then and there to attend to give account of the execution of this order. Given under my hand and seal this 2nd day of November 1745.

Geo. Conyngham

To the Constable of the Parish of Ardtrea.

Londonderry Militia Badge

As well as taking part in military matters, the stern George was much occupied, fifteen years after his succession, in building the village of Coagh beside his old corn mill. He called the principal street 'Hanover Square' in honour of King George the Second, and obtained a market charter for the little town, which caused him to be sometimes termed 'Provost of Coagh.' As at this time other towns were being built by landed proprietors – the newer part of Cookstown by Mr. Stewart of Killymoon and Stewartstown by the Caulfeilds and Stapleses – a certain amount of rivalry was in the air. Some years later one of George's letters give a hint of this feeling of competition and shews that he was anxious that Coagh should be a model town. This letter was addressed to Mr. John Watt, who was to have the tenement house then occupied by one Andrew Dunlop:

Above is a copy of the bargain made between you and your sons and me for Dunbar's tenement. I have given you for your encouragement to build all the time I could, but as Mr Stewart and others give the best leases they can, to take

Coagh Bridge
Courtesy of Ian McCullough

Hanover Square, Coagh
Courtesy of Ian McCullough

> advantage of the present prosperous state of the country to build new towns, I think it prudent I should do so likewise, or our town of Coagh may lye behind. ... This I think is such an encouragement for building the houses in the Square, as neither Mr. Stewart or Mr. Caulfeild and Staples can give in Cookstown or Stewartstown. If my son write to me for any further information, I will answer it and recommend it. You will find him either in Dublin, Summerhill, or Tullamore
>
> I am Yr friend Geo. Conyngham.

The building of Coagh had been begun about twenty years before the above letter was penned on Feb. 7th, 1753. It is a pretty village lying on the slope of a hill which faces south west: many of the oldest houses still survive and it is found that the walls of some of them are double, with turf fillings to give warmth to the rooms. There was an old mill beside the bridge long before the rest of the village was built, and, from time immemorial, pearls, for which the local name is 'squillans,' have been found in the river.

However, in spite of his building activities, George Conyngham's mind was chiefly occupied by military matters. At this time France was aiming at a descent upon England and gathered a Naval armament at Brest. There were but three regiments fit for service in England in 1756. The Seven Year's War had a disastrous commencement, though it brought great glory to England and had a far-reaching effect on the history of the world. In this War, William Conyngham, whom his father considered a ne'er-do-well, was to fight with great distinction. He was probably at the victory of Minden in Aug. 1759. But in this history more will be written of his prowess.

Accordingly, at this critical time, the minds of Ulstermen seem to have been obsessed with plans for the defence of the Country in case of a French Invasion materializing, and George Conyngham, who was wont to take the lead in affairs, was determined to be ready for emergency. He had by now been appointed to the command of the Militia, and we find that he has left a second list of the officers.

A REGIMENT IN THE BARONY OF LOUGHINSHOLIN

Field Officer	*Capts. & Lieuts*	*Ensigns*
George Conyngham Col. & Capt.	William Ashe Capt. & Lieut.	Tony Tracy
Thos. Ashe Lt. Col. & Capt.	Nich. Averall	Thos. Birkby
Daniel Carmichael Major & Capt.	James York	Wm. Man
Wm. Beaty	Wm. Ramsay	Samuel Ferguson
Wm. Jackson	Jack Clark	Wm. Jackson Junr.
Thos. Hammersley	Hn. Montgomery	Thos. York
Richard Forbes	Windsor Brown	James Houston
Geo. Downing	Richd. Taylor	Wm. Downing
Thos. Neve		David Campbell
	Grenadiers	
John Lawson Wm. Gage Jhn. Boyd	Jas. Hammersley Clark Jackson Edwd. Searson	Hen. Ashe Lawce. McAlister Geo. Shaw
		William Reynolds Adjutant.

About eleven years later, the following list was sent to Mr. Secretary Bonfoy, the 6th of March, 1756, by Col[l]. George Conyngham:

> A list of the present Field Officers that are alive and the names of such that are lately dead of the Regiment of the Militia of the County of Londonderry, so far as I can recollect them:

REGIMENT OF DRAGOONS

The Right Honble. William Conolly Esq. Col. dead.
Lieut. Col[l] Stratford Canning Esq. of Garvagh.
Major Conolly McCausland of Fruit Hill[19] Esq.

Regiment of Dragoons

Right Hon. Henry Lord Mount Charles Esqre.
Lieut. Col. William Scott of Dungiven Esqre.
Major Thomas Smith of Newtown Esq.

Regiment of Foot

Marcus Earl of Tyrone	Col^{l}
Lieut. Col.	Vacant
Major	Vacant

Regiment of Foot

Col. Rt. Hon. Horatius Langford Rowley of Summerhill.
Lieut Coll Edward Cary of Dungiven Esq.
Major

At Springhill George Conyngham kept a large store of arms, a few of which still remain, and he seems to have distributed weapons among his neighbours. Some letters are extant which shew this state of affairs.

To Coll George Conyngham

Oct. 30. 1745.

Dear Col.

The old arms you gave me has employed me ever since I had the pleasure of seeing you. I sent sixteen of y^{m} to Belfast to get new locks and stocks and ye rest I have Crosset at work at here, and though I attend constantly he cant clean one in a day and night. They'l really cost me more than they are worth. Since I writ the above I received the Express from Mr. Johnston w^{h} you'l see.

I think it is good news, for I don't expect the rebels will land in Ireland except some few to hide themselves, for I imagine the main body will endeavour to get into their own country if they can get shipping or boats. However we should have all the Arms we can in order and ready to march to the assistance of our Neighbours. Downing has enlisted both the Clark's companies ab^{t} Maghera & Tobermore & some few about Castledawson. I believe he intends to raise a Regiment, for he gives ym money and Drinks, but I believe as soon as yt is over they'l desert him, he at least has apply'd for an independent Company which I suppose he'l obtain, as no body opposes him & Mr. Conolly being in England.

I am dear Coll
Yrs. most sincerely
Abr. Hamilton.[20]

Military ardour seems to have seized the heart of George, and he was prepared for any emergency. But mutiny and insubordination among his own comrades he certainly did not expect, and hot anger possessed him when on a certain day in February, 1745, an untoward episode occurred.

On the previous day Col[l]. George had especially warned his Major, William Ashe Rainey, to have the Regiment ready to mobilize on the first disturbing news. Exciting tidings were evidently expected at any moment, and Conyngham probably looked on his important self as the defender of his home and district. His three sons were at this time aged respectively twenty-two, eighteen and seventeen. Mary was already married to the undesirable Sharpe, and the fair Anne's wedding with young Clotworthy Lenox arranged to take place in the following June.

Let us picture the girl of twenty-one on this chilly February morning, sitting by a turf fire in the parlour facing Slieve Gallion mountain. Her mother and grand-aunt – the two older Annes – were with her, and they were probably stitching at some of the wedding finery, while many a qualm troubled the girl's heart that those wicked Frenchmen might be coming to disturb the Province and postpone her marriage. Perhaps her handsome Clotworthy[21] ('Tatty' she called him) would have to fight and might be killed: woeful thought! Hark! What was that? – a shot! two shots! Heavens! had the French come already? Then her father's wrathful voice was heard through the side window; 'Father will take care of us!' cried simple Anne.

But George was not railing at French invaders, but at some of his own Militia officers, whom he surprised trying to take his precious arms by force from the little tower in the lower yard, formerly used for storing arms.

We can read of this encounter in a torn document which still reposes in Springhill's Oak box; It is a complaint addressed to

> His Grace John Duke of Bedford
>
> L[d] Lieutenant General and General Governor of Ireland.

> The humble memorial and complaint of George Conyngham Esqre Col[l] and Commander of a Regiment of Foot in the Militia of the County of Londonderry and Deputy Governor of the same County Humbly sheweth that, on the first notice of an invasion by landing of French forces in the County of Antrim, your memorialist immediately gave the necessary orders to the officers of the Regiment under his Command to have the several Companies of the said Regiment in the best order and readiness to preserve the quiet and peace of the County. Orders personally to William Ashe Rainey, who is Major, to be very diligent in his duty in having all the Regt in readiness for Service on the first emergency, which orders he promised to observe.

An account follows of the raid on his arms, headed by William Ashe Rainey, who tried to make off with a large store of weapons.

> An outrageous insult and mutiny then committing against His Majesty's authority and your Memorialist's command as Colonel and Deputy Governor by the said W. Rainey and his accomplices … and your memorialist did with as

> much haste as a violent fit of gout would permit, repair to the place where the said Riot and Affray was carrying on – saw two or three of the rabble carrying out firelocks in their hands, and at the outer door he found William Rainey and George Ramsay, an Ensign in the Reg^{t} and Jas Cranston with firelocks charged in their hands.

Then followed a struggle in which the robbers carried away some of the firelocks, but some time afterwards 'returned them on apprehending the consequences of what they had done'

We pity the poor outraged Colonel thus defied by his officers, and just as he was suffering from one of his attacks of gout!

Fortunately the French invasion did not materialize.

Protestant ascendancy was now high, and memory of past violence kept up a constant fear and suspicion of the Roman Catholic population. The enactments of the Penal Laws, which were in force for many years, were really infamous. Catholics were forbidden to carry arms, to acquire land or to sell it, to educate their sons either at home or abroad, or to enter into any of the principal professions. Any member of a Roman Catholic family who was base enough to abandon his religion was rewarded by being allowed to appropriate the property of his kinsfolk – the others being dispossessed, and all Roman Catholics, no matter what their rank or lineage might be, were treated as being socially inferior. In consequence of these laws, many secret organizations were formed to carry out the work of the Roman Church by stealth. Monks and priests, disguised as laymen, went in and out among the people, bearing with them instructions as to the maintenance of their church. Hidden groups of disguised monks and nuns were scattered in secluded places, celebrating the forbidden Mass in constant dread of detection, which would have led to the severest penalties.

A piece of slate which represented an altar-stone from penal times. Measuring seven inches by four it could be slipped into a saddlebag and carried around by itinerant clergy such as Father Fottrell. The original is in the Dominican priory, Drogheda.

It was in 1739, during this time of persecution, that a Dominican monk named Fottrell was captured at Toome Bridge on the shore of Lough Neagh and brought before the stern presence of George Conyngham to be dealt with according to the rigour of the law. No record remains of the form of punishment inflicted on this monk, but his little battered leather portfolio, gold-embossed and with faded ribbon strings, still lies in one of the hiding-places at Springhill. This contains very interesting documents, particularly for the Dominican Order in Ireland.[22] John Fottrell, on whom these papers were found, was the Provincial (or Head) of the Order in Ireland, and several of the papers consist of the proceedings of the Chapter of the Order. It would have been dangerous at this time for any Dominican Monastery to establish itself publicly as such. There were many such monasteries, some large, and some very small, all apparently living in a surreptitious manner, possibly under the protection and with the support of wealthy laymen. It is evident also that Fottrell going from place to place all over Ireland and having on him papers with many foreign references, came under the suspicion of being a spy. The monastic orders were specially suspect at that time, because their members were continually going to and from the Continent.

The papers in the small portfolio are mostly in Latin, and contain Proceedings of the Dominican Chapter, in 1722 and subsequently, with orders *re* parochial functions, examinations of confessors. In the latter, injunctions are given to each examiner to take two others with him suitable for this duty and to

> Enjoin each of those who are approved that on Sundays & Festive days they propound to the people something from the Gospel or Christian doctrine and endeavour with all their strength to promote devotion to the Holy Rosary.
>
> Those who return from abroad to be assigned to their native Convents unless the Provincial thinks otherwise, but let each brother know that he incurs the penalty of excommunication or imprisonment, if he publicly says that he cannot be moved from his native Convent or any other. ... The goods of deceased brother should be divided into three equal parts, one should be given to the original Church, the second to the Convent of Assignation, and the third for Masses for deceased's soul . , . only for those dying in Ireland. ... None of our members to contract debts, with persons outside ths Order, above 10/- without the express license of his Superior. ... To avoid the ills which we are daily experiencing we order that no Brother approach the City of Dublin without the express license of the Provincial or the Vicar of the 'Nation' to which he belongs.[23] ... We direct the Master of Students that at his Classes he expose to discussion the matters which are in controversy between Catholics and Protestants of this Country, in order that the students may be made more fit for the Mission.

There is a long letter from one Colman O'Shaughnessy, from Kilkenny, dated Oct. 11th, 1738, franked by 'Mount Alexander,' relating to a 'cringing little fellow named Shee who has been deprived of his Parish.' Also a letter from Rome Nov. 1738 to Father Patrick O'Diarmid, who had been to a post in the Convent of Seville. (This Patrick O'Diarmid was Professor of the Convent of the Dominicans at Coleraine).

And there are many other detailed epistles – one of these a long one referring to Ridolfi and written to Michael MacDonough, then titular Bishop of Kilmore, who was taken with Fottrell at Toome on June 6th, 1739.

There are many other interesting letters and papers in this little portfolio.

When Fottrell was brought before George Conyngham over two hundred years ago, we can imagine the scene at Springhill – these two determined men facing each other in bitter antagonism – each believing that he was acting according to his conscience. Judging from George's portrait in the dining room, I am afraid the sentence may have been a severe one.[24]

Fear and suspicion die very slowly in a Province which has suffered so long from internal strife.

It is curious to notice that although George Conyngham seems to have thus taken part in persecuting the Roman Catholics, he himself was under a religious disability. Being one of a 'plantation' family, which till then had adhered to the Scottish Church, he was obliged under the Test Act to partake several times a year of the Sacrament according to the rites of the Church of Ireland, and if this could not have been certified he would have been deprived of his public offices. Strange little papers are to be found among Springhill's archives, such as the following:

> We James Woods and Archibald Woods doe make oath that we were present and did see George Conyngham of Springhill Esq. in the above certificate mentioned, receive the Sacrament of the Lord's Supper in the parish church of Ardtrea on Sunday the first day of May 1737 immediately after Divine Service & Sermon, according to the usage of the Church of Ireland.
>
> John, Gordon, Clerk.
> James Woods.
> Arch. Woods.
>
> and nobis 3 die May 1737

If George Conyngham's mind was taken up with his country's danger, his private affairs caused him still greater concern, for anxiety and bereavement succeeded each other.

His eldest son, and heir – William – had joined the army in March, 1747, at the age of twenty-four. The Commission is signed by 'George Wade Esq. Field Marshal of His Majesty's Forces, Lt. General of Ordnance and Governor of Fort William' – and appointed 'William Conyngham, Gentleman, to be Cornet in General Sir John Ligonier's Regiment of Horse.'

At a later date another Commission was issued to William Conyngham Esq. to be Captain lieutenant in Colonel Henry Conway's Regt. of Horse, dated Dec. 10th, 1755, and signed by King George II, and by H. Fox.

The young officers of that period, who frequented the London Coffee Houses were notably gay and dashing blades, and it seems that this extravagant young man was no exception to those in the set in which he moved.

Did rumours of William's recklessness, which were his father's torment, disturb the peace of mind of the beautiful and devoted mother, who from the far away Irish home was in thought following his movements? A few years after he had joined the Army she left this world of mingled joys and sorrows, perhaps to watch over her much loved son from a home which we are too apt to call 'far away.' The Family Bible records in her husband's handwriting that; 'My dear wife died on Thursday, the 30th of May, 1754, of macaritis. Bury'd at Lissen.'

'Macaritis!' Apparently an obsolete illness. There is a theory nowadays that every disease has its origin in some particular disorder of mind – and we can only wonder what psychical disturbance can have caused an illness called 'macaritis'!

It was only in the previous year that a familiar and old-established member of the household, 'Old Aunt Ann,' had, after thirty-two years of widowhood, followed her husband, 'Good William' of the Siege, dying in her ninetieth year. These losses left a diminished party at Springhill, as John, the youngest son, had already followed his brother's example in joining the Army, and had taken part in the European War at the crisis when Charles Edward 'the Pretender' was leading his Highlanders to attack England.

John never married, but there is an old tale of his attachment – platonic or otherwise – to a lady at Buncrana, for whom he made a miniature spinning-wheel. He eventually died at Bath and left his goods to his elder brother, and some money to his bath-chair men.

The second son, David, was probably the only child left at home, not yet having adopted any profession, though twenty-seven years of age.

Anne, the younger daughter, was established at Derry with her husband, Clotworthy Lennox, and their young family, but Mary, her senior, who was a widow at the time of her mother's death, may have been a companion to her father before she too departed this life, at Springhill in the year 1756.

During the following lonely years, George's anxiety deepened. He seems to have been too much engrossed with pride of position and possessions, and the emptiness of his home may have caused him to brood more darkly over the money losses incurred by his imprudent son.

And yet William seems to have had a charming character, lacking in few virtues save thrift. His friends evidently bore great love for him, and in after life he was greatly respected. An affectionate letter is extant, written to him in gossiping vein by his cousin Elizabeth Rowley of Summerhill in Co. Meath, who was in 1776 created Viscountess Langford in her own right. This lady's husband, who refused a peerage for himself, was Hercules Langford Rowley, many of whose letters remain at Springhill. He was the son of Frances Upton, sister to Ann, the wife of 'Good Will' Conyngham: and as both places received their names at about the same time, we may be right in concluding that the Upton sisters may have agreed to call their homes 'Summerhill' and 'Springhill.' Elizabeth Rowley's letter to William runs:

> May. My dear Cousin
>
> With great pleasure I received your letter yesterday. I longed much to hear of you from London after a march which I was sure was both disagreeable and fatiguing, but I long much more for a letter from you from the same place after the Campaign is over. It has been said here that your Regiment was to go no further than England, but I suppose there was no foundation for this report, as you make no doubt of your going to Germany so soon. Wherever you go, my dear cousin, all Happiness and Safety attend you. I should be very glad to gratify you with a particular account of your family if there was any agreeable occurence had happened since you left us, but really we are in the same situation as at that time, sometimes in good spirits and at other times frights and terrors. When God sees fitt He will rescue us from this anxious state. Tatty[25] was in town a week lately and took the long lecture I had for him very well. I am sure his desire that everything under his care should be in greatest perfection occasion'd his erring in those points I mentioned to you. I am extremely con-

cerned for the accounts we receive of poor dear Lord Powerscourt. The very ignorance of all his physicians as to his case takes off any reliance one could have in what they say. I dont know if Mr. Rowley mentioned a case to you, in a letter he wrote to you last week, that I think Lord P's physicians ought to know. It was an Aunt of Sir Thomas Taylor's that had that complaint that Lord P. has for a year. None of the doctors could tell her disorder. At the end of the year she died and was open'd and they found the breadth of a shilling of the inside of her stomach quite raw. There could be no account given whether this was occasioned by a hurt or not. Perhaps the mentioning of such a thing to the Physicians might put something in there heads that wd. be of service. I fear the accounts he has from his brother wont help to establish his health. What I have heard for some time, is now certain. You never could believe me when I expressed my apprehensions that a certain Family in this town would draw him in – but alas, it is too true. God Almighty help my poor sister, for I am sure the imprudent match will be a great trouble to her. Mr. Rowley has insisted with him that he should not take any further steps in this affair till he hears from England, but I fear it is gone too far to be prevented.

I beg you'll give my affectionate love to Mrs. Donaldson. I hope she'll be so good as to let me know when Cosn Campbell comes to London. I also beg you will assure Sir William Rowley's family that our affectionate love attends them all.

Poor Mrs. Montgomery died last night.

Mr. Stewart was turn out of the House of Commons last Wednesday, for bribery. I suppose you knew before you left Ireland that old Fortescue had given Jemmy £1,300 a year over and above what he had settled on him.

I'll trespass no longer on your patience, but bid you adieu, my dear Cousin, and believe me to be

Your sincerely affectionate friend
E.A. Rowley

We are preparing for Summerhill.

Soon after receiving this letter the gallant but extravagant William went off with his Regiment to Germany to fight in the Seven Years' War, begun in 1757, and in which England supported Frederick, King of Prussia, against France, Austria and Russia.

* * * * * * *

Bereft by death and marriage of the companionship of his family, old George Conyngham still occupied himself with public affairs. In April, 1756, Bonfoy wrote to the 'Governor of the County of L'Derry' at the Lord Lieutenant's command, to ask for a list of such gentlemen as he should think proper to be Commissioners of Array for the County, and on the back of this paper, in Conyngham's handwriting, is the list of suggested gentlemen, arranged according to Baronies.

Barr. Kenaght	*Barr. Inisheran*
Hudson Gage	Andrew Knox
Tho. Smith	Edwd. Cary
Conolly McCausland.	Geo Ash
Marcus McCausland	William Thornton
Audley Canning	Henry McCullagh

Barr Coleraine

Stratford Canning
Geo. Cary
Richd. Jackson
James Do. Heyland
John Blair

City of Derry

Charles McManus
Alexr. Knox
William Scott
Will. Stewart

Loughinsholin

Abraham Hamilton
John Downing
James Mauleverer
Wm. Ash Rainey
Mossom Gamble
Hugh Miller

There is another list, also in George's writing, evidently a copy of the list which he finally sent to Bonfoy, Governor of Derry on April 24th, 1756. It runs thus:

Henry Lord Baron Mount Charles – Governor
Henry Cary Esq. Deputy Governor
George Conyngham Esq. Deputy Governor
John Dawson Esq. Deputy Governor
Edward Cary Esq.
Andrew Knox Esq.
Stratford Canning Esq.
Richard Jackson Esq.
William Scott Esq.
James Jones Esq.
Conolly McCausland
Abraham Hamilton Esq.

Charles McManus Esq. Mayor of Derry
The Sheriff of Derry
George Cary Esq. Mayor of Coleraine
Marcus McCausland
Hodson Gage Esq.
Hugh Hill Esq.
William Stewart Esq.
Dominick Heyland Esq.
Thomas Smith Esq.
John Downing Esq.
Audley Fanning Esq.
Geo. Ash Esq.
William Thornton Esq.
Alexander Knox Esq.
Mossom Gamble, Esq.
Joshua Swettenham
William Hogg Esq.
Nathaniel Alexander Esq.
Robert Church Esq.
John Blair Esq.

Meanwhile the unhappy, grudging feeling towards his eldest son continued to embitter George Conyngham's heart, and some of his letters to William are in sarcastic vein, such as the following:

> Springhill May 7th. 1756.
> Dear Will,
>
> I wish you joy of your purchase, and Will Buttle of his Cornetcy in Genl. Bligh's. Your letter was not the first intelligence I had of it. Mrs. Jones knew it ten days ago and the canal through which the scheme ran. So far as you have thought fitt to let us know of the matter I think you must have a good bargain. You may very reasonably expect both from duty and inclination all the assistance and information I can give you. I goe this afternoon to Coagh to find the names of the tenants and to desire them to meet me there on Monday with their articles of agreement &c. &c.

> Springhill. May 17th. 1756.
> Dear Will
>
> Since my last directed to Athy I had a meeting with all the tenants of Tamnaghmore, and now I send you a Rental as perfect as I could make it by comparing the tenants receipts with Mr. Buttle's return to Matthew Patterson. You will observe that Mr. Buttle began to sett this land at a very unlucky time for setting, being the year next after the Rebellion. As to treating with the

> tenants about renewing, I can by no means advise that measure, as it is now almost as unfavourable as the year 1747 or 46. The present embroil'd posture of our publick affairs has put a little damp on trade & made timorous people more indifferent to land. Therefore ... let matters stand as they doe. ... You will feel the benefit of your purchase. We are all well here but you may believe I am uneasy about poor Jack. Pray let me know the earliest intelligence you get from Minorca or wherever Jack may be. I am Dr. Will
>
> Your affect father
> Geo. Conyngham

This second letter reveals a reluctant tenderness towards a rather uncongenial son, and shews the better side of George's nature.

Yet, almost four years later, George Conyngham lost all patience with his eldest son and resolved to give him but little help in his money difficulties. He wrote thus to his lawyer nephew David Butle:

> Springhill, Feb. 22nd. 1756.
> Dear Davy
>
> By last post I had the satisfaction of hearing from you that my son David's affair at Belfast is happily finished as it now only remains to take out his Commission. ... Send it to me as soon as you possibly can and what money will be wanting to pay the Commission Secretary. If you speak to Kennedy Henderson he will get it for you from Mr. James Given who has a little of my money in his hands. ... The account you give me of my son William's affairs is so very loose that I can make no other judgement than that I perceive both he and all the innocent part of my family are likely to pay dear for all the polite fine company he has been keeping these sixteen years past, if I should run into all his measures. Let him know that I have received his several Letters, but that I do not care to answer them, because it must open a field for such discussion as I would at this time rather avoid until better times may make it less disagreeable. I will now tell you how far and no further I am content to embarrass myself, and I am induced to it more to vindicate my own character to the world than from any merit in him or satisfaction to myself in my private thoughts.
>
> I will be subject to no judgements of anything that may affect my person or my chattels, which I will not enjoy at the discretion of my son's creditors, because my son David is bound for this debt and must be discharged of it. I am unjustly consenting to punish my unoffending posterity for the error of one unhappy mismanager. Now you will observe that I propose that all those debts which will probably be most pressing are to be secured, & then there will remain 960 unsecured, as Mr. Rowley is engaged on the large sums. I am willing to agree that in case my son do not survive the present War with France that I will add an additional security for the 960, but, in case my son live, he must take that debt on himself, unless his future behaviour may give me more liking to him. Whilst I am writing this I have an Express from Mr. Staples, now at seven o'clock at night, that he this afternoon had got an account from the

> Governor of Charlemont that the French to the number of 1,500 men were landed near Carrickfergus. What will be the Issue, God knows, but it is no encouragement to undergo incumbrances
>
> I am in some hurry
> Your affec Unckle Geo. Conyngham

It is painful to read this harsh unforgiving letter from the father of a gallant son then fighting for his Country and to notice that father's indifference to the fate of one who was vastly superior to his commonplace second son David, for whose welfare so much solicitude is shewn. As to the landing on Feb. 28th, 1760 of the French at Carrickfergus, Horace Walpole playfully alludes to the episode:

> Louis XV is Sovereign of France, Navarre and Carrickfergus. You will be mistaken if you think the peace is made and that we cede this Hibernian town to recover Minorca or to keep Quebec. Indeed, seeing that the great mechanics of this age have not invented a flying bridge to fling from the coast of France to the N. of Ireland, it was not easy to conceive how the French should conquer Carrickfergus, and yet they have! Last week Monsieur Thurot landed in the isle of Islay. He had three ships which burnt two ships belonging to King George. When they had finished this campaign they sailed to Carrickfergus a poorish town situated in the heart of the Protestant Cantons. They immediately made a moderate demand of about twenty articles of provisions. ... If this was not complied with they threatened to burn the town and then march to Belfast, which is much richer. We were sensible of this Civil proceeding and agreed to it, but somehow or other this capitulation was broken, on which a detachment attacked the place. We shut the gates, but after the battle of Quebec it is impossible that so great a people should attend to such trifles as locks and bolts, accordingly there were none, and as if there were no gates either, the two armies fired through them. ... If this is a blunder remember I am describing an *Irish* war. ... The Irish army consisted of four Companies, but 72 men under Lieut. Col. Jennings, a wonderful brave man. Unluckily our ammunition was soon spent, for it is not above a year that there have been any apprehensions for Ireland, and as all that part of the country are most Protestantly loyal, it was not thought necessary to arm people who would fight till they die for their religion. When the Artillery was silenced, the garrison flung the town at the heads of the besiegers, Accordingly they poured volleys of brickbats at the French, whose Commander M. Flobert, was mortally knocked down, and his troops began to give way. General Jennings thought it prudent to retreat to the Castle, and the French again advanced. Four or five raw recruits still bravely kept the gates, when the garrison finding no more gun-powder in the Castle than they had in the town, and not near so good a brick kiln, sent to desire to surrender. General Thurot accordingly made them prisoners of war and plundered the town.

Referring to this incident, thus so jeeringly described by Horace Walpole, George Conyngham mentions in a letter of March, 1760

On Wednesday the 27 there was certain intelligence brought to this Country that on the day before the French had abandoned their enterprise on Carrickfergus and Belfast, that they had reembarqu'd their forces and that the danger of that country was apparently over.

* * * * * * *

But to return to the unfortunate William, we fear that the friends who made excuses for him made but little impression on the stern old father.

One of these was the Primate of Ireland, Archbishop George Stone, whose handsome person had gained for him the nickname of 'the beauty of holiness,' though historians have not much to say as to the beauty of his character, representing him as selfish and unscrupulous. At that period a Primate possessed great temporal power in the land in which he took a large share in governing, and his influence was very great. Archbishop Stone wrote to George Conyngham a charming letter, which goes far to show that history has treated the Prelate unfairly, as no one but a wise and kind friend could have penned the following:

Dublin 25th Feb 1760
Sir

I hope you will not only excuse but take in good part my troubling you upon a subject in which I have naturally no concern, and as it relates solely to your own family it is of that sort that the Interposition of friends is often thought impertinent. When the Regiment, in which your son William has a troop, received orders to prepare for going abroad, He came to see me and related the distress of his circumstances (all which was a new Story to me). He said that he had applied to you for Relief, upon giving up everything that he possesses and every Reversionary Claim into your Power, and to depend entirely upon your favour in the future. He told me that you were disposed to make Him easy for the present upon these terms, but that previous to it your son David must be put in possession of the Office in the Revenue at Belfast, and in order so that by which alone his immediate Ruin might be prevented He begged my Assistance. The thing was not easily to be done, but I promised to exert the utmost of my Credit, and had the good Fortune to succeed. But now I find that He had been mistaken in his expectations, and that His situation is as desperate as ever, and that unless you are so good as to lay aside former dislikes & to take his case into your consideration with the Indulgence of a kind Parent rather than the Severity of a strict Judge, he must be lost without possibility of Recovery. I do not mean, Sir, to defend his indiscretions in point of past Expence, but will only just observe to you how general that Excess has been, and in this careless dissipated age how few young men have escaped the Contagion. I have in the course of many years past just seen enough of Him to beget in me a favourable opinion of him with regard to his appearance and Behaviour, which are very becoming and proper, and his general character is extremely good. I cannot therefore but be much concerned upon His own account when I see Him so near Ruin, as He now is, and were He not personally known to me, I should be glad to be instrumental in saving Him, as He is your son. I am sure you will do yourself great Honour at present by acting kindly towards Him, and I will venture to say that it will certainly redound to your future satisfaction. I have no Right to ask anything as a Favour from you, much less a thing of this Nature, but there can be no offence in my saying that your kindness to Him upon this occasion will greatly increase my Regard for you, and will secure to the Rest of your Family every good office which my Situation in this Country may enable me to perform towards them.

I am Sir
With great truth
Your very faithfull Friend
and humble Servant
George Armagh.[26]

George Conyngham's answer, written one week later, makes excuses for his own but not for his son's conduct:

Springhill
March the 4th. 1760
My Lord

That you have not sooner had an acknowledgment of the Honour I have of your Grace's letter of the 25th of Feb. is because your letter by the Post Office stamp had not left Dublin till the 28th. which was Thursday, and that post does not come here till Monday which was the last post. I am now with all the gratitude and Respect I am capable of bound to return your Grace my sincerest thanks for your prevailing interest with the Commissioners on my son David's behalf. I know I need say no more to your Grace on that subject.

The part I have to act in my son William's case is of the last consequence to the very being of myself and my family. If I had no other child but him 1 think I could carry parental affection and indulgence as far as any man, but I have other children and grandchildren, from whom I have never received the least Disobligation and who have an equal right to my care. I think I have a hard card to play as the common Trustee of my whole family.

By a list of debts returned to me they amount to £4,000 besides £2,500 for which my small fortune is already engaged to Mr. Rowley for my son's former promotions in the Army. That his desperate circumstances should be unknown to your Grace I do not wonder, since he and his friends thought fit to make it a secret to me, who had a natural Right to be made acquainted with every natural transaction of his Life, if filial Duty or Respect had been regarded. As matters stand, I am unwilling to aggravate the Errors of my unhappy Son, and therefore in a Letter I wrote him last post, wh. I hope he will let you see, I have told him I am content to distress myself by subjecting so much of my Estate to a Rent Charge as will be sufficient to secure the Capital sum with an interest at

£5 per cent redeemable by a gradual reduction of the principal sum by the sale of lands or such other ways as may hereafter be prudent and beneficial to myself and children. Since from a general benevolence to all men Your Grace has thought fit to interpose in this particular case, I entreat the Favour of you to call for the letters I have written containing the utmost of what I can doe, and therein you you will see a fair scheme of securing these creditors on a real security instead of a very precarious one. As I think Your Grace will consider what I have consented to doe is not only very advantageous to the Cred^{rs} but a pretty large share of generosity to my son. As I need no new testimony of your Grace's goodwill to me it would give me the greatest content and peace of mind if my conduct in this whole affair shall have your approbation, wh. I the more hope for when I tell you that the payment of the Interest of the Debts will consume full one half of all the Estate of Inheritance I have in the world.

You see, my Lord, what trouble your goodness brings on you at the same time that it gives me the opportunity and pleasure of answering you that I am with the greatest respect and Duty

Your Grace's most obedient
obliged Hum^{ble} Ser^{vt}
Geo. Conyngham.'

It is to be feared that even the Primate's intercession did not cause old Colonel George Conyngham's heart to relent towards his eldest son, and that the old man took little trouble in helping William by settling with the Creditors. In the following year, 20th Aug., 1761, their kinsman, Hercules Langford Rowley, wrote from Langford Lodge – his second abode – when sending a receipt for a Bill drawn on Mr. James Given for £100. He reproached George, of whom he clearly disapproved, though loving and respecting his extravagant son. The letter runs:

I really expected you w^{d} have made more frequent payments according to agreement. I am much surprised that nothing has been yet done to carry into execution wh you and your son Cos^{n} Wm. Conyngham enter'd into; the delay injures me much & will vastly increase the money that is to be pay'd on that ac^{ct} ... If it be not soon done your son the Capt will be put to great difficulties, and I am afraid has no way of satisfying the debts but by selling his Comm^{n} and putting himself in a different way of life, which as I know him to be a man of the strictest honour, must be the greatest distress to him to sell out during the War in the place of Action, but he will do anything rather than any Person should be a loser by him, and the agreement between you and him. ... I spoke to David Buttle often about this, and he says he has sent everything to you long agoe that was necessary ... but that you have never done anything towards forwarding it. ... You are the sole cause of this delay, ... I heard, since I came to this Country, from Cos^{n}[27] Will which is the only letter I have had since the last Campaign began, he is extremely well and has not met with any accident either in health or Limb notwithstanding.

This excellent cousin, Hercules Langford Rowley,[28] has already been mentioned in these pages. Throughout a life of great integrity and prominence, he continued to take a lively interest in his relations at Springhill and to write many wise and affectionate letters, which are still preserved there. That he was especially fond of young Captain William Conyngham is evident. He wrote thus to him on June 26th, 1762:

My dear Will Conyngham

I heartily wish I could send you any good and agreeable ac^t from this Familly, as I am convinced no one partakes more of pleasure at the welfare of it than you, my Dr^est friend, but Providence has thought fit it should be otherways and we ought to be satisfied.

My son Hercules continues much in his usual way as to his disorders ... he is now at the Mountains of Moran (Mourne) drinking goat's whey to sweeten his Blood and to alter the scene for a little amusement. Clotworthy will be Captain in the Royal Irish Dragoons as soon as the King signs any Commissions, but it is not by purchase but by the natural rise of officers in the Reg^t he came to be Capt, he behaves extremely well and has been so in his health thank God. ... This great while Arthur improves & is a good boy. ... All the girls grow tall and are more agreeable to us every day. We have the Blessing of seeing every one of our children endeavour to act as we could wish upon Principalls of Virtue & Honour, & I am superlatively Bless'd in the chief and Principall wheel that keeps all in regular & proper Motion, my Dearst wife, who loses nothing of the many valuable Qualities you know her possess'd of – and every day adds strength and new ones to them. She wrote to you about Feby. last. Our sons & daughters joyne my wife and me in the most affect. Love and best wishes for your Happyness in every Situation both in War and Peace.

I am dear Will
Yr. most sincerely affect. Friend
& H^ble servant
Her. Langford Rowley.

(The address on this letter is:
Captn William Conyngham
of the Honble. Genl. Honeywood's Regiment of Horse
in the Allied Army, Germany.)

The Seven Years' War continued, and young William gained more and more experience of soldiering and hardship, while at Springhill his unhappy old father instead of following his son's movements with proud anxiety, never ceased to bemoan the debts occasioned by the youth's very pardonable carelessness.

There is no record that George ever resorted to 'strong waters to assuage his woe,' but in those so-called 'Good old days' it was the custom to consume much wine, and that Conyngham was no exception to the general habit is shewn in the following letter from his son-in-law, Clotworthy Lenox.

Derry 28th May 1760.
Dear Sir

I had the favour of your letter by the Bear^r and have done my best to choose the best wines this town affords. I have sent two dozen of Fronteniac from Rob[t] Fairly at 21[s] per dozen bottles included plain corks at the top of the sacks, which you had better have cross nick'd , as you unpack 'em, because there is one dozen of Mountain from Walker Marshall at 15[s] per dozen, bottles included, at bottom plain corks. They are the very best wines I cou'd get and shall be glad to know how you like them. I am very much vex'd I cannot get the Tincture of Benzoin to send you, as George Gordon has not any yet made – he is Kept so busie attending children in the smallpox that he has scarce a spare minit.

Thursday se' night Mr. Hamilton, our new member, made his publick entry into this town attended on horseback by a number of gentlemen and freedmen who met him at the Liberty post. They had drums, fidles and Ships colours carried before them … a vast crowd of mob and common people dressed out with orange ribbon & whin flowers, which made a great show, and in the evening had an entertainment in the Town Hall, several bonefires and his friends' houses illuminated made a great deal of noise that night, but since that have been very quiet and did not hear of any quarrels or disputes unless it was among the comon mob when they were drunk. I suppose you have heard that there was Bribery proved & that Mr. Stewart's friends deserted him, except Mr. Rowley, who stuck to him to the last. They say Mr. Stewart bore his disappointment with surprizing spirits, much better than his wife and family. Peggy Paterson writes from Dublin that it is thought he will be made a Lord, I believe he finds that he need not think of getting into the House of Comons.

Nancy and the little ones all Joyne in duty to you, and I am D[r] Sir
Y[r] most dutiful & affect Son
C. Lennox.'

Derry, and not Belfast, was evidently then the shopping centre for the Conynghams – both towns being just the same distance from Springhill. Derry City was also the seat of County business, and many old papers survive dealing with the affairs of the County in the days of old George Conyngham and his Uncle, 'Good Will' – such as the following account which George has left of business transacted in the County Town in March, 1762.

At an Assize held in Londonderry the sixth day of March 1762 the sum of £288. 6. 8 str. was ordered to be assessed on the Inhabitants of the said City and County at large in the following manner for the purposes in the Under Warrant.

Draper's Proportion	£17	0	6
Salters Do.	15	16	4
Vintners Do.	14	11	11
Mercers Do.	15	16	4
Ironmongers Do.	15	16	4
Mercht Taylors Do.	12	13	3 1/4
Cloth Worker's Do.	10	18	11 1/4

Haberdashers Do,	17	0	6
Fishmongers Do.	12	3	3½
Grocers Do.	17	0	6
Goldsmiths Do.	14	11	11
Skinners Do,	17	0	6
Manner (sic) of Limavady	28	18	1½
Mr. Dawson lands	3	17	10½
Mr. Gage do.	8	10	5
Sir John Rowley's lands	17	0	6
Drumbo do.	4	8	2
Captain Ch^s^ Philip's do.			
Sir Robt Staples do.	2	14	0½
Messrs. Conyngham & Richardson do.	2	18	10
Lady Cooke	1	7	2
Lands of Faughanvale	1	14	0
City and Liberties of Londonderry	17	0	6
Town of Coleraine	9	14	6
Liberties of Coleraine	14	11	11¼

From the large number of papers referring to County affairs, from 1721 to 1764, which George Conyngham has left at Springhill, it can be seen how keen an interest he took in local matters – even when he reached the evening of life. But the old man was failing fast. For years he had suffered from gout and in 1765 his days were numbered.

George's son David left work at Belfast harbour to be with his father, and his sister Anne and Clotworthy Lenox, her husband, came from Derry and did all in their power to help the invalid in his last illness, though they were then much engrossed in equipping their eldest son, John, for the army.

George's two soldier sons were with their Regiments, and Capt. William received several letters from his brother-in-law and sister acquainting him with what was passing at Springhill. Here are some extracts:

> 12th Feb. 1765
>
> To Captain William Conyngham
> of General Honeywood's
> London.
>
> Dear Brother
>
> I had the pleasure of your letter of 31st. ult by yesterday's post and another of the 2nd inst by express from Derry which bring the agreeable news of my son John's being an officer. His mother is a little shocked with the thought of his going to America, but as she consented to it is now resolved to behave with courage. By his letter to me he seemed to be in high spirits. I hope in God it will turn out for his good and our satisfaction, and think ourselves much

obliged to you for your affectionate care and assiduity in this matter. … The full sum you mention for his Commission is £460 English 21 days' sight. … It is not to be expected Jack can have any notion of the disposal of money. I will write to Col[l] Maxwell this night, on whose friendship I have great dependence.

You see we are at Springhill. On receiving a letter from my father's servant ab[t] ten days ago, and one from Mr. Laird of Machrafelt, who at that time attended him, we came here the next day and found him ill of a violent cold he got by going out in the Post Chaise after being confined with a fit of the Gout in his hand, his appetite is very bad and gets but indifferent rest, he has taken two pukes but does not think his cough any better. He has pretty good spirits at some times, & at others seems to think himself growing weaker, and indeed we and all that see him think him declining fast.

Davy is here with us, and we wrote to Jack last post, but as we did not know where to find you, we desired Jack might let you know my Father was not well. Your sister is in great distress at present between her duty to her father and her son; her father cannot bear the thoughts of her leaving him, & her presence in Derry is absolutely necessary to get things ready for Jack's departure. I realy do not know what we shall do if it is absolutely necessary for Jack to be in London by the middle of March. … I propose going home to-morrow or next day & must bring Jack here to see his g[d] father, who is vastly pleased with the bargain you have made for him & says he will give him 40 guineas to buy Regimentals. I believe it will be sufficient to write a letter by Jack by way of introduction to his Uncle Robert.[29] Your sister and Davy join in affectionate love to you. I am Dr Brother

Your sincerely affectionate
Clot. Lennox.

Another letter of Feb. 26th runs:

Dearest Brother

I had the pleasure of yours of the 14th which I received in Derry where I returned for a few days, at my father's desire, to bring my son John here to see him. I hope you have rec[d] my letter of the 12th £400 enclosed. I then let you know of my father's being in a very bad state of health that we thought him going very fast, he has grown worse every day and is now so very low that his life is not to be depended on an hour. He has made a Will, which he has never read to any one except Mr. Workman, with whom he has lodged it. Davy is here and we all join in begging your presence with us as soon as possible both for your own & our satisfaction. … Concludes with joining your sister & Davy's affect Love and my Son's Duty. …

I am my Dr Brother
Most sincerely affect
C. Lennox.

Clotworthy Lenox was only a brother by marriage to William, but the latter's own brother – John Conyngham – was at the same time writing to sound him as to his plans – from Cirencester, on March ye 14th, 1765. It is addressed to

> Capt. William Conyngham, St James' Coffee House, London.
>
> My dear Brother
>
> I had a letter this morning from Davy & he tells me Brother Lennox wrote to you. My father continues extremely ill & cant get out of Bed, & so ill that I think we may very soon expect to hear of his Deceas. I find he has settled his affairs & what he could leave he has done equally between Sister Lennox, Davy & I – except some legacies to my sister's children – Nancy, George and Beck; he has given Jack Lennox forty guineas. Davy says he has not been consulted in anything, only my Brother & Sister Lennox has been consulted. They are all very desirous that you and I would go over. ... If you go over you can take care of any affairs of mine and I should be very glad that you were there now, as Davy tells me he is obliged to go to Belfast upon his own business.
>
> Adieu my dear Brother
> Yours affectly
> Jno Conyngham.[30]

William's sister, Mrs. Anne Lennox, also wrote to him at this time, her thoughts divided between solicitude for her brother's affairs and motherly care for her young son Jack, just about to join the Army. The old father had died by this time.

> April 2nd. 1765 L. Derry
>
> Dear Bros.
>
> I wrote you the 24th, the day after we came here from Springhill, as you had been wrote to ye 8th of March of my Father's death of ye 6th & Jack also wrote ye same night. I concluded you must be on your way over, so I enclosed my last letter to Davy Buttle, in case you were not come to Dublin, to forward it to you. Bro. Jack writes me that you were obliged to attend ye Aprile Muster &, in hopes of seeing you before ye 15th., fixed that day for ye Cort (sic) at Springhill as we coud not think of moving anything there till we first knew your mind or what things you would be inclined to keep, But my not hearing a word from you distresses me vastly. ... Neither Davy or I can stay at Springhill to take care of any thing there, all is left to servants whose times are all out at May, & at present supporting 8 of them at a very great expense, and a number of cattle, which will not sell for more than half value after May, and it is very necessary you should be there immediately on every account to dispose yourself of your demesne, gardens, Medows etc. before that terme. I have got ye Garden sow'd and plough'd, just what my Father intended if He had liv'd, and is to sett the same quantity of potatoes, which will make your land more valuable. I long most impatiently to see you. ... We have at last got my Son ready to set out tomorrow for Dublin & to sail in ye pacquet as soon as possible. ... In Dublin

he is to lodge at Mr. Robert Colvill's, opesite ye Indian warehouse in Abbey Street. Couzon Bob Maxwell lodges in that house, who I hope will give him a letter to his Bro. ... Tatty writes this post to Bro. Jack to meet him in London if he is well, ... He shall carry a letter to Tatty Upton and one to his Uncle Robert.[30] I have furnished him with everything I cou'd get for him here, I think very sufficiently. He carried a Bill with him for forty guineas. We have done everything in our power to send him of in a comfortable way & has all reason to hope he will turn out deserving, and trust that God Allmighty will preserve him & bless our schemes with success. Will Stewart[31] is just left us, he has been here these several days at our Assizes.

All this family are well & join in duty & love to you & believe me to be my D[r] Bros.

Ever sincerely Affectn. Sister
Anne Lennox

Anne's next letter to her brother William is addressed to 'Capt. William Conyngham at Mr. David Buttle's, Ann Street, Dublin.'

I have ye long and much wished for pleasure of finding my Dearest Bros. is safely landed, but greatly concerned that you have not seen our boy yet, hoping to hear that ye friends who have seen him have it in their power to give you an agreeable description of him, had you known the child I have parted with I am sure you wou'd pity me, but what is done was by my own consent, and hopes for his future good, therefore shall endeavour to be content & put my trust in providence for his preservation and happiness. His father wrote to Tatty Upton by him, to whose care I do most gladly recommend him. I had ye pleasure of Jack's arrival by last post, which I scarce expected, and not in my power to be with him at Springhill as soon as I wish, as my servant and chairhorse are gone to Dublin with Jack's trunk, which I hope is sent after him to London, directed either to Couzen Upton or Sam Smith. Ye poor fellow Wd be quite broke if he shou'd not get it in time.

Matthew George[33] wrote me this morning ye hay is so scarce he has been obliged to sell part of ye cattle; my Bros. neither know nor considers these things, yet I would be as far from doing ye least thing disobliging to any as any in ye world, and when we have the pleasure of all meeting makes not any doubt of everything being settled to our mutual satisfaction. If I know myself, covetousness has but a small share in my composition & has often felt by painful experience that natural affection was predominant, which I pray God may always subsist in a family which hitherto has never had reason to suspect each other of ye contrary. I shall write to Davy to have ye Cort adjurn'd to Monday ye 6th of May, and thinks we sd. all meet some days before that time. Tatty and ye children are well and join in affect Love and Duty to you, dear Bros.

Ever affect sister
Ann Lennox

My love to Davy Buttle and tell him Tatty and I return him ten thousand thanks for

his great care of our son. I shou'd write to him but cant get a frank & does not think anything I have to say at present worth postage.
L[n] Derry 19th April 1765.

Kind, gentle, simple Anne! her warm heart and domestic outlook speak through these artless letters.

There is another letter written from Springhill at this time by Captain John Conyngham, William's youngest brother, and it shows that he was doing his best to take the family affairs in hand until the procrastinating William should return.

Springhill
May 14th 1765.

My dear Brother

My sister and I came here this day. Matthew George recd your letter of the 9th May with the power to take possession of Mullaghnahoe, and this day he has been with all the tenants, who gave up their possessions very quietly, and also gave security that they will not pay any rent to any but you – except John O'Haggan and James O'Haggan. There is no dependence to put in those Haggans. … I hope you'll have no trouble with them. … My sister gives her Love to you and hope we shall see you on Monday.

Adieu my dear Brother
Yours most affectly Jn. Conyngham
Our compts to the Buttles.

George Conyngham's will runs thus. I give it in abridged form:

In the name of God I George Conyngham Esqre this 9th day of February in the year 1765, being minded to make the best Provision for my younger children & their children w[h] my Chattels real and personal can enable me to make.

First I bequeath to my second son, David Conyngham now of Belfast, & to my third son John Conyngham, now a Captain in His Majesty's Army, and to my only daughter Ann Conyngham, wife of Clotworthy Lennox of the city of Londonderry Esqre, all my right, title Interest in the two townlands of Ballydally and Crosspatrick in the County of Londonderry wh I hold by Lease from the See of Armagh. … the said lands to be enjoyed jointly by dividing the Rents & Profits thereof among them.

After my death my Executors shall sell by Cort or otherwise all my Chattels personal, my Household Furniture of all sorts Plate, Pictures, Books & also all my stock of cattle of all sorts and my Carriages & horses & Horned Cattle & also all the Corn, Malt, Meal & grain of all sorts which I shall have at the time of my death and also what Wine & other Liquors shall remain after my Funeral, except such of any of my Children shall desire to keep for their own use, and the money arising of the Sale of the said goods I do hereby direct to be added to such Ready Money as I may have at the time of my Death.

Item. I do hereby nominate my said son David Conyngham & my sd. son John Conyngham & my sd. daughter Anne Lennox executors of my Will, & in regard my sd, children are much dispersed in their places of Residence & have no experience in the business of Executorships, I do make it my earnest Request to my good neighbours and friends the Rev. Mr. James Lowry[34] & the Rev. Mr. Arthur Workman that they will give the said Executors & such servants as it will be necessary to employ as much of their Advice & assistance as they can spare in the best manner of disposing of my goods & Chattels. I hereby bequeath to my granddaughter, Anne Lennox, the sum of £300 sterling on her marriage, provided she shall marry with the Advice & Consent of her Father & Mother ... and if she shall marry without such consent ... in that case I bequeath to her the sum of five shillings & no more.

Item. I bequeath to my grandson, George Lennox, the sum of one hundred pounds & to my granddaughter, Rebecca Lennox, the sum of fifty pounds. I bequeath to my servant, Rachel Weir, in testimony of her long & faithful service about me, the sum of twenty-four pounds over and above what may be due to her at the time of my Death – provided she render up to my Executors a just & true account of all the several goods & Articles committed to her Care.

Item. I bequeath to my servant, James Kennedy, the sum of Ten pounds. ... I leave to my servant, Jane Marshal, the sum of six pounds ... as a token of my opinion of her Fidelity. ... To my servant, John Skinnader, five pounds. I desire my Executors may from the time that they shall discharge my old Cook-maid, Jane Barker, take care that out of the yearly rents of Dolusky she shall be paid the yearly sum of forty shillings. ... I give my daughter Anne Lennox the curtains and Materials of a wrought Bed in Dimity with the wrought hangings & silk for chairs and also the Dutch Ebony cabinet in my own room also the picture drawn for me by Lowry the painter. I leave to my son David my two original Pictures of King William and Queen Mary, drawn by Sir Godfrey Kneller.[35]

Item. I order all the old firearms in my hall and in and about the house (except the hundred Firelocks and Bayonets given me in a particular Compliment by the Earl of Chesterfield) to be sold to the best advantage for the use of my Executors. ... I also order all my wooden vessels, Tools & Instruments in Husbandry and all my Corn and Meal Chests or Arks and all Timber or Lumber lying in or about any of my Houses to be carefully gathered and sold. I order that the said three Legacies should be out of the aggregate sum of my effects when converted into money. ... I empower my s[d] Execut[rs] to employ such proper persons to be assisting to them & to reward them for their trouble.

Dated this Twelfth day of February, 1765, & declared to be my last Will and Testament.

Published in presence of Theodore Martin[35]

Geo. Conyngham.

Matt. George. Alexr. Staples.

George Conyngham's portrait looks down disdainfully from the walls of

Springhill's present dining-room and shews a thin-featured elderly man with powdered hair, small clever eyes, florid nose and a firm unamiable mouth.

Many letters and documents exist which refer to this stern parent; his Marriage Settlements, dated 1721, his Will of 1760, a Mortgage to Mr. Rowley 1744–46, his Commission dated 1744 in which he is styled 'Provost of Coagh,' a Deed of Bond dated 1732 – a protest from the Irish Society of Co. Londonderry, in 1731, to George Conyngham for having cut timber for a building which he wished to erect without having asked leave to do so, the Irish Society having the monopoly of the trees on the lands of the London Companies. There is a letter from The Revd. Thomas Staples,[37] Derrylauren, 1747, referring to a Bond for £50 said to be due to George from him & the Revd. C. Caulfeild, the authority being a note in Lord Templetown's pocket-book. He adds:

> Grace and Molly joyn in our best respects to Cosin Conyngham and all your good Family – I wish you a happy New Year and am your
>
> affect humble servant
> Tho. Staples
>
> Molly Maurice was very ill at Lissane or would have waited on you at Springhill.

During the forty-four years of his residence at Springhill George had shewn himself to be clever, active and capable: but his nature was warped by a harsh, censorious outlook, and though respected and feared, little affection can have fallen to his lot.

The dovecote in the lower yard

Colonel William Conyngham

VI

William Conyngham

SOLDIER AND POLITICIAN
1723–1784

DURING THE FIRST FEW YEARS of William Conyngham's succession to the property the Springhill family were no longer to be seen in the old home, but though deserted, it was not silent, for the noise of stone-hammer and chisel could be heard there for many a long day. The new owner was determined to add to his house, and, as in those more elaborate days things were not done hurriedly nor cheaply, neither time nor money were begrudged in making the necessary improvements. A West wing was added, containing what is now the large drawing-room, which was built as a dining-room wherein to entertain William's many friends – the 'polite fine company' so scornfully alluded to by his sarcastic old father. This room is forty-three feet long and each of the boards in the floor extends without any join to the full extent of the room. Another bedroom is said to have been then added to the East wing, part of which had existed in the first years of the house's early history – as marked in the old drawing of 1722. Over these lower bedrooms are the day and night nurseries, one of these having perhaps been built at this time, though William never had any children to occupy them.

Another alteration, which was probably made in Captain William's first years at Springhill, was the removal of the Bawn behind the house and of the walls and gate enclosing the front Bawn, or 'Court,' as these were no longer needed for protection.

At this time the following letter was addressed by William Conyngham to his steward, Matthew George, who, as well as his son who succeeded him, was for many years the trusted employé of the Conynghams.

The letter is written from Walworth, Limavady. July, 1770.

> Matthew
>
> The bearer, Mr. Carter, is so very unfortunate in his application for the mill of Coagh. He has proposed to give one hundred and four pounds a year, to pay half a year in advance and to be allowed £30 for putting her in repair. I have told him I expect one hundred guineas and to have my own grain ground toll free. … Let me know your opinion after you have treated with him. He has the character here from Mr. Sterling and other people of an honest and industrious man, and of some substance, and a good miller and mill-wright. Such a man I think wou'd be a proper tenant & a useful man in the Country. … Let me know if the Chimney-Piece[38] is put up and how other things are proceeding. I hope you'll begin the meadows as soon as possible. We have a great deal to mow. If you go to Derry while I am here, you may return this way, it is but little about and we may agree with this man or be off, as we see.
>
> Yrs. Wm. Conyngham.

Diana's sister-in-law Gertrude Clements with Mina in the large drawing room, built by William as a dining room. The chimney-piece mentioned in the above letter is clearly visible.

William was at this time Colonel of the Black – or 4th – Regiment of Horse (now the 7th Dragoon Guards). He was a great favourite in Society, and his ever genial character was mellowing into greater wisdom and stability.

In depicting William Conyngham's life, it is necessary to go back to a few years before his father's death, when the young man was winning laurels in the European Campaign, known as the Seven Years' War.[39]

Painting of the rear of the house with the smoking room

To this conflict went the gallant William and had occasion to shew his military skill. A little journal written during the campaign is still preserved at Springhill. It is, however, a dry record of marches and halts as the following short quotation will shew: –

> We halted there, the weather excessive stormy and wet. The 23rd we proceeded to our cantonments between Munden and Göttingen to Janosia and Gunterson near Dransfeld and Pembroke's quarter. The Head Quarter at Horst, very severe duty and bad weather. We remained in the cantonments the 9th of December, the weather so excessive bad that we were obliged to retire from the enterprise against Göttingen for the present, ... The duke's Quarters at Usler & Meringen.' &c.

Four years before Conyngham had joined the Regiment, the Black Horse, under Sir John Ligonier, had been prominent in the battle of Dettingen, at which the French were defeated. Another North of Ireland officer, young Cornet Henry Richardson[40] of Richhill, Co. Armagh, had won great fame in this engagement by his gallantry and mother-wit in having saved the Standard, which he carried, defending it stubbornly when surrounded by French horsemen, who cruelly wounded him. It is said that Richardson remarked in Irish fashion; 'If the wood of the Standard had not been of iron it would have been cut off.'

This Regiment was largely officered by Irishmen, having been stationed in Ireland until 1741, and it had a high reputation. 'The majority of the men consisted of the younger sons of old and respected families,' writes Holt Waring, 'and it was no uncommon thing for would-be recruits to pay from twenty to thirty guineas for the privilege of serving in the Corps.'

In 1742, on Hounslow Heath, the King (George the Second) reviewed regiments which were about to go to the War.

> The Black Horse had received the unexpected orders when the thin and wretched horses were at grass and the clothing of the men in shabby condition. The King's dragoon Guards and the Blues stood to the right and left of the King in smart new uniforms, while Ligonier's Horse cut but a sorry figure. Turning

> to the dejected Colonel, the King said: 'Ligonier, your men have the air of soldiers – their horses indeed look poorly, how is it?' 'Sire,' replied he, 'the men are Irish and gentlemen, the horses are English.'

Later on, Conyngham's Regiment was commended by General Conway. A very frail and crumbling paper is still extant:

> Capt. Conyngham's Muster Roll, ending the 31st March. 1759. The Right Honble Maj. Genl. Conway's Regiment of Horse.
>
> William Conyngham Capt.
> William Lovett Lieut.
> John Staples Cornet
> Thomas Shortt. Qr. master
> Thomas Hunt Trumpeter
> William Kennedy Corporal
> Matthew Evans Corporal
> William Robinson
> Robert Junck
> James McCullagh
> George Lamb
> William Cunningham
> John Foxwell
> Theophilus Eaton
> John Strange
> Sprained ankle Edward Coughlan
> Michael Culbert
> Edward Collins
> Jeremiah Connor
> John ———
> Henry Monroe
> William Miller
> Andrew Cunningham
> Humphrey Thomson
> William Dyer
> William ———
> Matthew Davis
> Robert Freestone Donaghmore
>
> April 11th 1759
>
> Mustered men–Capt. Conyngham's Troop in the Right Hon. Maj. Genl. Conway's Regiment of Horse, the Capt. Lieut. Cornet & Quartermaster with their led Horses, two Corporals, one Trumpeter and twenty one Private men mounted.
>
> N. Burscough.

General H.S. Conway, Conyngham's Commanding Officer, was none other

Reproduced from *Ulster Journal of Archaeology*

than the constant correspondent of Horace Walpole – that inveterate gossip-monger, who during the Campaign, sent him long epistles retailing all the London scandal. Conway had been in Ireland in 1755, as Secretary of State to Lord Haddington, then Lord Lieutenant. After the War he was Groom of the Bed-Chamber to George the Second, and was made a Field Marshal. He married the widowed Lady Aylesbury. In 1763, on account of his opposition to Government, he was dismissed both from Court and from his Regiment but on change of Ministry in 1765 he became Secretary of State.

There is no doubt that William Conyngham distinguished himself in the War. For a time he commanded his Regiment in Colonel Honeywood's place, and he must have been a fine figure mounted on his black charger caparisoned with the splendid gold embroidered saddle-back and holsters, which to this day repose in a cabinet at Springhill. Nor can there be any doubt that Conyngham was popular in his Regiment. Many letters survive which were written to him by brother officers and by members of the Allied Army. Some of these give a vivid picture of the conditions then prevailing. There is one from P.E. Count of Schaumburg Lippe written in broken English. It runs:

> Sir
>
> I have the honour to receive your letter of the Feb. last with the Attest you've done me the honour to send me and I take the liberty to explain to you the circumstandies better. … Upon the accounts that are sended to you for your Regimt and the Blewes there is no body upon who has received receipts and those that are here I send you them hereby. It are 5, but as well of your Rgt. as of the Blewes … but these poor inhabitans have received nothing. … If you or if your regiment could have the least desagreement of producing the receipt I would not do it for the whole world, & the inhabitans may then loose what they eitherwise would have so delivered had pay'd. … Here all is tranquil in the Quarters, there is fallen so deep Schnow in this Country the past weeke that different People, horses and Wagons are perished, and I fear it will give a great quantity of water. I hope you've receivd my last letter … with one other to Lord Pembroke. Our English Commissaire, who makes the Revue of the Artillery horses & dined yesterday with me, told that you not only would stay in Germany but be reinforced by 6 Regiment horses and 3 Dragons & 3 light

> horses … so I hope to make you against my Compliments by mouth so as I do here by writing of me and my whole family – being for ever with true mind and esteem Sir
>
> Dearest Friend
>
> Allverdessen Your P. E. Count of Schaumburg Lippe
>
> Feb. 15th
>
> 1762
>
> P.S. – I beg leave humbly for the faults by writing and in the explication having written this in *haste*.

William Conyngham has also left letters from Colonel C. Lyon, from Coblenz, written in French, two from Josias, Comte de Waldeck, written in 1762, and four or five from Lord Pembroke, a brother officer who appears to have been warmly attached to him and grateful for his help and advice during an unfortunate and discreditable affair to which Horace Walpole alludes in his letters, i.e., Lord Pembroke's elopement with a Miss Hunter, who accompanied him abroad. Walpole, writing on Feb. 22nd to Geo. Montagu, remarks in his vivacious manner:

> In all your reading true or false have you ever heard of a young Earl, married to the most beautiful woman in the world, a lord of the bedchamber, a general officer, & with a great estate, quitting everything, resigning wife and world, and embarking for life in a Pacquet-boat with a Miss? I fear your connections will but too readily lead you to the name of the peer, it is Henry, Earl of Pembroke, the nymph Kitty Hunter. The town and Lady Pembroke were but too much witnesses to this intrigue last Wednesday at a great ball at Lord Middleton's. On Thursday they decamped. … The Earl has left a bushel of letters behind him, to his Mother, to Lord Bute, to Lord Ligonier (the two last to resign his employments) & to Mr. Stopford, whom he acquits of all privity to his design. In none he justifies himself, unless this is a justification that having long tried in vain to make his wife hate & dislike him, he had no way left but this. It may not be the worst event that could have happened to her. You may easily conceive the shock that such an exploit must occasion.

In a subsequent letter, of February 25th, Horace Walpole adds:

> No news yet of the runaways, but all that comes out antecedent to the escape is more and more extraordinary and absurd. The day of the elopement he had invited his wife's family and other folk to dinner with her, but said he must himself dine at a tavern, but he dined privately in his own dressing-room, put on a sailor's habit and black wig, that he had brought home with him in a bundle, & threatened the servants that he would murder them if they mentioned it to his wife. He left a letter for her which the Duke of Marlborough was afraid to deliver to her, and opened. It desired that she would not write to him, as it would make him completely mad. He desires the King would preserve his rank of Major General, as some time or other he may serve again.

A few days before the elopement took place. Lord Pembroke wrote the following letter to William Conyngham:

Wilton House, Feb. 12th 1762

Dear Conyngham

I am literally so lame a writer that I can scarce scrawl enough to ask pardon for my long & unpardonable silence. I have got a bloody hand by parting two dogs, one of whose teeth has made a largish orifice between my first and second fingers. If ever I meddle in frays again unnecessarily!

As I hope you do me the justice not to doubt the pleasure I should have of being of use to you, I will tell you my mind openly & that of more knowing ones whom I have consulted. After having lavished away Brevets, they (by 'they' always are meant the Great) have stoped their hands & seem resolved to give no more. For my own part I should think one for a majority might still be had. though not a Lieut. Colcy. … If you have the mind to try the Majority, to muster your forces & command me, put me at the head, rear or centre of them, as I can be most usefull, I shall be very happy to do my best. I hope all ye Blacks are well. In spite of motions, protests &c. I shall soon have the pleasure of seeing them again en bivouac. I have called, *en ceremonie & hors de ceremonie*, on Mrs. Toby, but *kein* admittance. I am not certain whether she has not gone to Ireland. A strapping well-hung young countryman of yours is said to have taken possession of her out and in posts, & will admit of no company there. Staples[41] is gone to Ireland from Bath, where he left his Cash with the Sharpers and his heart with Miss W —— , his old toast, both I fear at very low interest. I hear Osnaburg is a petit Londres, the bodys knocking down & picking pockets as in our Capital. The expedition is going out, & another soon to Portugal, of 12000 men, with Lord Tyrawley & Waldegreve. God knows where the men are to come from. Poor Germany is indeed voted on, but the Devil of a Permit for it yet provided.

Pigot's medal was easily explained. I shewed it to an antiquarian, who read it pat and laughed at our ignorance, as if soldiers were obliged to know at all how to read! On the medal is

Fides Siles inf
vratis D xxxi Oct
M.D. CCLXI

The homage of the lower Silesia – Breslau the 31st Oct. 1761.

N.B. The medal was struck at *Breslau* which, in modern German Latin, is called Wratislavia. …

If you approve of trying this majority I should advise you to send me four memorials, one for the King, of course, to Ld Granby, under whose immediate command you are, to Lord Ligonier as a Black, to a Commander in Chief & to Capt. Townsend, Secretary of War – to prevent opposition. Excuse my dictating this, but you would have it so. Adieu, D^{r}. Conyngham. Remember me to all friends & believe me most sincerely & obedly Yrs. Pembroke.

The books for the Court of Alverdessen shall not be forgot. This letter is addressed to Capt. Wm. Conyngham

Com^{g} the 4th Horse in
the Allied Army
Germany.

Less than ten days after this letter was penned, the writer eloped with Miss Hunter.[42]

William's early Command of his regiment is explained by a letter written to General Honeywood shortly before:

Schwarzoff Jan 1762

Sir

The absence of your Lt Col. and Major at this time gives me the honour of the care of your Regiment & also an opportunity (which I have long wished for) of addressing myself to you.

Before this time I have had no right, now I claim some little, as Commanding your Regiment & hope you will permit me to trouble you with a letter as often as everything new happens in these parts, either in respect to your Regiment or any Movement of the Army. In either case I shall not fail to give you the best intelligence I am capable of, if you will do me honour to accept of my letters. Lt Col. East left us the 27th of last month, & carrys every return of the deficiencies of the Regiment to you, till that time; there is nothing since then to acquaint you with except one man Lyon of the Lt Cols group being returned unfit for further Service, by the Captain sent to the Hospital from the Brigade, having lost the use of a leg from a hurt he received last Campaign. We thought all these invalides from Bremen were to have been sent from there. We have applied to General Conway & hope he will put us in a proper method of sending them to England without putting the poor creatures to the expense of the journey through Holland out of their own pockets. General Conway has been for some time at Hildesheim at the Head Quarters. … We expect some orders at his return which may give us some little hint whether we are to have an Expedition this Winter or not, it is variously talked of. If we are ordered forward, your regiment, I'll venture to say, both officers and men, will be as strong at least as any of the Brigade of Cuirassiers. We have now ten officers (exclusive of Capt. Webber who is Major of the Brigade). We should choose (if it depends upon us) to remain where we are for some months longer, but if we *must* go, we are all ready. I beg leave, Sir, to present my best compliments to Mrs. Honeywood & to wish her and you & your young gentlemen (besides the common compliments of the season) every happyness you can wish, & beg you will honour me with any Commands you have, which you may depend shall always be most punctually observed by, Sir, your most obedt. & Most Humble Servt.

Wm. Conyngham

From Col. Lyon to W. Conyngham at Willingholtshausen, Osnabruck.

Thursday

Dr Conyngham

I shall enclose L^d^ P's last letter, though I expect him here every moment, he will be with you almost as soon as the letter. … I hope you will all escape this Damn'd Distemper, I have been myself very ill with it. ... I hope once more our Quarters are near you, for I shall want some comfort after being so long in this solitary place. Adieu

Yours C. Lyon.

There are letters written at this time from the delinquent, Lord Pembroke, mentioning the troubles and anxieties of his escapade. One runs as follows:

Tuesday night Ap. 13. 1762

Utrecht

Dear Conyngham

I am this moment come back here & receive your's, for which I return you ten thousand thanks. You are very good to me. Since I saw you I have recd but one letter from England, viz. from Stopford. He says he has many for me, flatters me with everything I could wish and y^t^ he will be with us immediately himself. Since that I've heard from no one. The wind indeed has been ever since constantly East. I hope to see you soon. The first Army people I shall see will be at Osnabrugge. The Conway's & Taylor's houses are probably the only ones I shall enter there, & as the latter is a talkative fellow & sees everybody, you'll much oblige me by seeing him yourself as if by chance as soon as possible, and doing & saying the same there in respect to me as you did at Conway's you'll very much oblige me.

Finding the way a little paved after so many misrepresentations as I find have been sett about on our account, will take off a little from the feelings you must suppose I have, & prevent people's unthinkingly saying what they would perhaps not say before me. Miss Hunter[43] goes away this week, she begs her compts and feels more oblig'd to you than she can bid me tell you. I trust too I shall see you soon & all be as well as can be after such a shock. I dont, wonder people's blaming me severely, even such as are not nice, yet if it would not seem vindicating one's own conduct, which I dont intend to do, I should be glad to know how the nicest of them would have acted in my circumstances supposing the step taken & its unhappy consequences taking place, as was our case, for I cannot help thinking that few, very few, would have resisted such a temptation.[44]

Adieu my dear Conyngham, dont forget Taylor's & believe me

Ever yours most sincerely & affectly

Pembroke.

Did you ever receive mine?

Remember me to the Blacks, pray.

Another letter runs:

> Dr Conyngham I trouble you very often, quite shamefully I own, but' tis your own fault. I cant believe the Cavalry will be settled differently to our wishes. ... M.H. is waiting for a passport, which she has great hopes of. ... We shall never meet more certainly, but she shall allways have the greatest care & attention from me every way. She has received a very unexpected letter from England. Nothing, my dear Conyngham, would make me happier than your being so good as to give me your company. I was allways attached to you from acquaintance since we met & have served together.
>
> Remember me to the Mess & believe me,
>
> Ever yrs
>
> Pembroke.

Lord Pembroke also wrote to his dear 'Leo' (Col. Lyon) on the subject of his difficulties. Two letters still exist in which he mentions the large annuity he was settling on the young lady, whose friends appear to have forgiven her bad conduct, and he alludes to his affection for and indebtedness to Conyngham 'which will ever bind me to him.'

The letter runs:

> Dr Lyon
>
> One word & little more. I am on the German Staff. Ld Ligon'r has rd the King's orders for it, & yng Lig. has just wrote me word. All M.H's family are willing to be reconciled to her & want her to come home immediately, on a supposition she is not ... at least they take no notice of it. When I say 'all,' I may say except her father & *he*, by what they say, is coming in & keeps out more from what he feels. I have settled on her 800 per annum & 200 fr child for life, & much wish her, in case of accidents, to keep up that independency, which they of course would prevent, but as she is resolv'd not to stir & I think with great reason ... there is time enough to settle that, & I hope even her friends will by that time grow cool & reasonable enough for her sake. I advise it, though they must for ever curse me.
>
> ... Ever yrs. My dear Lyon
>
> P.
>
> Pray shew this to Conyngham. Kitty begs her compts. to you.
>
> 24 April 1762.

The following letter has been found among old papers at Springhill, which must refer to Lord Pembroke's elopement with Miss Hunter. It is to William Conyngham from J. Fortescue,[45] one of the Fortescues of Co. Louth, and is written from Dublin on May 4, 1762:

> My dear Conyngham,
>
> I received yours of the 6th last week, but the hurry of the close of our sessions and of our Ld Lieut's departure prevented my answering it directly. I am very

> glad you are well & that you have had so agreeable a tour through Holland[46] as your letter to Lady Clan: mentions. As to mine, I do not know how to answer it. I read the same goodness of heart in it I ever loved you for, and you are not deceived in me, but what can I do for that unhappy girl whose fate has cost me so many uneasy moments, I should say days, I am at a loss to conceive. This, were she entirely penitent, which I much doubt, (having seen a letter from her to my wife lately), is of all others the most improper country on earth for her to come to – the region of scandal, vanity and prejudice, As for me, I am, I hope, pretty free from the latter, but that makes me a more quick-sighted looker on of other's. I have just opened two letters from England and find her friends have try'd to get her over, but failed and will think no more of her. They have sent me copies of all the letters that passed. I did most sincerely love her and sincerely lament her unhappy passion for that damned villain, which I fear is too strong still to suffer her to think as she ought, & must be entirely got over before we can be of real use to her.
>
> Her Aunt Gray, I find, has done everything in her power to make her return as smooth as possible, but she now gives her up, & will hear no more of her, as she says, at least *till sorrow has brought her to a sense of her crime*. My wife is most deeply afflicted, and, had not the secret been most wonderfully well kept, it would have killed her. She is now very well & can talk with composure about it to me, but it has made a deep impression.
>
> We leave town in a few days for the Country, where I propose to stay till after next Christmas, and I hope we shall have the pleasure of shewing a very jolly recruit for you when you have got a Regiment, as I flatter myself you will come and see your friends when Winter comes on. I have often intended to write to you for some time past, but I still waited till I cou'd tell you your affairs with your father were settled, but I fear we must force him by law but I suppose you hear enough of this from others. My lovely cousin[47] has been the subject of talk for some days. Ld Boyle & Sir John Mead, and I hear another great fortune, were at her feet, but unfortunately Lord N. came up from Quarters while I thought everything looked well for Lord B. and has determined her in his favour, but he has not married her yet. I wish it was done, for fear he will not be able to resist his father's commands, tho' he vows he will disobey them if he refuses his consent. Lord Shannon & his son have behaved in the handsomest manner. My wife desires to be remembd to you and our comp^{ts} to the Staples.[48]
>
> Ever yours most affectionately J. Fortescue.

It seems fairly clear that Capt. William Conyngham had exerted his influence with Lord Pembroke to free Miss Hunter from her unhappy entanglement.

A year later, Horace Walpole revealed later developments of this affair in a letter to George Montagu, written on March 29th, 1763:

> Lord and Lady Pembroke are reconciled and live again together. Mr. Hunter would have taken his daughter too, but upon condition she should give back her settlement to Lord Pembroke, and her child. She replied nobly that she did not trouble herself about fortune & would willingly depend on her father, but

> for her child she had nothing left to do but to take care of it and would not part with it, so she keeps both.

William Conyngham seems to have been a wise and true friend, even in such disgraceful circumstances as those in which Lord Pembroke found himself. We believe the advice was good and that there was no condoning of the crime.

There are other letters which give an impression of the affection which Conyngham cherished for the regiment which he commanded – the 4th, or Black Horse. The officers are alluded to as 'the Blacks' – and the names of those mentioned in letters are; G. Burdett, Col. East, Roberts, Colclough – 'John' (at Kilkenny) Colonel Holmes at Tullagh, Pigott, in Dublin, Purefoy, the General and Webber, Major Medows 'Our old friend Mick Hinds in Derry,' Vaughan, &c.

These long ago events, escapades and the historic campaign, are shrouded in the mists of the past, and we are only reminded of them by a bundle of faded letters and papers.

The Seven Years' War having been ended by the Peace of Paris, and our army having returned to England, William Conyngham was stationed in that country, and letters of his which are still extant are addressed to 'St. James' Coffee House, London,' much as present day officers have theirs addressed to the 'United Service' or 'Naval and Military' Clubs.

William was evidently in no great hurry to return to his inheritance in Ulster,[49] but subsequent letters to him, addressed to Springhill shew that after a while he took up his abode there.[50]

His brother David's work lay in Belfast, where he married, in July, 1773, Ann, the daughter of the late Margetson Saunders of that City and Catherine, his wife – then a widow. This lady[51] was apparently not approved of by David's relations. Her miniature reveals a stout good-humoured dame, homely, with a *nez rétroussé*, and probably a busybody. There were no children of this marriage, but Anne Lenox, the only remaining sister, had a family of six, five of whom lived with her and Clotworthy in Derry city. Their soldier son, John, having survived the wars, was not much mentioned in after years and is said to have lived and died in Portugal. Of Anne's other sons, George, Clotworthy and William, more will be said in due time. The daughter, Rebecca, married a Mr. Stafford and was mother of a Mrs. Mauleverer, but of the younger Anne Lenox little is known, and we may wonder if she married with her parents' consent or was cut off with 5/- according to her grandfather's will.

As for William Conyngham's brother, John, who was also on foreign service during the War, (at Minorca among other places), he never married, but died in Bath in 1774. The only relics he has left are his will,[52] a silver watch, the spinning wheel and the tattered remains of his portrait as a baby Cupid in a pink dress.

For ten years after his father's death, Colonel William Conyngham remained a bachelor, but at length, having reached the age of fifty-two, he decided to embark on matrimony. His choice was a beautiful widowed lady – Mrs. Hamilton[53] – whose first husband had been John Hamilton of Castlefin, and her father John Hamilton of Brownhall, in Co. Donegal, a finely-timbered demesne, watered by a river where curious caves exist.

Mrs Jean Hamilton d. 1788

In the dining-room at Brownhall her portrait as a girl hung not long ago, and explains why she was always known as 'the beautiful Jean,' as does her lovely face in a diamond-mounted miniature, painted in after life.

Of Jean's first husband, John Hamilton, but little is known,[54] but there is an old story that he was often in a debtor's prison, where his wife and four daughters used to visit him, bringing with them his fresh linen which they had beautifully laundered.

William Conyngham was averse to the idea of the four daughters coming with their mother to live at Springhill. Evidently he could not see himself in the light of step-father to half-grown girls. This problem worried him excessively, and at length he asked his nephew, George Lenox, to use his persuasions with the lady to make other arrangements for her children. George was at this time Mrs. Hamilton's agent for the Castlefin property, so was thought to have some influence with 'the beautiful Jean.'

Shortly after the marriage, William penned the following letter to his nephew:

> Dear George
>
> I write from Castle Upton on my way to Belfast, where I have some particular business with my brother, & I hope to satisfy him with respect to you, but if you come to Springhill before I return there, I would have you come over for a day to Belfast. … I suppose this will find you at Derry, returned from Brown Hall. … When you go to Springhill I would have you mention to Mrs. Conyngham the proposal I made to you some time ago with respect to the future arrangement of her Family, but you must sound her with the greatest delicacy. When I know from you how she seems to relish it, I can then better talk to her myself of the particulars of my motives and sentiments. You may let her know that we talked of this matter some time ago, but, till Tatty[55] was removed, the scheme was not ripe for communication. You must lay the advantages before her that must ensue to her Family from such an arrangement, but I must repeat it to you to talk to her with the utmost delicacy and by herself. Your usual rapidity is too much for the fineness of her feelings upon a subject of such a

> nature, for probably it may at first appear to her as separating her Family from her, but her good sense and cool reasoning I hope will soon conquer that natural weakness. Digest well in your own mind the advantage both to them and to you and to the Estate, and they evidently will appear to you all; for the retired way of life the girls must live with me, they have very little opportunity of meeting with matches suitable to their situations, which I look upon as a very material consideration at their time of life, and I cannot alter my manner of life upon their accounts, nor can I either afford or think it proper to take them into the world among my connections, where I should be happy to take my wife sometimes.
>
> Yours sincerely and affectly Wm. Conyngham.

What a change must have come over the once gay and dashing blade!

> Not that in truth when life began
> He shunned the flutter of the fan,
> He too had maybe pinked his man
> In beauty's quarrel.
> But now his fervent youth had flown
> Where lost things go, and he was grown
> As staid and slow paced as his own
> Old hunter Sorrel.

There does not seem to have been very much romance in this elderly marriage – an affair of sober affection, comfort and convenience. William seems to have been something of a diplomatist, and also somewhat jealous.

It is amusing to find a letter on the same subject from the other point of view. It was written to the bride by her friend M. Cole.

> I received my dearest Jenny's letter, and I am much obliged for the Almanack, but shall expect a very long letter from you soon to tell me of the courage you had, and that you was not afraid of shewing your affection to your children on your meeting them, and at every other time, for believe me, my friend, whilst you continue a restraint in shewing your feelings for them you never will be happy. I wish you happiness at any rate consistent with your character. You have sacraficed a great dale for your children and been an affectionate Mother, & in my opinion if you would exert a proper spirit and be constant in it you would preveall. Harry thinks as I do and is sure you could get everything you please if you would but do it. Let me hear a good account of you, have you got any servants at Belfast? Beware of not having your children sufficiently with you, for from what my Aunt Price[56] said, if your company does not see you make companions of them, they will not think themselves the least obliged to ask them. Certainly no company is so fit for them as yours, & I would insist on what was reasonable and keep to what you say, or you give hopes to a certain person that he may yet preveall in his own way yet by persisting. Tell me the reception you met with at Belfast – if they asked for the girls. Give my love to them.

The Dutch garden

I have got a cold. I had a little spice of it, but went out in the Cabrioly with Harry to Down, & have been lay'd up since with a soar throat. My Uncle and Aunt intreated him so, & his Horse being lame both contributed to make us happy in his Company longer than he intended. Indeed my poor Uncle has great pleasure in him, he is a good creature, tho' a very great cheat at Codrill,[57] tell him I say so, & he'll tell you how he cheated me.

We have had no variety since we saw you. Are the Stuards returned, if they are, pray present my Compliments to them. They are both favourites of mine. We expect Crum to-morrow or Tuesday. I write so far tonight, as I dont know but Harry may leave us tomorrow, so I would be ready, but I'll not finish till I'm certain. Its my only request to you, my D^{r}, to have a will of your own & to persist in what you think is right to make yourself happy. Tell me you are so and love me as usual and you will contribute materially to your Mariana's happiness. Adieu for the present.

Harry I am sure will leave to-morrow, so I will finish this … were I to write another it would be in the same straine. … The more you submit in a certain circumstance, I main the children, the more he will encroach … & by degrees he'll find its as good to give up. Its impossible to leave Hollymount as soon as one intended, I now don't leave it till the middle of Aprill &. then go to Dublin. … I hope to meet with a lodgen or house to my mind, have you thought of taking a trip there, if you do … you would meet with so many of your friends that you would be very happy & it would do you good.

Adieu, my dearest friend, & believe your happiness is very dear to your

M. Cole.

Sunday ye 31st (continued)

I begin a third time. At last Harry is determined, or rather they would if he stayed till tomorrow give him leave, tho' with regret, to leave them – his portmanteau has been hid, everything don to make him stay, I am sure we shall miss him very much.

My sister says she has wrote to you about Jinny Logan who has quit her place & is now at liberty to attend you … I feel very much for the distress I know you must have been in – I wish you had a Cook. I know Jinny is not equal to both plaices, so dont depend on her for anything of cookery. I wish you may be happy in her. I think she will ease you of a great dale of trouble & you may look on her as one of your own people. What have you don with Molly, will she be housemaid. I wish to Got you had a sett of Servts that would make you easy as to your House. I often wished I could be one week with you, had I wings I would have flown of directly to my Jenny & given her all the comfort in my power. Tell me how your day passed of that your quality sister did you the honour to spend with you.

I desire you will burn all my letters or I shall allways write with restraint. My love to your Husband, & tell him the happier he makes you the more I will love him. In my last I told you I go to Dublin. Monday fortnight I leave this. You may direct to my brother's for me & you know anything in my power I will do for you.

Ever truly

Your M. Cole.

Warm-hearted, strong-willed 'Mariana'! (to use her *nom-de-plume*, adopted in accordance with the custom which prevailed among sentimental young ladies of those times). Her dearest Jenny did not, however, do as she begged. She did not 'preveall' in persuading the nameless one to relent in his decision, and she certainly did not comply with M. Cole's desire that she would burn all her letters, seeing that this letter has survived for a hundred and seventy years still unconsumed!

Poor Mrs. Jean Conyngham! Did she wander disconsolately in the Beech walk and 'Green Garden,' lonely and craving for the companionship of her children? or did her deep affection for her masterful husband prove sufficient solace? Perhaps she was after all, not unhappy at Springhill during her nine years there with Col. William 'in a retired way of life.'

From William's letter to his nephew, it seems that an arrangement was made for the four young ladies to reside in Derry City under the roof of George's parents, Clotworthy and Anne Lenox, the latter's death not having occurred till June, 1777. In an old account book in George Lenox's[58] handwriting such entries as these occur;

Paid to Mr. Flanagan, the dancing master, for one year's tuition to Miss J. Hn	£4 11 0
By cash pd John Shannon money due him for instructing Miss Bess Hamilton in the guitar	1 2 9
By Mrs. Conyngham pd Miss Bess Hamilton's subscription for the Assembly	– 11 4
Pd for making a riding habit for Miss B. Hamilton	– 6 0
By one half year's diet and lodging due this day for Miss R.H. and Miss E. H. 22 days at 1/6 ye day	– – –
By Wm. Conyngham pd for 2 hattes for yr postillions	– 7 7

A long letter is extant, written in Feb. 1776, to Mrs. Conyngham from Greenfield by the Revd. Mr. McGhee, presumably a parson living near Castlefin. He mentions a lady who was probably destined to be governess to the Miss Hamiltons.

> Miss Barclay's indisposition of body & the intenseness of the frost were the only hindrances to her going to Springhill since you mentioned her to me in your last letter … so I had prepared horses to carry her & the servant.... I prevailed on her to stay till to-morrow morning. She will set out early & will deliver the purse I send by her with 40 guineas safe into your hands, if she will get passage over the Alps that are stretched between Dungiven & Maghera without molestation from robbers … I send you the two volumes of Addison's works wh I hope will be carefully read by Bob Patten's little friend & her sisters, who I am persuaded will do everything within their sphere to please Mr. Conyngham and you – & to improve themselves.
>
> Your truly sincere and faithful humble Servant
> Robert McGhee.[59]

Colonel and Mrs. William Conyngham seem to have been a much attached and a very happy couple.

We can imagine their stately mode of life – driving in their coach-and-four into the Court at Springhill, ascending the steps, and passing through the panelled hall to the great oak staircase, with its wainscotted sides and twisted oak rails; William stalwart and distinguished, with fresh-coloured face and white wig, its queue tied behind with a black ribband bow, and the lovely Jean, elegant and dignified, with sweet pale face beneath the towering powdered headdress or *tête* worn by dames of that period. Let us watch them passing into the passage of the east wing, and to the left through the strange little latched door to the oak panelled 'Gun room.' Then on through double doors to Mrs. Conyngham's Dressing-room (for in olden times it was the wife and not the husband who owned the dressing-room). This room is spacious and pleasant – sunbeams stealing through the three windows of the bow and playing on the chintz hangings and carved pillars of the four-poster bed. A deep peace hovers around the old four-poster. It was once hung with curtains embroidered by the deft hands of 'the mistress,' which are now folded in an ottoman, the colours unfaded, but the linen ground-work somewhat tattered. These may indeed have been the 'wrought bed on dimity with the wrought hangings' alluded to in old George Conyngham's will.[60] Many a peaceful happy dream have those hangings enclosed – the six curtains all carefully drawn at night, as was customary, to exclude any breath of the dreaded night air. A door at the far side of this room opens into the large bedroom, which looks out on to the back of the house, where the great Cedar once spread its branches.

No doubt the Conynghams of 1775 constantly interchanged visits with their friends and neighbours who lived within driving distance. Of these, the nearest

were the Staples' of Lissan, a family which twice intermarried with the owners of Springhill, and the ancient houses Lissan and Springhill are only four miles apart. Lissan House stands high among finely timbered woods, threaded by a trout stream, which spreads into a musical waterfall below the curious irregular mansion. At this time the owner was the handsome and wealthy Right Hon. John Staples,[61] a son of the Revd. Thomas, Rector of Derryloran, who had written to old George Conyngham as 'Cosin Conyngham.' John had been in the Black Horse, and though we know from Lord Pembroke's letter that he was gallivanting in Bath in 1762, he had since those days married twice, having, in 1774, brought to Lissan as his second wife the charming eldest daughter of Richard, 3rd Viscount Molesworth. This peer, owner of Breckdenstown, Co.

A recent photograph of the staircase showing the yew bannisters.

Lissan House, home of the Staples family
Courtesy of Mrs Hazel Dolling

Dublin, had been A.D.C. to the great Duke of Marlborough, and at Ramillies had saved the Duke's life by lending him his horse in a moment of peril.[62] Afterwards Molesworth was Commander-in-Chief in Ireland, and married Dublin's fairest toast – lovely Mary Ussher, whose tragic fate in 1763 had thrilled the country with horror. The tragedy will be recounted later in this history.

Her daughter Henrietta – or 'Harriet' – had beauty and charm, and a strong character which caused her to triumph over misfortune, and she left behind in the family circle the mark of her personality to a remarkable extent. Many of her letters, books, diary and other possessions, are at Springhill in the keeping of present day Conynghams, who descend from her daughter Charlotte.

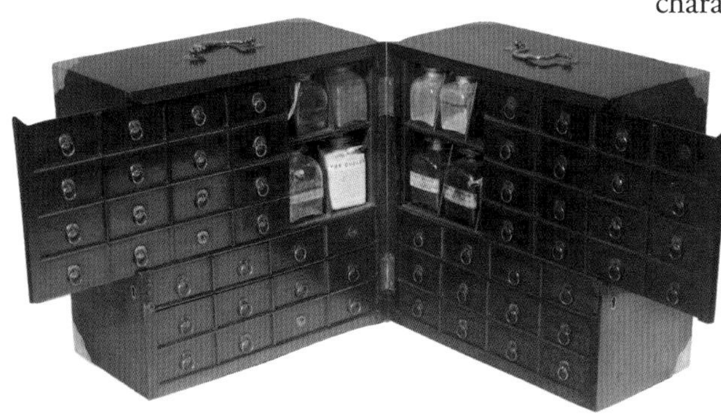

Medicine chest carried throughout the campaign for the Spanish Succession by Viscount Molesworth.

It is probable that this spirited lady and Mrs. Jean Conyngham were congenial to one another and that they often met, for in spite of being crippled with a wooden leg, Harriet Staples seems to have driven all over the Country in her 'Cabriolet,' often recording in her diary that she had driven to 'Killy' (moon) to see her sister 'Bess and her brats,' also to the Hewitts at Derryloran Rectory, to the O'Neills at Shane's Castle, and to Tullymore.

Other friends of the Conynghams were the Lindesays of Loughry, Stewarts of Killymoon, Lowrys of Rockdale and Pomeroy (which the Revd. James Lowry built soon after this time, for his two sons) the Castlestewarts of Stuart Hall, Caulfeilds (Drumcairne) and Richardsons of Drum as well as, of course, the Castle Upton cousins.[63]

Many letters from members of these families to William Conyngham and his wife survive at Springhill. Shortly before William's marriage, Lord Castlestewart wrote thus to him:

Stuart Hall 2nd Sept. 1774

A thousand thanks to my good friend for his care and perfect execution of the business I gave him the trouble of at Omagh. … I am extremely happy, my dear Conyngham, at the very pleasing and satisfactory Tour you have had, as it affords me the prospect of your being in a few months to be disposed of so certainly to your own Happyness, & also that I shall in some degree be a Sharer of it by the acquisition of so amiable a neighbour. But after all let me tell you you will experience Regret, but it is of this sort, that you and I have idled away so many days without that domestick real happyness at length you find yourself possessed of.

The great Blessing is to know where to fix with some assurance of happyness, so soon as I shall be able to obtain that, no time shall be lost, on my side, in following your good example.[64] I am as always, bound to you for your friendship & which I always reflect on with pleasure, and shou'd be very happy in any opportunity of shewing you how truly I am

My Dear Friend
Your faithfull
and affectionate
Castlestewart

Harriet Staples *née* Molesworth 1745–1815, second wife of John Staples MP of Lissan, or Harriet Conolly, his first wife, by William Hoare of Bath. She is painted as 'Personification of Spring'.

I shall be here all this month and shall certainly expect the pleasure of your taking this on your way home, particularly after your having felt Lord Clanbrassil's[65] pulse, to whom if you think proper, I beg you will do me the honour of presenting my congratulatory compliments.

C. St.

Stanhope St. April 11th. 1774.
Dear Sir

Nothing can flatter me more than your goodness & friendship for me. The news Mrs. Buttle told you is, I believe, very true. I imagine the affair is now settled, but as yet no steps can be taken in writings, as Miss Foley's father has been

> out of Town at his son's Election at Droitwich, & will not return before next Saturday. It is no secret now, and indeed I wonder it was not talked of sooner, as some steps were taken on my side towards it last year. I do not know what to say to express my gratitude for the very flattering things you say, but that I shall only wish for every opportunity of proving the very great Truth & Esteem with which I am
>
> Dear Sir
> Your most Faithfull affecte & most Obed^{t} humble Servt
> Clanbrassil
>
> I wish you would come this way. Your room's empty. My best comp^{ts} to your brother.

Some-months after his own hopes were fulfilled, Lord Clanbrassil wrote again to Conyngham, this time to send congratulations in similar circumstances;

> Tollymore Park. Sept 2nd
> Dear Sir
>
> I have this very moment received your very obliging letter of last night from Dundalk. Ly Clanbrassil desires her comp^{ts} to you and joins in wishing you all the Joy & Happiness you deserve, which I have no doubt of your having from the choice you have made. We are both extremely sorry we were not at Dundalk to receive you, & to have the honour of being made known to Mrs. Conyngham.
>
> I am Dear Sir
> With truest Regards
> Your most Faithfull
> & most obed^{t} humble Servt
> Clanbrassil.

In later years there are other letters from both Lord and Lady Clanbrassil[66] to the Conynghams, one alludes to a proposed visit together to the Giant's Causeway and mentions a Mr. Winnington and Lady Clanbrassil's sisters.

The allusions to Dundalk in the foregoing letters refer to the fact that William Conyngham sat in the Irish Parliament for that Borough, consequently he and his wife were frequently in Dublin, which made a variation in their quiet life when at Springhill. When in the country Jean spent much time in needlework and embroidery. For many hours this gentle lady must have sat at Springhill plying her needle. How many women of the present day leave behind them such lovely and lasting mementos of their skill and patience? Many loving thoughts must have been woven into Mistress Jean's *petit point* and cutwork, relating to the four young daughters who were so dear to her.

Her husband had objected to their residing at Springhill, giving as an excuse the plea that the girls were unlikely in so retired an abode to meet with suitable husbands! But young George Lenox, his nephew and heir, to whom the excuse was made solved the problem for Jane, the eldest Miss Hamilton, by marrying her himself. This marriage was apparently a great joy and interest to the elderly couple at Springhill, and it seemed indeed an ideal arrangement. We find William writing to his brother-in-law, Clotworthy Lenox, broaching the subject of his son's marriage, and though Conyngham probably felt some coolness towards the father, he evidently loved young George, and at that time, and later on, wrote to the impetuous young man letters of wise and affectionate counsel.

This is shewn by letters from William Conyngham to George's father Clotworthy Lenox.

My dear Lenox

I had the pleasure of receiving your very satisfactory letter yesterday. Indeed it was no more than I expected from your tender affection & generous treatment of your children. My dearest Wife is very much pleased with your prejudice in favour of her and her Family, and We have no doubt this connection we have in view will turn out to the advantage & satisfaction of all partys. For my part I confess to you the Prospect of such successors will make the remainder of my time in this world easie and Happy. My wife writes to George, so I will not answer his letter. I have just now a messenger from David. He is laid up in the Gout. … I am, my dear Lenox, with sincere affection

Yours very truly
Wm. Conyngham

Springhill Jan. 26th. 1779

My dear Lenox

Your son George left me this morning after passing as much time with me as to give me entire satisfaction of his worth, good sense and amiable disposition. … You may suppose that my observation of him was pretty accurate and more minute than it would have been on a Common visit. … He will acquaint you with the plan I suggested to him after having some knowledge of him. … I must tell you he has answered my utmost wishes as to propriety & delicacy of conduct so much, that he has gained the good opinion of my Wife and her family & prejudiced them much in his favour. I think there is little wanting to complete our plan but your approbation. … You and I, my dear Lenox, are both advancing in the vale of Life, and it is natural for People of thought and Prudence to look out for a worthy successor to the goods of this Life, in whom they may hope to have pleasure & comfort as long as they remain in it, and good grounds to think they will be worthily represented hereafter. There is very little Prospect of my Brother or Me having Children, & of course my next view is to your Family, if They merit my distinguishing them. I have great pleasure in seeing such qualities in George as point him out to me as the object of my wishes as a Successor. I remember some time ago I mentioned to you the propriety of George settling himself … to attach him to some settled mode of Life.

… You said nothing woud give you so much pleasure. … The scheme He is now upon occurred to me as the most advantageous to your Family and the most agreeable to me that could happen. ... It waits only for your sanction to compleat it. I know you will do everything in your power that George will ask, to forward his Happyness. … I never heard any young man express more affection for a Parent than he does for you. The choice he has made has been sensible & prudent. … She is a girl of an amiable disposition, cultivated by the example & instruction of, I will venture to say, one of the best women in the world, who has from their infancy instilled into her daughters every virtuous principle the Human Mind is capable of receiving. They have been trained in innocence, modesty and economy, which in this dissipated world are qualities rarely to be met, with, and I think preferable to every consideration of fortune or ambition. There is a pretty little Estate among them, which will be every day growing better, and by the management of a man of prudence & business … will be a pretty thing. In the meantime I know you will do your best to make your living together happy. Her desires will be very moderate, and I think it will make the remainder of your Life – which I hope will be long and happy – more easie than anything else could happen to you. … George also, I think, must be looked on as the representative of your family in Derry, where you have been so long established with so much credit and Regard. I cannot see by candlelight to write, but wou'd not delay, to tell you my mind on so interesting a subject, till next post.

Ever yours my dear Lenox sincerely & affectly

Wm. Conyngham.

Either Harriet Staples *née* Molesworth (1745–1815), second wife of John Staples MP of Lissan or, possibly, Harriet Conolly, his first wife, by Francis Cotes.

George and Jenny – as she was always called – were married in 1779 and continued to live in Derry city near George's old father, by that time a widower and taking charge of the delicate younger son, Clotworthy or 'Tatty,' whose mental balance was uncertain.

Jenny's mother was indeed devoted to her son-in-law, and her letters to him abound with expressions of love and confidence. Here is one written shortly before the marriage in her small pointed handwriting:

Dear George

I heard with pleasure yesterday that you got safe to Derry and found your Father well, he is a worthy man, & I'm convinced will leave nothing in his power undone that can contribute to the happyness of you and my Dearest

Jenny. As your Uncle writes to him by this post there is no necessity for my saying any more on a subject which I need not tell you is very near my heart and which I trust in God will contribute to the happyness and satisfaction of all parties. My good opinion of you, joined to the goodness of your worthy Uncle, leaves me not the least shadow of doubt. Accept of my thanks for executing my little commission so carefully, but your Uncle desires me to tell you you forgot the hayseed.

Jenny begs I may thank you for your obliging letter & the tender affection you express for her & wishes to deserve it and to comply with everything your Uncle and I recommend to her. She has no doubt of your doing everything in your power to contribute to her future comfort & happyness, and flatters herself your Delicacy and Tenderness for her will greatly alleviate the feelings of her heart in parting (tho' for a short time) with a tender mother and sisters she loves with the greatest affection. I pray God give you every Blessing I wish you and make you deserving of the Peculiar Care of Providence. This you may feel assured is the ardent & hourly prayer of

My D[r] George
Your sincere & affectionate Aunt
J. Conyngham.

Beck, Bess and Isabella beg, I may assure you, of their Love, & make my compliments & good wishes to your Father and Brother.

Tuesday. Springhill
Ye 26th Jany. 1779.

The young ladies at this time seem to have been installed at Springhill. Did Jean adopt her friend 'Mariana's' advice? and did she indeed 'preveall'?

The young couple, George and Jenny Lenox, must have greatly contrasted in looks, he being a tall, powerfully built man, and Jenny small and fragile with a little pale face full of dignity and gentleness. Though forty-two miles of mountain road lie between Springhill and Derry, George seems to have thought nothing of frequently covering the distance on horseback. He was still agent to his Uncle and Aunt and was beginning to take his place in County affairs. He was High Sheriff of the County when his Uncle wrote to him:

Dear George

If it is possible for me, I will attend you at the Assizes, but Wednesday at Dinner is the soonest I know I can be with you. My brother and sister are here, and I expect Mr. Rowley and his son Hercules and Lord Templeton to-morrow – if they leave me on Tuesday, or even Wednesday, so that I can set out early, you may expect me, and I will give you every assistance in my power with respect to your Grand Jury. I daresay you will have a great attendance of County gentlemen. I know Mr. Jackson will attend and Counse[lr] Rowley and Mr. Staples from this country. … You'll tell Sir Hugh Hill … how I am circumstanced. … I also told Staples

Ever yours affectly
Wm. Conyngham.

George's young wife was eager that her husband's term as High Sheriff should be a success. Though still very young and inexperienced, she enlisted her younger sister Rebecca's help, and arranged and acted as hostess at a supper at which she entertained the Grand Jury.

Her mother penned the following charming letter of congratulation:

My darling Jenny

I really cannot express to you the delight I felt in hearing the account of your Supper, the eligance of it & the Propriety altogether of every thing was such comfort and satisfaction to me as you can only conceive (from the knowledge I hope you have) of the anxiety I feel for everything that concerns you. When I think of you two, my poor young creatures, without even a female friend to consult or a proper cook to assist you, how genteel and cleverly you managed everything, & made all the sweet things yrselves. You are charming girls. I'm delighted you had it in your own House. … You have got such credit, I know very well you wd have every thing as nice as possible, all my uneasiness was your being too much fatigued for want of a proper person to assist you, which I know very well Derry would not produce. I wish with all my heart I could have seen your supper set out. Mr. C. seemed highly pleased with everything. How sorry I should have been if he had not gone. I have been as brisk as a Bee, & my heart has felt as light as a feather since I got your letter yesterday. God bless you my D^r^ child, & grant you success in all your Little undertakings & the same credit & Honor in every material scene of your Life.

Every one so pleased too with the behaviour and conduct of the *sheriff* that I cant tell you, my Dr Jenny, how happy I feel. I intend to lay by your Bill of fare, it will help me if ever I have occasion to give a public supper. Poor Harriett Hamilton! I am really sorry for her, when I think of her Poor Mother it checks the happyness which I have so much reason to feel myself and to be thankfull for. Mr. Conyngham got an account yesterday of Major Rowley's Death, I think a very happy circumstance, tho' it will distress poor Lady Langford & Mr. Rowley. Will you put on mourning for him – I believe it is only three weeks, but you may make it longer if you chuse it. I cannot help telling you, my Dr Jenny, of Mrs. Campble & Mrs. Oliver. They were both in Church yesterday, came flisking in together, Mrs. Campble with a Hat *Litterary* speaking not much larger than a breakfast plate, & the little rim turned down, & her Hair flying in Ends – poor Mrs. Oliver without even a little Pudding over her Hair, but the string of her Hat tighed tight round her Head & all the Hair she had, I suppose, she bundled together to make one large stout Curl, which she had stuck behind her ear on one side, the other as bare as if she had shaved it, what would have become of you, Jenny, if you had seen them flisking in, & jostling one another to get foremost, as if to shew us all how handsomely they were dressed, dont you wonder how I kept my countenance? Bessy was ready to die —

Poor Mrs. Martin[67] has been very ill of a violent cold. I enclose you a letter I got from Mrs. Gillespy yesterday. I think, my D^{r}, I have no more news to tell you. Will is grown the sweetest little husband you ever saw. Jin and he delight in one another, & she is sitting on three eggs. Unfortunately one of them was thrown out of the nest & broken. Strange alteration this matrimony makes. Tho' Bess is writing to Beck, I must give her a few lines & give her credit for her assistance at your supper. Mr. C. wants me to go to the Garden. A thousand Blessings & Loves attend you all.

believe me my Dearest Jenny
Yr truly affect. Mother
Be sure my love to George. J.C.

And so the happy years rolled on, William Conyngham, though childless, being the centre of a genial family circle, taking a useful and leading part in public matters and giving sage advice to his nephew George Lenox. Portions of some of these letters will serve to shew his wisdom and good feeling. In one he reproves George for his carelessness and procrastination in furnishing his accounts of the property:

August 31. 1781.

Jin told me a long time ago I might expect a remittance of jointure. I expected when you were some days so near us as C. Dawson & M. felt you would have spared an hour to have talked to us upon our affairs, your punctual attention to which I must remind you will be of more real advantage to you than any trivial ...'s which at present may serve to amuse you. I cannot think it prudent for you, a Married Man, with a great deal of business on your hands both from your own employment and your family affairs, upon a moderate income, to be among the foremost in every Scheme of Pleasure and Expence. These are my sentiments which my real regard for you and wish to see your conduct in every circumstance irreproachable, draws from me, and I'm sure when you consider a little cooly you will perceive that its worth your while to pay some attention to them. Depend upon it, George, the solid character of prudence and economy in a settled station of Life is both more honourable and desireable than that of the gayest Bon Vivant in Society & in the end will in every particular prove more really satisfactory to a Man's Private feeling.

'I am, dear George, your sincere Friend and affect. Humble Servt
Wm. Conyngham.

In November, 1779 he writes; 'there never was so much money in Ireland as at this moment, however unwilling they are to part with it.' In another, having given caution as to avoiding a Chancery Suit in connection with the Castlefin property, he ends with these words:

> These matters require all the *cool & solid thought* you can give to them, it is not momentary or offhand thought that will do. I congratulate you, Dr George, on the recovery of your wife, I'm sure her sufferings and Patience, Poor thing, ought, and I daresay will, endear her to you more & more, & call for every tender sentiment and attention that is possible to give her; even the least appearance of coldness & indifference, tho' without real foundation, is distressing to a Delicate and Feeling heart. Endeavour to make Home agreeable to each other by making your amusements more domestick. Two people who really love each other can never be at a loss for amusement together. Time can never lye heavy if you wish to employ it to each other's satisfaction. Besides the more a young man in your Situation, beginning the world I may say, lives a domesticated life the more Credit and Reputation he will acquire from all whose good opinion you would wish to cultivate,
>
> Yours affectly
> Wm. Conyngham.

Much can be read between these lines. George was evidently impulsive and thoughtless, and his Uncle, being profoundly happy in his own marriage, had learned to understand the sensitive and delicate mechanism of a woman's feelings, which his kind heart felt might be wounded by a seeming indifference.

Little Jenny was far from strong, and each hope of bringing a tiny new life into the world was frustrated time after time. There are many letters which dwell on her repeated disappointments and severe illnesses, some of these coming from neighbours of the Conynghams.

In previous mentions of these neighbours, enough has not been said of two families which were in close touch with the occupants of Springhill – the Stewarts and the Lindesays.

About seven miles from Springhill, beyond the market town of Cookstown, were two beautiful and well-wooded demesnes, situated near to each other and watered by the same winding river. These were Killymoon and Loughry. In bygone times, when old George Conyngham was building Coagh, the Stewarts of Killymoon were adding to Cookstown and planting trees along the long street so as to give the effect of an extensive boulevard. Later, when William and Jean Conyngham were living at Springhill, their old friend, Will Stewart, M.P., was still alive. His son James, in the year of her sister, Mrs. Staples' wedding, married Elizabeth Molesworth, second daughter of the unfortunate lady who was burnt to death in 1763; and the young couple lived with James' father in the old house of Killymoon. Later in the century, Colonel James Stewart, who like his father, was a member of Parliament and extremely rich, erected an imposing castle beside the older building at the cost of £100,000[68] and also built the church at Cookstown, in both cases employing the famous architect, Nash.

James Stewart was an influential politician and received the freedom of the

Killymoon Castle, Cookstown, designed by John Nash, 1803.

City of Dublin. He did much to lighten the burdens of the Presbyterians of Ireland, and we are reminded of their gratitude by a number of handsome silver trays and presentation pieces now in the keeping of James' great-grandson, Colonel Marcus Clements [69] of Ashfield, Co. Cavan, as are the splendid diamonds, interesting Molesworth MSS. and other family relics from Killymoon.

The Stewarts were often at Springhill, as were Robert Lindesay of Loughry and his wife (*née* Jane Mauleverer) who were married in 1777 and held the lands granted to Bernard Lindesay during the plantation of Ulster.

Loughry demesne abounds in beauty and romance. Its river flows through tree-clad ravines, and there is a 'Lover's Leap,' where a frantic youth leapt to his doom, the white owl – Banshee of the Lindesay family – no doubt having given warning of the impending tragedy. Near the mansion is a Summer-house, built on a wooded crag above the river, where Dean Swift used to sit at his writing during his visits to Judge Lindesay.[70]

Mrs. Lindesay wrote, *circa* 1780, to Mrs. Jean Conyngham mentioning Jenny Lenox's severe illness.

> Dear Mrs. Conyngham
>
> I have wished to write to you some time, but was prevented by a report that you was expected daily at Springhill, till yesterday, when I was informed that Mrs. Staples had received a letter from you mentioning your intention of staying sometime longer at Derry.

> I assure you it gave both Lindesay and me very great concern to hear Mrs. Lenox had been so ill, and we felt greatly for you, who I am sure must have suffered much during your attendance upon yr Daughter. It would give us both very great pleasure to hear she is recovering as you cd wish and that your Health has not suffered by your great anxiety.
>
> We dine tomorrow at Killymoon, & I hear Mr. & Mrs. J. Stewart and their little ones are returned from Brown Hall. I will not seal my letter till I can inform you how they left all yr Friends there. Mrs. Lowry is recovered, tho' she looks rather delicate. She has not been abroad yet except to take the Air. I was with Lindsay in Dublin at the time Mrs. Lenox was so ill that we did not hear of it till some time after, or I should certainly have wrote to you then. Lindsay begs to join me in best Compliments to yr self, Mr. & Mrs. Lenox & Miss Hamilton, and I am, Dr Mrs. Conyngham
>
> Affect Humble St
> J. Lindsay.
>
> Loughry August ye 14th
> Sunday night
>
> Just returned from Killymoon where there was a great company of Hewitts,[71] Stewarts & Staples's. Mr. J. Stewart told me he left all Fds well at B. Hall & Major Hamilton amongst ye rest. He also said He brought a letter for you wh he put into ye Post Office at Strabane.

George Lenox was evidently much attached to his charming mother-in-law, 'the beautiful Jean Conyngham.' He preserved a little packet of twelve of her letters to him. They are carefully folded and dated, and on the back of the first he had written '26th Jany. 1779 Mrs. Conyngham, previous to my marriage to her daughter Jane.' As these letters give a vivid picture of the times, extracts from a few of them must be given. One of these deals with the servant question. It is dated Jany. ye 7th, 1780:

> Many thanks to you, dear George, for your obliging and affectionate letter. There is not at present anything that I can think of that I want from Derry, or you may be certain I wd trouble you to bring it to me. I'm well convinced of your disposition to oblige everyone, but particularly a *friend* who, be assured will always have real pleasure in serving you as far as lyes in her power. I dont know what to do about this unfortunate Miss Count, besides this girl who has apply'd to you, there is another exceeding pretty sort of woman & would either hire as a nurse or Lady's maid. Now as I have no occasion *myself* for a person in the former station, suppose I was to think of her for some *friend* of yours? I have already apply'd to *one* in her favor, whose only objection is her appearing to be too fine a Lady – for my own part I like a genteel-looking woman in that Station. What is your opinion? I confess her appearance and her motives for going to service has prejudiced me much in her favor, & if upon further enquiry into Character we find her what we wish, I think you & I between us will be able to satisfie her expectations tho' they should exceed the common run of

Vulgar, ugly *Moggys*. As to the girl who lived with Mrs. Knox, it was Kitty that mentioned her first to me. I told her I wd have been glad to have heard of her before I engaged Miss Count. ... I was apprehensive the other would not continue long with me, as she was ignorant of everything but plain work, if the poor wretch had not sent her cloaths I would not scruple so much puting her off, but I think it would be a sort of cruelty now to disappoint her, though I daresay I shall loose a good servant by my consideration of her.

I fancy I have now sufficiently tryed your patience with a subject you would willingly excuse the reading of, but you must learn to accustom yourself to these *little matters* of female importance. We all long much to see you; Jenny I know writes about Ticken, Gotten, Damascus to you. We have heard ye Damascus washes very ill. Contrive to bring the Ticken with you, I shall have Feathers to fill it.

Friday Feb ye 11th

My dear George

I find you have got neither Paper nor Cotten yet, & William in his letter yesterday to Jenny does not seem to know when he will have an opportunity. I wish with all my heart he had left them with Beck to send with all the other things. ... I was certain from his hurry to get them from Mrs. Price that he had sent them to you long ago. I'm only anxious about the paper, as I think it will be more prudent to have the Cotten cut out when Jenny & I are in Derry. If you and she can make yourselves comfortable for a few nights in your old bed, indeed I think it will be much better for you both to sleep in the room off the dining-room, & Bessy, Bell and I can sleep in the room above stairs with the two beds. I find, George, Tatty remains with you, indeed I judgd it woud be so, it was easie to see through their schemes from the beginning & how Mrs. Stafford's[72] *very* great anxiety and *affection* would end towards her favorite Brother. I am much mistaken if she has not gained her point by her friendly visit to Derry, & the burthen of all is to be left on you. I can not help feeling some resentment at this, therefore if I do not behave to some of your relations, as I should wish to do to everyone connected with you, dont suppose it is for want of that sincere esteem which I'm sure I shall always have reason to feel for you on every occasion. ... The addition which I must unavoidably give at times to your family I assure you woud give me uneasiness, if I did not think I coud in some measure make it up to you. You and my poor Jenny are but young housekeepers, therefore I think *Fathers* & Mothers should deal gently with you in the beginning. I am apprehensive the former will have very little consideration in that particular (for you two at least).

I will send the bed L[n] towards the latter end of next week. I have sent this morning to make enquiry for something to carry it in. I have it filled these some days past & airing every day, its a most delightfull bed, I hope in God my D[r] Jenny and you will enjoy many peaceful comfortable sleeps upon it. You may believe my anxiety on the approaching event is equal to your own. I flatter myself it will not happen till the end of March.

Jenny writes herself, therefore I need add no more than to assure you of the Love & good wishes of Bess, Bell and your affectionate *Mother*.

J. C.

... Your father's behaviour vexes me. I must request, George, you will in Future consider yourself & family, for I'm pretty certain he will not assist you. You must excuse me for speaking my sentiments so freely. I want you very much at present to mend my pen, for its a most horrid one.

Adieu

Sunday morning. Feb. ye 20

Tho. we all long to see you, D[r] George, yet I hope the bearer may find you in Derry on Tuesday, as I know you will give proper directions about the things he carrys. Inclosed is the Key of the large Chest wh contains the Bed bolster, three pillows Blankets &c. which are pined up in a sheet & need not be opened till I go to Derry, two ban boxes a little Trunk a little Tea Chest & a little bundle, you will be so good as to order Kitty to have those things taken out & brought upstairs to any room you think proper. The Blanket that is sewn round the bed desire her to rip off, but not till she carrys it up, & then let her put the bed into the new bedstead, & Cicely shake it extreamly well & throw the Blanket & a coarse sheet over it. There also goes a large Trunk, a small one, a Horse and a Chair. You will laugh at the idea of sending a Chair for myself. But you know I have a particular passion for a low seat, & all yours are too high for me. You will be so good to give Kitty a charge about everything till we go to Derry, which I begin to grow very impatient for ... anxiety makes one have a thousand fears. ... I hope, my D[r] George, William has long before this sent you the paper. If the room was paperd I woud soon get the curtains for the bed ready after I went to Derry. I have got as much of the lining prepared as I coud without having the cotten— . I propose, please God, leaving this on Tuesday or Wednesday seven night, will it be convenient for you to come to us next week? & will you let Ross of Newtown know that we shall sleep at his house Wednesday the first of March, & to have beds ready for us, it woud be too far for Jenny to go in a day. We have had a great fall of snow since yesterday morning, but I hope it will not Lye.

'Jenny Bess & Bell all Joyn in sincere Love & good wishes with Dr George

Your very sincere

and affect. J.C. in a great hurry.

The bearer is not to be payd till he returns to me.

Other letters refer to business matters connected with the Castlefin property – and in most of the correspondence there are affectionate references to her daughter Jenny, George's wife.

On March ye 9th 1782 she remarks:

> It makes me very happy to find my Dr Jenny is better than she has been, & have no doubt of your doing everything that is necessary to contribute to her health, which I trust in God will soon be as good as ever, her complaints I know proceed from weakness. I believe none of the Horses carry Double, if they did she coud ride sometimes behind Esther, Charles or Henry, for she does not like to ride single but when she can have you with her. Moderate exercise on Horseback I know woud be good for her, & I wish she coud get some bathing this Summer without the disagreeable inconvenience which attend Fahan; it certainly takes away the advantages that attend those sort of places, when one is not accomodated with the necessaries they want. What sort of bathing is there at Magilligan? … It was a disagreeable business the prisoners breaking out of gaol, I wish you had not given yourself any trouble about them. No news but that the papers will inform you of & that I think we have no great reason to brag of. We have a Recess for about 3 weeks. I long to get to the Country, but God knows when that will happen.
>
> My love and Blessing & every good wish attend you all.
> I have a very bad pen.

This excellent mother-in-law does not scruple to advise her Dr. George tactfully as to the conduct she expects of him. On August 10, 1783 she observes:

> I find your Uncle intends going to the Derry Assizes, dont you think it woud be well to write to him by return of post and ask him if it is his intention & where he woud chuse to sleep? You know the objection he made before. I cant tell whether it still continues, but this I am pretty sure of that he woud expect to be asked by you. You'll excuse me reminding you of what perhaps was unnecessary, as I daresay you were intending writing next Post. … Jenny tells me that she baths delightfully. I'm sure it will do both her & Beck a vast deal of good. I hope you take a Dip sometimes yourself? … Your Uncle & Aunt David have been at Lissan since last Monday, we expect them this day.

Mrs. Jean Conyngham, we can observe, had no great liking for the sojourn in Dublin, which her husband's Parliamentary duties often demanded. In a letter, of ye 27th April, 1782, she declares:

> I must put you in mind of the £20 Bill you promised to send me and I'm much affraid that will not be sufficient to take me out of Dublin. I confess I'm heartily tired of it. The Parliament is to adjourn to-morrow for a fortnight. How long it will sit after is not yet determined. Great expectations from our new Ministry & hope we shall not be disappointed. Woud you wish at any time to get a Dublin paper I will send it to you – either Falkener or the Evening Post. … This is a tolerably dry morning, your Uncle is out walking the Streets. We are to dine with Sir Hugh Hill to-morrow.

The new ministry to which she refers was what was known as 'Grattan's Parliament'.[73]

Henry Grattan was one of the wisest and most disinterested of Irish patriots. He had been induced to enter Parliament by his friend, Lord Charlemont, in 1775, had sympathised with the Americans in the struggle for independence and advocated self-government for Ireland, bringing forward this aim in his famous 'Declaration of Rights.' Eighteen of the Counties and all the Grand Juries supported him, and finally Lord Buckinghamshire,[74] the Lord Lieutenant, announced the consent of the English Parliament. At this time the hated Poyning's Act was repealed. For centuries it had crippled Ireland's progress, having enacted that no Statute could be passed without the sanction of England.

Grattan's grateful country granted him the sum of £100,000, but he had no spirit of self-seeking and declined the offer, though later he accepted a portion of this sum.

At this time Dublin could boast of a political circle of much brilliance and dignity, and though some of the gentlemen who composed it may have been swayed by selfish motives, there were many among them who were truly patriotic – persons with an inherited sense of responsibility, and who, in loving their country, regarded the welfare of its people. At the end of the century many of these proved their integrity by rejecting the shameful bribery employed by Lord Castlereagh to induce them to vote for the Union.

As well as the genius of Grattan, there was another circumstance which indirectly helped to obtain an independent Parliament for Ireland, on the principle that 'Might is Right.' This was the formation of the Irish Volunteers, from 1779 onwards. Those were the days of the War with America, and, as most of the British troops had been withdrawn from Ireland to take part in the conflict, fears were entertained of a French invasion, and also of rebellion breaking out in the island when left in an unprotected state. Accordingly the gentlemen of Ireland once more rose to a critical occasion and with great spirit raised and equipped Volunteer Regiments.

In this effort Springhill played its part manfully, and though most of its activities belong to a somewhat later date, its Corps was probably first enrolled by Colonel William Conyngham,[75] and the fine old Banner may have been begun by the clever fingers of 'the beautiful Jean,' whom we know to have been skilled in needlework. We have noted that this lady disliked the bustling life in Dublin during the parliamentary sessions and enjoyed a quiet existence in the country.

The long dark winter evenings may have seemed wearisome, and the dim light of wax and tallow candles must have but faintly lighted the large rooms of Springhill and have made reading difficult. But William left many books behind when he died – far more than the slender list allowed by the poet to the 'Gentlemen of the old school':

> His books, and they sufficed him, were
> Cotton's 'Montaigne,' 'The Grave' by Blair
> A 'Walton' – much the worse for wear
> And 'Aesop's Fables.'

A recent photograph of the library showing the portrait of Sir Albert Conyngham.

Springhill has many leather-bound volumes bearing William's signature and book-plate on the fly leaves.

As to the newspapers of those days, these were few in number, each containing two small sheets and giving the news of two days at a time. William has left us a bound volume of *Lloyd's Evening Post* for the years 1769–70, 71 and 72. Each page contains three columns of badly printed poems and advertisements, and each copy of the paper cost twopence halfpenny. The contents of these newspapers are in many cases so quaint that a few specimens may be given:

> A few days ago was married at St. Giles in the Fields Mr. John Borrick, Coal Merchant, to Miss Molly Maxfield, a most accomplished young Lady with every requisite necessary to make the marriage state truly desireable, a genteel fortune being the least of her qualifications.

* * * * * * *

> We hear from Dublin that Beef and Mutton now sell as dear in the market of that metropolis as in London, though beef was formerly sold for 2d and mutton for 2$^1/_2$ per pound.

* * * * * * *

IRELAND

We hear from good authority that a Gentleman has discovered a method of preparing seed instead of manuring land whereby Ireland may become the Grainary of Europe.

* * * * * * *

At Chelmsford Assize seven persons received sentence of death for sheep stealing. The following were convicted to be transported, James Allen, for stealing a handkerchief, Paul Dunn, for stealing a Laced Hat, Elizabeth Bird, for stealing a shift.

This morning Robert and Richard Belchier, for a robbery, were conveyed in two carts from Newgate to Tyburn, where they were executed. They seemed extremely penitent and behaved with great devotion. They were very personable young men. A new Gallows of an uncommon construction was erected. The execution was attended by a prodigious concourse of people, the greater part of whom were females.

* * * * * * *

Dec. 27. 1769.

We hear from Dublin that a poor man who had been for many years afflicted with the Leprosy, having broke his leg was received into the Meath Hospital in that City, where he catched the Smallpox, on which the Leprosy entirely left him and has not appeared since.

Leeds. June 1770.

On Wednesday last ended the match of Cocks at Wakefield betwixt the gentlemen of that town, Smith feeder, and the gentlemen of Leeds, Culdred feeder. The main consisted of twenty battles.

* * * * * * *

A VOYAGE ROUND THE WORLD

in His Majesty's ship the Dolphin, commanded by the Hon. Commodore Byron, in which is contained a faithful account of the several Places, people, Plants, Animals as seen on the Voyage and a minute and exact account of the Straits of Magellan and of the gigantic people called Patagonians Together with an account of the seven Islands lately discovered in the South Seas.

This day is published, price 1s, 6d. sewed, embellished with three copper plates. Aug. 17. 20

* * * * * * *

Yesterday morning about five o'clock, a Gentleman and Lady in a one horse chaise were stopped at Epping-Forest near the tenth milestone by a single highwayman on a black horse and a crape over his face, who robbed them of three guineas and the Lady's watch.

THE DESERTED VILLAGE
A Poem by Dr Goldsmith

Printed for W. Griffen at Garricks Head in Catherine Street, Strand. Price 2d.

* * * * * * *

A few days ago died at Rathfarnham, in Ireland, aged 84, the celebrated Mr. Plunket, famous for curing cancers by external application.

* * * * * * *

How happy are we in the hands of so just and moderate and merciful a Prince as George III.

Such was the form of news published every second day, and read by William Conyngham, sitting perhaps in the old Cock-fighting chair, by dim candlelight over a turf fire in his oakpanelled chamber, where now his successors sit in electric light near a telephone and listen to the most recent news of the world spoken on the wireless.

* * * * * * *

Though allusions have been made to George's brother, 'Tatty' – or Clotworthy – no mention has been given to a sad happening which had occurred soon after George's marriage to Jenny Hamilton. It seems that Clotworthy Lenox junior was very unbalanced and had tried to take his own life. This horrified his relations, who did not know at first that the attempt had been unsuccessful. George's Uncle William wrote thus of the affair in a letter which reveals his delicacy of feeling and warmth of heart, and also his poor opinion of his brother David's wife.

Dear George

You may conceive I was much shockd by the account of the melancholy catastrophe of that poor unfortunate young man. I feel for your poor Father with the tenderest compassion. My love to him and tell him so ... on such a subject the less is said or thought the better. ... They were much offended at Henryville [76] that they were not immediately acquainted with the event, particularly Mrs. D— but ... I softened the matter as well as I coud. At first I determined not to tell the unhappy circumstance lest it should be the topic of conversation among all her gossips at Belfast, but upon consulting with my Dear Wife, we thought it better to tell my brother than that the account should come otherwise. ... I begged him to caution his Wife not to talk of the matter

> at all, it is not the business of our Family to publish such an event in it … curiosity always delights in wonders be they ever so unhappy. … I told him your wife did not even mention it to her Mother in a letter she wrote after the misfortune happened – & that you delayed informing us. … This all does not seem to satisfy Madam D., as to the punctilio I dont think it much matter. I see a mixture of Pride and insincerity there that is not very amiable.
>
> We go from hence to Castle Upton on Thursday, stay there about a week and so home, where I shall let you know our further schemes. … My dearest Wife, I believe, writes a note to her daughter, thank God she is very well, except her feet which have been very troublesome, but I have hopes of procuring her release from that troublesome complaint from Doct[r] Halyday who I have prevailed on her to consult.
>
> Yours my dear George
> very affectly Wm. Conyngham.

A constant anxiety to Conyngham were the family affairs of Clotworthy Lenox, who, as time went on, worried his good brother-in-law with his many difficulties. In one of William's later letters to Lenox he remarks; 'I wish to spend the evening of my life [77] in ease and happyness and not be disturbed by dissentions.'

But alas, ease was soon to be broken, for bad health was seizing him in its grasp. Many letters to and from his devoted friends shew that his days were numbered. To his friend, Judge Lindesay of Loughry, he wrote in 1784:

> My dear Lindsay
>
> You know our motions already from Mrs. Lindsay, I know, I shall therefore say no more than that I continue tolerably well and much the better for Springhill air, though nothing but snow to be seen. I received your most friendly letter from Belfast yesterday. I can only say, my Dearest Friend, I am most perfectly sensible of all your goodness to me, and the propriety of your sentiments in every part makes a deep impression on my mind. When you come to the country … with your friendly & judicious assistance I hope we shall do everything to your satisfaction and my own. We heard from Mrs. Lindsay yesterday. We rejoyce to see her and all her little family so perfectly well – God grant you all long life and good Health to be a comfort to each other and support to your dear little Family. Writing is not quite easie to me yet, but it grows more tolerable, especially when I write to such a friend. My wife joyns me in sincerely affectionate Love to you.
>
> Ever yours most affectionately
> Wm. Conyngham.
>
> Springhill Feb. 17th. 1784.
> I saw Staples yesterday and Hamilton.

This letter is addressed to Robt. Lindesay, Esq., No. 18 Gardiner's Row, Dublin, and franked by H. Rowley.

To his brother-in-law he wrote on October 13th (no date).

> My dear Lenox
>
> I am much obliged to you for your affectionate anxiety about me. I have had a three weeks severe attack of that confounded hereditary disorder. I am now, thank God, pretty well recovered, but have not left my room yet. I am quite free from pain, the weakness alone confines me at present. That Bond shall not prevent my paying you soon, but really at this present time there is such scarcity of money in the country that I can scarce get sufficient to pay my weekly expences. I hope times will get better soon. My dear wife has had a troublesome confinement also, by a rheumatick complaint in her head & jaw. She is, thank God, a good deal better, but still muffled & confined with me to our Bedchamber and Her Dressing-room. She desires her Love and best compliments to you
>
> Ever yours affectly
> Wm. Conyngham.

Several other letters refer to the grievous state of health into which William Conyngham had fallen. An amusing epistle from Mr. R. Jackson written at Forkil, December, 1783, is as follows:

> My dear Conyngham
>
> I am very sorry to hear of your ill state of Health occasioned by your being a Disciple of that foolish Dr Cadogan. It is not fit for you and me at our Time of Life to drink Water &c. He was a Drunkard. We never were. Sometimes we may have exceeded, as who of a good-natured Temper have not often. I beseech you not to drink less than a Bottle of good Claret in condition after your Dinner and a Pint of old Port after your Supper. Experto credo, Roberto. If you encourage me, I will see you in perfect Health next Summer, please God. You have answered, I am just informed, for my Honour to Lord Clan: as I am sure I woud have done to any man for yours.
>
> Adieu, my dear Sir, & believe me most truly
> Yrs. R. Jackson.

William's old friendship with Lord Castlestewart remained firm, and the latter at this time wrote to express his regret at his friend's bad health:

> Many thanks, my dear Friend, for your affectionate letter & friendly condolence with Lady Castlestewart & her deeply afflicted friends. . . . You can well conceive poor Mrs. Lill's distress to be immense, for I well know your tender feelings on such afflicting events. The obliging part you have always shewn where my interest has been concerned, ever marked your warm friendship. The only Will yet found was made in July /82, it is but a few lines, and vests the Judge's whole real and personal estates in Mrs. Lill without limitation. I can

perceive my dear Conyngham, what you write relative to yourself to have been imagined when your spirits were low – this I hope earnestly to be the case, as the account Staples gave of you here w^{d} not well admit of so rapid a change. As you do not come to Town, I am very happy to think you have determined putting yourself under the care of Dr Halyday, whose professional abilities are so well established. Might I have the satisfaction of knowing how your journey to Belfast agreed with you. We leave town on Saturday for the North, but shall halt a day at Mrs. Doran's in the country. I shall be much obliged if you direct a Line to Stewarthall inform me *very particularly* how your travelling agreed with you & whether the supposed swellings were diminished or increased by it, or what you understand from Halyday[78] of your case. It is, I should think, almost impossible your situation can be so precarious (for that is your word) as you seem to conceive, as you have been so lately so strong as to determine on a journey to Dublin on horseback, & that by Summerhill. Your travelling with blisters on your back must be most distressing. It is likely Halyday will prescribe something less tardy and more forcing. God send you, my dear Conyngham, what will be efficacious to a restoration of perfect health. My best wishes shall ever attend you. Lady Castlestewart joyns me earnestly & to Mrs. Conyngham. I beg my best compts to David and his small fireside, not forgetting Halydays. Adieu ever my dear Conyngham

Yours most Sincerely & affectionately

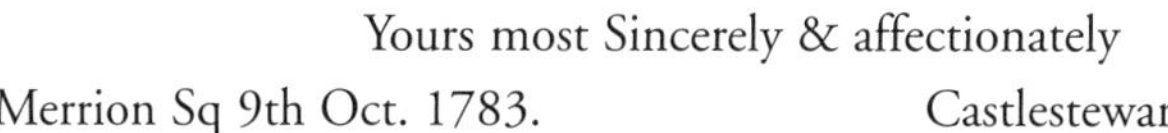

Merrion Sq 9th Oct. 1783. Castlestewart

The coat-of-arms in the black seal of this letter is as fresh and clear as if imprinted yesterday. The address is; 'William Conyngham Esqr. at David Conynghams Esq. Belfast' (and franked Castlestewart).

It may be noticed that at this period persons of importance usually wrote on gilt-edged notepaper, about 7 by $8^{1}/_{2}$ inches in size. No envelopes were used, but the paper was folded over and sealed: and as stamps were not yet used, the letters had to be franked by peers or members of Parliament, if not paid for.

There is no doubt that William Conyngham knew that his end was drawing near. On September 23rd, in a letter to his nephew George, he writes:

The Lenox Conyngham Coat of Arms

My health continues so bad that I find it necessary to ask the best advice, and for that purpose I intend, as soon as the weather settles a little, to go to Dublin. My Situation is so very precarious, I am anxious to see all my own & my Dear Wife's affairs on the clearest footing. I have been bled this morning and can write with difficulty.

Springhill Sept. 23rd

There are more letters of enquiry dated from this time, from Clotworthy, Rowley and others, but the most sincere of all these is from his old cousin Hercules Langford Rowley, whose affection for William had never waned during all the years which had elapsed since the Seven Years' War. The letter is written from Summerhill:

> My Dr Conyngham
>
> I am much concerned to hear you have been, ever since we parted, so indisposed and that your complaint still continues so strongly to affect you. Be assured that the affecte Love and Esteem I have for you make me feel this with great Regret and Affliction. I should have long agoe expressed my friendship, & my anxiety for your welfare if I had been able to write, but realy I have been prevented from puting Pen to Paper ever since Sept. last by a swelling in my hand occasioned by an eriscipulous Complaint, that it is with difficulty I undertake it to manifest my affection for you & let you know you cannot have a better friend or more hearty well wisher for yr happyness than myself. ... The most comfortable & relieving advice I can give, is what I am convinced you practice: Patience & Submission to the Will of Providence ... sincere endeavours will be assisted by that powerfull Director of Universal Nature, whose mercies & goodness are over all his works. My wife & I joyne in praying that God Almighty may influence you & support you in y^r^ Duty to Him, that you may have this Blessing & every other Satisfaction fit for the situation you are in, is the hearty & sincere wish of Dr Conyngham
>
> Yrs. very affect. Friend now & for many years
> Her: Langford Rowley.
>
> My wife & I send out best Loves & consolations to Mrs. Conyngham.
>
> Summerhill, 5th of the beginning of a New Year, wch God grant may be spent in noblest virtue & absolute Submission to the Will of God, confidence in His Aid, our weak but sincere endeavours to make our latter end acceptable in His sight. Then all will be Happyness and comfortable to us.

This cousin was evidently devoted to William and was much in touch with Springhill. His letters to three generations of Conynghams still remain and they imparted affectionate interest and wise counsel.

At the time of writing the above letter, Hercules Langford Rowley and his wife (nee Frances Upton [79]) had celebrated their golden wedding. They were married in 1732 and their homes were Summerhill in Co. Meath and Langford Lodge on the shore of Lough Neagh, which H.L. Rowley built – or, at all events, added to.

But all the love and solicitude of Conyngham's friends were powerless to prolong his life. On the 27th of March, 1784, he passed away at Springhill, aged 61, having been devotedly nursed by Jean, his wife. He was laid to rest in the old tomb up against the East wall of Lissan Church, and there a headstone bears his name and coat of arms.

William had made a will earlier in that month, of which an abridged version is here given:

> I desire that all such debts as I shall owe at the time of my decease, except such as are due by Mortgage, may be in the first place paid by my Executors … and as to my Estate … I dispose thereof as follows: Whereas upon my marriage with my present Wife, Jean Conyngham, an annuity or Rent charge of two hundred pounds was settled upon her for her life in full of her jointure, and whereas I am indebted in the several following sums of money for which my estates are bound by mortgage viz. three thousand pounds due to Richard Olpherts of Armagh Esqre in trust for the Revd William Lodge, also the sum of five hundred pounds to Archibald Hamilton of Mullinagore Co. Tyrone Esq. in trust for Andrew Woods of Ballygoney in the County of Derry Gent. also the sum of two hundred and fifty pounds due by bond to Miss Susan Lennox, of the city of Bristol, also four hundred pounds to Clotworthy Lenox of Londonderry Esq. … charged upon the marriage of the said Clotworthy Lenox with his late wife, and whereas my meaning is to provide for the full payment of the principal to the sd purpose that my said Estates may remain clear of all debts and incumbrances whatsoever to the person or persons to whom the same are limitted.

William appointed, as his trustees, James Stewart of Killymoon in the Co. of Tyrone and Robert Lindesay of Loughry, requesting them to pay his wife's jointure, the interest due on the sums aforesaid mentioned, and then to pay the residue to his brother, David Conyngham of Belfast Esqr., during his life, and no longer

> my express intention being that no part of the same shall remain to my sd brother's wife for her life in case she shall survive her late husband … she being already sufficiently well provided for.

After all debts were paid, he bequeathed all his estates to his nephew, George Lenox, in trust – the third trustee being Clotworthy Rowley, Esq. In case of George dying childless, all was to go to George's brother, William Lenox, and failing him

> to Arthur Upton, third son of my friend and relation Lord Templetown, and all such persons respectively as may inherit to take the name and bear the arms of Conyngham.
>
> I desire … part of the income of the estate to be used in keeping in good repair the house and improvements of Springhill.

He appointed his wife and Robert Lindesay his executors, and the will is witnessed by Thos. Fields, Anthony McReynolds and M. George. A codicil was added, appointing Major Henry Hamilton of the 56th Regiment and his own brother David joint executors with his wife Jean, and Robert Lindesay. He left to his

> dear wife all the arrears for the Castlefin property – all rings & ornaments of dress whatsoever to and for her own use with use for life of all my pictures,

View of the house from the Dutch garden

plate, books and household furniture with full power to remove the same or any part thereof whensoever and wheresoever she shall think proper, my desire being that no part thereof should be sold or disposed of, but should remain to the use of such persons respectively after her death as shall be entitled to the possession of my real estate.

I also bequeath to Matthew George, of Coagh, Co. Tyrone, the sum of fifty pounds sterling, also to my servant William Clerk ten pounds sterling, to my servant Mary Kane, ten pounds sterling. Also my will and desire is that the house, gardens and demesne of Springhill shall be occupied and enjoyed by my dear wife, Jean Conyngham, for whatever time she may find it necessary to reside therein, and whenever she shall think proper to remove from thence and reside elsewhere, then my will is that the said house, gardens & Demesne of Springhill shall be occupied and enjoyed by my brother David Conyngham, during his life, provided he shall chuse to reside therein. As for all the residue of my goods and chattels, coach and horses and all my cattle and stock whatever, all my house linnen, ready money and arrears of rent, and all other my personal Estate, not otherwise disposed of by this Will, subject to the payment of my just debts due by Mortgage I bequeath to my said dear wife for her own use and benefit.

Signed 20th of March, 1784.

What a contrast was William Conyngham's will – so full of love and thought for his wife and heirs – to that of his stern old father George, whose aim had been to deprive his eldest son of as many possessions as possible! But George did not after all succeed in impoverishing Springhill, for, by a curious turn of fate, all the money and property bequeathed elsewhere came back again, David and John Conyngham dying childless, and the son of Anne and Clotworthy Lenox succeeding to everything.

The *Belfast Newsletter* of 2nd April, 1784, records:

> Died on 27th inst, at his seat at Springhill in the County of Londonderry, William Conyngham, Esq. in whom every amiable disposition and social virtue necessary to constitute the perfect gentleman and agreeable companion were united. In the early stage of his life he devoted a series of years to the service of his King and Country, held a high military rank, which he filled to publick approbation and oftener than once acquired fame and honour on the Field of Mars. A numerous circle of all ranks and classes who were favoured with his acquaintance have just cause to regret his death, as thereby Society has lost a valuable member, the poor a generous benefactor and his tenants a tender-hearted and indulgent landlord.

VII

The Widow Jean

d. 1788

Jean Hamilton of Brownhall, wife of Colonel William Conyngham MP, from a miniature at Brownhall.

SPRINGHILL WAS NOW OCCUPIED by a sorrowing widow, whose wish was to remain in the place so dear to her late husband and to carry on his wishes as to payment of debts and care of the demesne. Her task was no easy one, as the following letter[80] will shew. It was written to James Stewart of Killymoon, her husband's old friend, and goes far to shew the delicacy and unselfishness of the writer:

> Your very friendly and obliging letter, dear Sir, merited my grateful thanks much sooner, but the truth is I really am unwilling to trouble you with my letters when I can possibly avoid it. I hope I need not repeat to you how highly sensible I am of your goodness and kind wishes to serve me so far as lyes in your power. Indeed I would not have Hesitated one moment about the payment of the Bond Debts as soon as my affairs would have enabled me to discharge them had I not been so Certain that my Dr Mr Conyngham never intended they should fall upon me, however if the Law says it must be so I shall endeavour to pay them. I have some days ago discharged Mr. Hanyngtons out of the first I received of my jointure. Mr. Henderson's and old Matthew George's debt are still unpaid. …
>
> There are some young cattle still to sell, but Matthew George tells me if I was to dispose of them now they would sell at great disadvantage. You were so kind,

Dear Sir, to ask me if there were any circumstances I woud chuse to mention that you woud have them laid before a lawyer. … Your worthy friend's kind intentions towards me woud, I fear, in the opinion of the Law avail but little, this I can assure you of that his earnest wish was to settle every relation to me so clear as not to admit of a doubt hereafter, which made him anxious to write the Codicil in his own hand. After it was signed, he hoped every matter was now settled as he intended, wished he coud do more for me, that he woud to his last moment bear testimony of my tender care and attention, and asked me if I wished for any part of his Estate. I would indeed have been an unreasonable Creature to have even thought of such a thing, and I can with truth affirm that if he coud have put me in possession of more than I will name, I would not have been tempted to have had him again disturbed for any consideration whatsoever.

At another time, in talking of his Brother, he told me he intended to Limit him very much, & gave me his reasons, but that he woud leave him sufficient with the addition of his own income to make him easie and comfortable during his Life, that his intention was to leave his Estate in the hands of three worthy men, whose Honor and integrity he could Depend upon, & then told me his trustees hoped I woud live at Springhill. I will own to you, Dear Sir, I coud not stay to hear the conclusion of this very distressing conversation, and at that moment, without making any answer, left the room. I saw he was afterwards cautious of entering on the subject with me, for really my spirits were so very much oppressed at that time with anxiety that the subject was more than they were able to support.

I know it was not his intention that his brother should live at Springhill, his wife and her connections he never coud reconcile to himself their having any command here, indeed I have had strong reasons for several years past to believe it was his intention to settle Springhill on me during my life, if I survived him, I only mention these particulars to yourself, Dear Sir; the high opinion and sincere friendship my Dr Mr Conyngham so often and so warmly expressed for you on every occasion, joyned to my own knowledge of your goodness, encourage me to repose a confidence in you, & also I fear to be too troublesome but the subject I hope will plead my excuse. Have not the Trustees a power of disposing of the dutys as they think proper? The Duty work will be a great loss to me, at the season for bringing home Turf &c.

Mr David Conyngham when last here left a *message* with Matthew George that as he intended to leave his four Horses at Springhill during his stay in England, that he woud for *that time* order the duty to be brought to me. I certainly woud have pleasure in serving Mr Conyngham as far as I coud with any degree of convenience, but I thought it a little strange that he woud not mention to *myself* his intention of leaving so many horses with me during his stay abroad. These sort of things make me wish to have matters settled as clear as possible for the satisfaction of all parties & to prevent my being troublesome to you in future, for I need not tell you that the Georges are rather more inclined to serve Mr Conyngham than me, nor can I condemn them for their attachment to the family.

> I own my anxious desire … to continue at Springhill, for I shoud feel real concern to be under the necessity of quitting it entirely. The expense of labourers I confess alarms me, I have already pay'd to them above one hundred and sixty two pound …
>
> I really feel ashamed at giving you the trouble of reading such a letter, & shall only add my most affectionate good wishes to Mrs. Stewart yourself & Family, & believe me with the highest Esteem
>
> Your very sincere and much obliged
> J. Conyngham.
>
> My brother left me about a week ago, I feel a great loss of him. My daughters beg their best compts. may be acceptable.
>
> Springhill
> April ye 11th. 1785.

Not much is known of the last days of this little lady, who died in 1788 and was buried in Lissan Churchyard, as recorded in the Family Bible. She has left a fragrant memory at Springhill hovering round delicate pieces of needlework and packets of charming letters in her clear pointed handwriting. And her pale, oval face, beneath a widow's veil, looks down gravely from her portrait by Francis Cotes, in whose studio the great Romney worked his way to fame.

VIII

David Conyngham

A SHORT SOJOURN

1727–1788

Ann Saunders – wife of David Conyngham

DAVID CONYNGHAM AND HIS UNPOPULAR WIFE lived for only a short time at Springhill, but they certainly made their abode there for a while. A pencil portrait of 'Madam David' still occupies a foot of wall space in the old house, and her miniature shews the same stout figure, wide mouth and 'snub' nose – so different from the aristocratic features of other members of the family, who are most unlikely to have brought the much disliked lady's portrait into their home.

David's wife did not long 'have command' at Springhill, for her husband died early in 1789, a few months after the death of his sister-in-law 'the beautiful Jean.' He seems to have expended some money on the place, as his widow afterwards tried to recover compensation for this from the nephew and heir, George Lenox: and there is a list of household and farm implements which were taken over at a valuation by George from his Uncle David's, widow. It is interesting to know what plenishings were in use in an Irish country house a hundred and fifty-six years ago, though no furniture is mentioned, as this went with the house, after Mrs. Jean Conyngham's death.

George Lenox Esq. to Mrs. Ann Conyngham.
Ammts. of goods, cattle &c. of the late David Conyngham taken at a valuation & bought 6th of April 1789

Dairy	*£*	*s.*	*d.*
to Two wooden butter bowls		2	2
to 6 milk pans			
to 4 milk crocks			
to 4 cheese vats			
to 3 butter crocks			
to 2 cream do.			
to 1 churn		2	2
to 1 new do.		4	4
to 2 milking cans & 2 piggans		2	9
to 1 strained milk barrow & dish		1	2
to 1 Piggan			7
Lumber Room			
Old barrels		2	2
Brew House			
1 Cheese Press	1	2	9
1 Stone trough		4	4
4 tubs		12	0
to 1 small do.			6
Slaughter House			
to 2 Beef trees		2	3
To Turf valued at	4	0	0
Barn			
to 2 oak arks	3	0	0
to 1 fir dale (deal?) do	1	10	0
to 2 meat sieves	1	1	0
to 1 Beam and Scales[81]	1	2	9
to metal weights	4	4	0
to 13 Boles & 1 quart Seed oats at 18 /- per bole	11	14	6
to Granary Oats 36 Boles at 14/s	25	4	0
to 1 dale vat Bin & 1 bushel & half 1 peck & half peck		6	6

Garden	*£*	*s.*	*d.*
to one old spade & 1 scythe & 2 new spades		7	7
to 2 Barrows		6	6
to 6-hoes		7	6
to 1 Saw & axe		1	1
to 1 Milton frame with 9 lights and 1 small 3 light frame	7	4	0
to 1 new light frame & 1 small old 2 light do & 11 small frames	2	16	11
to 18 Bell glasses		16	6
to old Matts			6
Stable			
to 1 Oat binn		11	0
to 1 Horse Car	2	0	0
to 1 do Strawberry			6
to 1 grey mare	2	5	6
to 1 Dunn mule	4	4	6
to watering bridles sadles &c. also brushes fetters & locks	1	4	4
to 5 old carrs	2	5	6
to 3 do. for mules	1	0	0
to 2 ploughs	1	0	0
to 2 brake harrows		11	4
to 2 single do		9	9
to 7 wheel barrows		7	7
to 4 steel hatchets		6	6
to 3 sledges		5	5
to 1 pick axe			6
to 4 Crow barrs		8	3
to 2 old Shovels			6
to 3 pr. sand boxes		3	3
to 2 sacks		6	6
to 2 winnowing cloths		8	6
to 2 Riddles		1	1
to 6 Turf Creels		1	1
to 6 wooden rakes & 1 stone slip		5	5
to 2 small do. 1 foot spade & 1 drag		3	9

Stable cont'd	£	s.	d.
to 1 Coal rake 3 pr. Clips & 1 stubbing crook		3	9
to 1 Bill hook & 2 hatchets & to 1 cross cut		9	2½
1 large cart	1	15	0

Cattle

	£	s.	d.
to 5 draft Bullocks	28	10	0
to 5 milk cows at £4	22	3	0
to 8 year old at 10s.	4	0	0
to 6 calves at 5/5	1	12	6
to 30 sheep at 17s	27	15	0
to 2 pigs		16	0

Corn-Meal

	£	s.	d.
to 8 boles of Barley at 1/6	10	9	0
to 31¾ Barrls. of oatmeal at 1 2 9	36	2	3
to 4 ton of Hay at £3 per Ton	12	0	0
to 65 Bushels of Potatoes at 6½	1	15	2
to 1 Heifer	1	10	0
to 92 flax 22 ton at 10d.	3	17	6
to a lott of green edged ware	3	0	0
to 1 glass jugg		11	4
to 2 glass Butter screens		13	0
to 2½ dozen glasses at 5s. 6d. pr.		13	9
to 1 Liquere Stand		5	5
to 2 Wine and Watter glasses		2	2
1 1 pr. Decanters		8	0
to 1 PlateWarmer[82]		13	0
to 2 slices, egg-spoon Cheese cake & curd		3	8
to 1 Blemonge Shape		2	8
to 26 Patty pans		5	3
to 12 tin cups		2	6
to 1 tin can & coffy pot		2	2
to 6 Earthen plates	2	2	8
to 2 preserving pans	1	0	0
to 1 Sopha cover & cushions in the dressing room	4	11	0
to 1 Tea Board	10	0	5
to 17 of double refined Lump Sugar at 16d	1	2	0
to 8¾ lbs. single refined do. at 1s. 11d.		9	6
to 10 Coffe at 22d. per lb.		18	4
to 19½ Barley at 3s. 3d. per stone		4	6

Corn-Meal cont'd	£	s.	d.
to 2½ of Sago at 1s. 8d.		4	2
to 2⅛ of Vermicella & 27 macarons		12	1
to 1½ of Rice at 4d.			6
to 11 lbs. of Currants at 7d		6	3
to 1 lb. 3 oz. of tea		6	6
to 16 lb. of Raisins at 9d.		12	0
to 10 oz. Saltpetre at 1s.		10	0
to 20 lb. of Jamaica Sugar at 7_		12	6
to 1½ Almonds at 2/6		3	9
¾ of Citron at 1s. 7d.		1	7
¾ of Isinglass		6	6
¾ of Starch			9
5 of Powder		7	2
1 lb. of Powder blue		7	8
½ Stone do.			4
2 do. of Anchovies		4	4
2 do. of Olives		4	4
3 do. of Brandy fruit		10	10
3 do of Oil			
1 Box Wax Candles counting 16 lbs.	2	5	4
2 of mould candles at 7½		12	6
63 of Scale Sugar at 3. 14. 0 per cwt.	2	1	9
Oil Cloth & Stair lanthorn	4	5	6
Cheese knife		2	2

Cellar

	£	s.	d.
2 Barrels of Porter at £3	6	0	0
1 Cagg rum 16½ gall at 10/10	5	13	9
8 gallons of Vinegar	1	1	8
1 hhd of Port Wine	13	18	3
do. half full	6	10	0
1 do. Clarret in bottles	30	5	6
5 doz. Sherry	5	0	0
10 doz. French Clarret in bottles at £1 7	13	10	0
2½ doz. of Frontiniac at £1 6s	3	5	0
3 Casks of Cyder			
2 Barrels & 2 butts of do.	2	1	3
to 67 bottles Ale at 4d. per bottle including bottles	1	2	4
9 Barrels	2	5	0
4 doz. of Beer at £1	4	0	0
3 qr. casks		12	0
4 do.		13	0

Cellar cont'd	£	*s.*	*d.*
2 Hhds & 1 small Cask		14	0
2 Porter butts		10	0
4 brass cocks		4	4
3 gross & 1 gr. of bottles at £1	3	5	0
1/2 cwt. & 19lb of			
Hung Beef & Bacon at £1.10	2	8	4
Herrings		7	0
Odd Beef & Pork		5	0
Delph ware		8	7
Amt. of Auction Bill	19	6	6
	396	11	9

	£	*s.*	*d.*
2 Cows	£8	2	0
2 Bullocks	6	16	6
1 Jaunting car	2	17	0
1 Wheel	£1	11	0
Six fatt Bullocks	60	0	0
	456	11	9
to plowing & harrowing	2	5	6
	458	17	3
Deduct price of Butter screens		13	0
	£458	4	3

By Ballance due to Mattw George Senr
by Mrs. Conyngham
as per acct. agreed to be credited to Mrs. Lenox

Sig. Received from George Lenox Esq. the above
sum of four hundred and fifty-eight pounds four s.
& 3 pence sterling, this 10th of April 1787.
Ann Conyngham present Wm. Lenox

IX

George Lenox-Conyngham

THE VOLUNTEER COLONEL

1752–1816

George Lenox-Conyngham

Lenox-Conynghams were now for the first time owners of Springhill, George Lenox, its new master, having added Conyngham to his surname, under the terms of his uncle's will. This stalwart young man and his little fragile wife Jenny made the old house their dwelling in the year 1789.

They had been married for ten years and were still childless, but were not alone, for Jenny's three sisters, Beck, Bess and Bell Hamilton, lived with them at Springhill until their respective marriages – matches which their late stepfather had considered unlikely to occur in a place so retired!

George Lenox-Conyngham, who had already shewn himself to be energetic, warm-hearted and impulsive, was quite ready to take part in public affairs at this changeful period of history. Though Ireland had been undergoing almost a decade of peace under Grattan's Parliament, a spirit of unrest was spreading in many parts of the world. The American War of Independence had awakened a craving for freedom and for the amendment of injustices: and now France was entering the furnace of revolution, which was to scatter incendiary sparks far and wide.

As we know, the American War had led to the war with France and Spain and to the forming of Volunteer Regiments in Ireland, which had been denuded of regular troops: and it was the menace of this strong Irish force which led England to concede an independent Government to the sister island and to repeal laws which had been as oppressive as those which caused America to revolt. The Irish Volunteers raised a storm of patriotic enthusiasm throughout the country. We read in the *Belfast Newsletter* of March 29th, 1786:

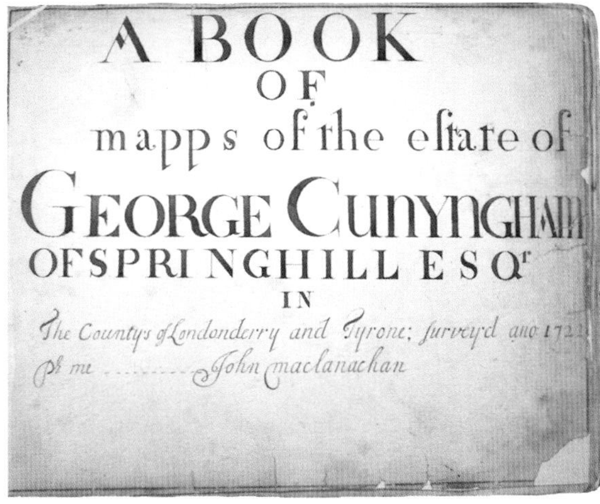
A BOOK
OF
mapps of the estate of
GEORGE CUNYNGHAM
OF SPRINGHILL ESQr
IN
The Countys of Londonderry and Tyrone; surveyd ano 172
P me .... John Maclanachan

PRONI

> Every lover of peace and good order, every man who wishes to see the laws duly maintained, every man of property in the realm, every man that calls to mind the glorious aera of /79 /80 and /81 when tranquility reigned throughout the whole nation, when rapine, murder and robbery were unheard of must retain a lively gratitude for those glorious and ever to be revered Sons of Freedom & Saviours of the land, the Volunteers of Ireland. Every man who now contemplates the rapid strides to returning barbarianism made within the last year, the numberless robberies, outrages and murders daily committing, must join in fervent prayers to the Deity to reanimate the supporters of that Divine Institution with the same fire of /79.

In these after days it is hard to realise the warmth of feeling which was caused in Ireland by the raising of the Volunteer Force.

Some corps existed as early as 1778, when the Armagh and other corps were already drilling. They supplied their arms and equipment at their own expense, and, though self-embodied and self-disciplined, were very law-abiding. Volunteer rank was coveted by all Irishmen. At first they were independent Companies, but soon joined into battalions with different uniforms. The Londonderry Bn. held a Committee in Derry City on May 1st, 1780, Capt. Bateson, Chairman, and Messrs. Lecky, Murray, Moore, Patterson, R. Houston Balfour and Acheson taking part. This Corps was reviewed in Derry on the 26th and 27th of July, 1781.

> Every Corps immediately arriving at Derry is to draw up in the Diamond. The Volunteer Army to be divided into 2 Brigades, one will be reviewed on Thursday and the other on Friday. The lines to be guarded each day by the Brigade which does not then pass in Review. At 10 o'cl. precisely a Cannon will be fired from the Ramparts, on which signal the whole are to march immediately to the Review ground, bayonets fixed and Colours flying. Twenty rounds of cartridge are to be used for the Review.

Organizing meetings had been held in Dungannon on December 1st, 1778, and on February 15th, 1762, when an epoch-making assembly was held in the Church[83] – when a large number of civilians trained to arms attended, and another on September 8th, 1783, with Colonel James Stewart of Killymoon in the Chair, when various resolutions were passed, one being:

> That Freedom is the indefeasable birthright of Irishmen and Britons, derived from the Author of their being, and of which no power on earth, much less a delegated power, hath a right to deprive them.

Resolution III laid it down that the majority of our House of Commons

> is not chosen by the people but returned by the mandate of peers or Commons, either for indigent boroughs where scarcely any inhabitants exist, or considerable cities, where the elective franchise is invested in a few, who are thus suffered to place the highest trusts of Society against the interest and will of the many, in the hands of men who seldom act as if they considered themselves accountable for their conduct to the People.

Another resolution thanked the Ld. Bishop of Derry[84] 'for his attendance and for his warm attachment to the Volunteer Cause.'

There were 272 Companies at this meeting (on September 8th, 1783) – and a Committee was formed of five persons to each Company to represent this Province in a grand national Conference to be held in the Royal Exchange, Dublin, on the 10th of November next. The following gentlemen were accordingly nominated;

Antrim Delegates. Col. O'Neill, Lt. Col. Sharman, Capt. Todd Jones.

Armagh. Earl of Charlemont, Lt. Col. Brownlow, Sir Capel Molyneux, Col. Sir W. Synnot, Capt. Jas. Dawson.

Cavan. Lord Farnham, The Hon. J. Maxwell, Capt. F. Saunderson, Col. G. Montgomery, Capt. Henry Clements.

Donegall. Col. Alex. Montgomery, Col. Jn. Hamilton, Col. Alex. Stewart, Col. Robert McClintock, Col. C. Nesbit.

Down. Col. Robt. Stewart, Capt. M. Forde-Crawford, Col. Patk. Savage, Capt. Gavin Hamilton.

Fermanagh. Col. Irvine, Col. S. A. Brooke, Capt. A. C. Hamilton, Jason Hazard, Esq., Capt. J. Armstrong.

Monaghan. Col. Powell Leslie, Col. J. Lucas, Col. J. Montgomery, Capt. Wm. Forster, Col. Jas. Hamilton.

Tyrone. Col. J. Stewart, Lt. Col. Montgomery, Col. Jas. Alexander, Capt. Eccles, Lt. Col. Charlton.

Londonderry. Ld. Bishop of Derry, Col. Right Hon. T. Conolly, Col. Right Hon. Ed. Cary, Capt. Lecky, Capt, Ferguson.

(It is to be observed that William Conyngham of Springhill is omitted from this list, because at this time he was nearing his death and incapacitated from engaging in public affairs).

Elaborate language was prevalent at this time, as shewn in stilted addresses presented to the Commander in Chief, Lord Charlemont:

> The Officers of the Volunteers express satisfaction at being reviewed by Your Lordship – Our pride is gratified & our esteem & veneration heightened by renewing our connection with a character whose affection, magnanimity and animated zeal on behalf of the preveleges of Ireland have been so eminently distinguished. …

Tribute is also paid to Colonel Stewart,[85] who played a prominent part in this Movement;

> Distinguished by your military abilities and animated zeal for the Volunteer Cause you acquit yourself with dignity and reputation. You always have discharged the trust reposed in you with honour and credit.

Colonel Stewart was held in high esteem. In an address to him at this time it is stated:

> The purity of your principles with respect to your conduct in the Volunteer Cause, by your early and persevering attachment to which you have been conspicuously distinguished … you, Sir, are one of those steady, upright Senators to whom the nation is much indebted for her regained privileges & for her glorious animating prospects. … We are thoroughly convinced you will never in your parliamentary conduct depart from the dictates of honour and integrity.

In his reply Colonel Stewart responds:

> The declaration of your approbation of my parliamentary conduct is a reward the most Honourable to me that the world can afford.

Of Colonel Stewart it was said that 'without place or pension, one shilling of public money has never found its way into his pocket or that of any of his friends during a period of 44 years.'[86]

As early as 1779 a Volunteer force had been founded at Moneymore, probably by William Conyngham – five years before his death, early in 1784. These 'the Moneymore, or Drapers' Volunteers' had been in a manner dissolved, but according to the *Belfast Mercury* of October 1st, 1784, had then raised themselves from their listlessness under the name of 'Moneymore Independents': and it also relates that 'this Company is formed of men of all religions, and a union is on the tapis between them and Coagh.' The latter corps was founded also in 1779 and commanded by Col. William Conyngham.

The union between these two corps was named the 'Springhill Union,' and its members presented the following petition to George Lenox Conyngham shortly after he had taken up residence at Springhill:

> May 14th. 1789, at a meeting of the Springhill Union assembled by public notice, the following resolutions were unanimously entered into
>
> 1st R. That in conformity to our original Institution this Corps are determined to keep up the Volunteering Spirit as formerly and to appear in military array occasionally for the purposes of Celebrating the annual returns of Certain memorable days, & also of co operating (if necessary) with Magistracy in the Execution & support of the Laws.
>
> 2nd R. That George Lenox of Springhill Esqr. be requested to accept the Command of this Union.
>
> 3rd. R. That if Mr. Lenox shall be pleased to Comply with the above Requisition, this Corps would wish to Express their Esteem & Respect for him as their Commandant by waiting upon him some evening at Springhill to congratulate him on his arrival at the antient seat of his worthy ancestors.
>
> 4th. R. That Capt. Lenox, Lieut George, Ensign Lawson, with our Chaplain, be as deputation of our number to wait on Mr. Lenox with a Coppy of the above Resolutions.
>
> Signed by Order
>
> Robt. Brown Secy.

George threw himself with his 'usual rapidity' into the training of the Volunteers, and Springhill was evidently a centre of this activity.

Many contemporary relics testify to this. The old house contains badges of the local Corps and Stewartstown and Lissan Infantry, regimental buttons, a 'Volunteer jug' and lists of local Volunteers. But the firelocks, alas, were given in to the Government at the time of 'red licenses' and were never restored.

Regimental buttons

The banner of the 'Springhill Union' still hangs over the wide oak staircase. Its colours are faded and its silk tattered, but through its present net covering can be seen the Volunteer Arms – Crown and Irish harp and wreaths of laurels and Shamrocks, and Scrolls bearing the words 'Springhill Union' and 'Pro Rege Patria et Lege.'

Beneath that colour hearts have throbbed with valour and patriotism, tenants and retainers flocking round the standard and following the lead of their beloved landlord. He has left some of their signatures written on a scroll of long strips joined by wafers. Many of these names are in the Colonel's handwriting, each marked with an X, for very few in those days could wield a pen as deftly as they could handle a sword.

At first sight it may seem strange to find so many Roman Catholic names in these lists – Quin, Devlin, etc., but though these may have been excluded in other Corps, it must be remembered that the *Belfast Mercury* had stated that this Company was formed of all religions. The explanation is that one of the chief leaders, Lord Bristol, Bishop of Derry, had insisted on their admission to the Corps in Co. Derry, which was one of the Counties to admit them. He was ahead of his times, for not till 1792 were Roman Catholics or Dissenters allowed to vote or to worship openly.[87]

The Earl of Charlemont was Commander-in-Chief of the Volunteers. This able and spirited man was an ideal leader and much respected. Old letters mention his tours through the country to hold reviews. It is interesting to note that, 132 years later, his descendant – the present Viscount Charlemont – showed even greater spirit and patriotism and fine self-forgetfulness by joining as a Private the Volunteers of 1912–14. He is descended from the Houstons of Castlestewart, who were such great friends of Good Will Conyngham, and the present owners of Drumcairne and Springhill are respectively descended from the sister-heiresses Grace and Alice Houston.

Springhill House in 1789 must have looked much as it does to-day, but the large dining-room, Cedar Room and 'Little Parlour' had not yet been added.

We can imagine little Mistress Jenny and her three sisters sitting together, their powdered heads bending over their *petit point*, or perhaps Miss Bess warbling to her guitar, her sister seated at the harpsichord.[88]

And now suitors began to appear on the horizon. Elizabeth, or 'Bess,' married a Mr. Colthurst,[89] Rector of Desertmartin in the Diocese of Derry, Miss Rebecca eventually following her example. She attracted a friend of George, her brother-in-law, a certain James Galbraith of Urney in Co. Donegal. A few of Galbraith's letters over a long period have been kept, and though some of these refer chiefly to business, they indicate coming events.

A jubilant one from Derry runs:

> My Dr Sir
>
> Rejoice with me, for this day the Chancellor pronounced a most elegant Decree in our favour. Before dinner I had not an instant to write and I write this at the table where I dined with Sir Hu. Hill. ... I shall see you in Derry on Wednesday and tell you all. My duty attends the Ladies. I hope they will be prepared to pay me my 'Fee.'
>
> Most faithfully yr servant J. G.

Military gorget

The gallant James Galbraith wrote from Dublin about a law case in connection with the Miss Hamiltons' Donegal property (which a certain 'Cowan' had mismanaged) and he wound up thus:

Be so good as to give my Complements to Mrs. Conyngham, Mrs. Colthurst and the young Ladies. I bought them very handsome hats, I wish I could find any mode of conveyance for them. 1 cannot conclude without expressing my obligations for your kindness & attention to me of w^h believe me I am truly sensible. I have seldom in my life spent so much time in such comfort & quiet, even tho' not freed from business, and seldom so happily. Believe me Dr Sir with Real Regards.

Yr. Sincere & faithful Servt Jas. Galbraith.

It is probable that Miss Rebecca's bright eyes were responsible for this effusion, though Galbraith did not marry Beck till some years later, and in 1812 he received a baronetcy and sent a cordial answer to George's letter of congratulation.

The fourth Hamilton sister, Isabella (or 'Bell'), also found a husband, later on, in a Mr. Fox, but little is known of this gentleman save that he was described as 'a villain,' so we may assume that poor Bell was not happy in her marriage. George's wife continued to be disappointed in her hope of motherhood. She was a gentle, fragile creature, evidently interested in housekeeping. Her brother-in-law, when planning a visit to Springhill, wrote that he 'hoped Jenny would give him a cut of the great Cheese.' And no doubt she added to the presses in the house-keeper's room new stores of capers, anchovies, olives and Jamaica sugar, commodities which were mentioned in the list of 1789.

The family friendship with the Stewarts of Killymoon continued. Mr. James Stewart wrote to George L. Conyngham in 1791 as follows:

House of Commons Feb. 9th. 1791.

My dear Sir

I had particular pleasure in reading your kind letter to-day. It gave me great pain to hear, on coming to town, that there was any likelihood of a Law Suit taking place, though I have no doubt but it might & would have been carried out in the most amiable manner; yet I should be concerned that there were any proceedings with a Friend I so highly esteem & love, wh could have been even an appearance of want of mutual Confidence and attachment. I was surprised indeed at the appointment of Mr Galbraith .... I thought every man in the County of Tyrone was pleased at the prospect of your being our Sheriff – to you I know it is a matter of indifference, for I shall always remember the obliging & Friendly offer you made me when the subject was first mentioned. Mrs. Stewart unites in Compliments and best wishes for you and Mrs. Conyngham – with My Dear Sir

Your Sincere Humbl Servant

I sent your letter to Mr. Torrens. Jas. Stewart.

(This letter is labelled by George L. Conyngham: 'relating to the Bogg in Mullinahoe').

A letter from George to Mr. Stewart from Dublin, in 1794, alludes to money matters, and that he had not seen Mr. Rowley since writing last, and that

> getting possession of my Estate is highly gratifying to me – and the more so as by your advice I have so happyly accomplish'd it. Thank God my days of vexation and Torment are nearly over. ... As it is possible the present parliament may be dissolved next August, I think it will be highly necessary for us to be prepared. I woud be extremely glad to have all my freeholders registered at the next Sessions in Dungannon. 1 have written to Mr. George on this subject &, if you will assist him with your advice, I will be much obliged to you. My Olivia joins in affectionate compliments.

George was meanwhile experiencing much worry over his youngest brother, William Lenox's unworthy conduct. This William has left behind a great many letters to his father and brother – all very plausibly and piously worded, but which display a disagreeable cunning, avarice and duplicity. He seems, however, to have been kind-hearted and affectionate, and this is shewn in a letter describing the death of his friend George Knox (probably of Prehen, near Derry). William had sat up with him all night, and writes:

> From his attachment to me and mine to him it was his anxious wish, as indeed my own, to be with him as much as possible, which caused me to sit up with him every night & remain with him then till, I may say I closed his eyes. But to describe to you the misery of his wretched family I am not equal to – at one instant in a stupour, the next in the most Violent state of absolute misery.

George Knox must indeed have been a favourite with his family, which William Lenox tried to help at this time by 'taking the Parlour furniture to the Dining-room and getting some beds from Pump Street.'

In 1778, Lenox writes that he had been at Springhill and found his Uncle confined to bed with gout. In the next year, when in Dublin, he describes an exciting scene:

> Yesterday morning there was a most outrageous mob assembled in the Liberty, from whence they proceeded, armed with swords, to the Four Courts in search of the Attorney General, who had declar'd his Sentiments against a short Money Bill, but he had luckily made his escape a few minutes before. Being disappointed at not getting him, they went to his House and broke all his windows, &c., after which they went to the Parliament House and swore several members, before they went in, that they would vote for a short Money Bill ... to obtain Free Trade. A Guard of the Black & Green Horse & part of the Highland Regiment were ordered to disperse them, but it was thought more prudent that they should return to the Barracks, as many innocent people might have been killed if they had fired, and shortly after the mob dispersed of themselves.[90]

In 1763 William Lenox wrote to his father remarking on the Bishop of Derry's entry into Dublin at the head of the Volunteers – 'escorted by the Derry Troops. Tis quite the talk of the town at present & people think it a very spirited thing of them.'

In 1789 Lenox refers to 'Fitzgibbons' becoming Chancellor and imagines that this will put some pounds in his brother's, George Lenox-Conyngham's, pocket in point of costs. In the August of that year we find him applying to the Lord Lieutenant for a post, through Mr. Hobart, the Secretary, and mentions William Molesworth as first clerk in the Secretary's office. He had previously gone to Abbeyville near Dublin to visit Mr. John Beresford who had been very civil to him.

In the following year, a letter from Derry gives a woeful account of a severe epidemic in that City. Here are some extracts:

> Derry Sept 20. 1790
>
> Dear George
>
> We have for some time past had a most dreadful sickly Season – a fever which the medical people call nervous in the beginning and putrid in the end – has made sad havock among the lower class of people, and among the better sort has carried off poor Marechel of the Free School, Alick Stewart, the Curate, and Betty Montgomery, Sam's daughter; and yesterday morning Mrs. Ash of Ashbrook and the widow Thompson's son were taken ill. Mr. J. Barnard's & Capt. Lecky's deaths I suppose you have heard of. Every body here almost takes a Wine glass of the tincture of Bark an hour before Breakfast as an antidote against infection. George Sampson and Dick Babington and Sam Montgomery are candidates for the school. Dick Babington has got the Derry Cure in the room of Stewart, & John Bateman succeeds Babington at Burt. Notwithstanding the sickliness of the times we have had great entertaining work to the Marquis of Waterford, Lord Tyrone and Lord John Beresford who arrived here on Saturday last. I took the King's boat across the water for them and shewed them the different parts of the Bridge, which Cox had got dressed out with all the Ship's colours he could muster. They staid a considerable time on the water, observing the process of sinking the piers. The Marquis was highly pleased and assured Cox that nothing on his part should be wanting to have a similar Bridge … erected at Waterford. There are now but 17 piers to sink, and Cox declared he would have it passable by the first of November at furthest. … The Marquis was entertained by Sir Hugh at dinner on Saturday & by the Corporation in the evening, who had in the morning all met them at the Ferry Quay; and this day the Gentlemen of the Town gave them Dinner at the Inn. … They have just gone away after paying me a visit & have been, ever since they came, very civil & obliging to me. … Alick Knox is on the look out for a House I can assure you, and has a hope of getting Venables. With affect. remembrance to Jenny & Beck, believe me to be, Dr George,
>
> Your Sincerely affect Brother
> Wm. Lennox.

This strange fellow seems to have been in perpetual money difficulties, which he recounts in smooth hypocritical language. Writing from London, in 1794, he told that he was

> staying with Will Babington at Guy's Hospital and that Willy himself, his sister Angel, Murray Babington & Capt. Arthur Buttle, who came up from Chatham, are the only acquaintances I have seen since I came to London. Public amusements I have not gone to nor the inside of any Public Buildings save St. Paul's Church.

'Tatty' – Clotworthy Lenox
1707–1785

In a long letter, dated August, 1785, Will Lenox announces his father's death – or, as he described it, that 'the Almighty God thought proper to put a period to his existence.' All the circumstances are set forth in detail. Old Clotworthy Lenox was staying in Cavan, when a cut in his foot caused blood poisoning. 'He wrought on himself with some plaister and some salts from an Apothecary's shop,' till the Inn-keeper's wife insisted on calling in Dr. Reily and 'an express was sent to Mr. Saunderson, of a place called Clover Hill, for Dr. Wilson, a physician of great consequence.' All was of no avail, and Clotworthy 'expired with scarce a perceivable sigh, just as Dr. Reily was holding a cup of Bark to his lips.' Dr. Cottingham[91] lent his friendly assistance. Clotworthy's daughter, Beck Stafford, came hurriedly to Cavan with 'Jemmy,' her husband, and soon the body was brought to Derry to be buried in the same grave as 'Their Dearest Mother.' The Mayor and Alderman Thomas Lecky and Mr. Swettenham, as his oldest acquaintances, and Mr. Alick and Mr. Henry Scott as relations, 'tho' very distant' were considered to be proper bearers. 'The Greatest Respect we can pay his memory without preposterous Parade we are in duty bound to do,' and so on.

Thus died Clotworthy Lenox – once the handsome young 'Tatty' who won the heart and hand of Anne Conyngham in 1745. His good-looking face and slim figure encased in a gay waistcoat can be seen on the wall of the dining room at Springhill, near to the portrait of his wife, the placid Anne.

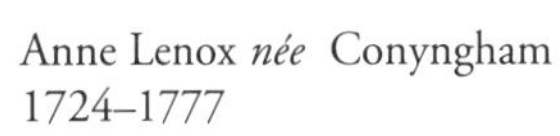

Anne Lenox *née* Conyngham
1724–1777

* * * * * * *

Time passed by and at last the much desired event took place. On January 9th, 1792, when in Dublin, Jenny Lenox-Conyngham presented her husband with an infant son, and the child was named William after George's good Uncle Conyngham, from whom he had inherited the Springhill property. George's happiness was unbounded. He thus announced the good news to his brother:

Dublin, 10th of January 1792.

My dear William,

I have only time to inform you of an event that from the goodnes of your heart will rejoice you almost as it does me. Know then that Jenny was safely delivered yesterday morning at six o'clock of a fine strong Boy. Doctors Evory and Clarke both attended Her, and by patience and leaving all to Nature, the business was happily effected without more than usual assistance. She and the Child both remarkably well, this is considered here as a singular case, and her Doctors have got such applause that it will make their fortunes particularly Evory, who was the man that actually deliver'd Her. Believe me to be, Dear William,

8 Great Denmark Str.
Rutland Square.

Your ever affectionate
Brother Geo. L. Conyngham

William Lenox's reply expressed admirable brotherly feeling – though, from what we know of his character, it is only too likely that he was deeply mortified by an event whereby he ceased to be his brother's heir.

Derry, Jan. 13th 1792.

My dear George,

Had I reason to consider you in a different light from that of a most affectionate Brother, there might be a kind of apology for my not feeling as I do from the late immense addition to the happiness of you and my Dear Sister, but be assured of it, that from the point of view I consider you both in, I sincerely congratulate you on the occasion and truly wish you every happiness that my Dear little nephew may ever have it in his power to give you. *Your* joy I think may be conceived, but that of poor Jenny, after so many and such dreadful sufferings, must surely far exceed imagination. My old friend Evory's consequence will certainly be greatly established by such a proof of his professional knowledge, after the unsuccessful efforts of so many men, hitherto considered of the first ability, and I sincerely hope his merit will result with that reward in the world which it deserves. Let me hear from you, when you have time, how Jenny and her *little pet* (which if there can be any excuse of making of him she surely has it) get on, and be assured of it, my Dear George, that I must be very much chang'd

> when anything that can add to your joint happiness will not most truly do so to that of
>
> Your ever affect. Brother
> Wm. Lenox.
>
> Remember me affectly. to *Aunty Beck* and *Aunty Bell.*

But George Conyngham's joy at his son's birth was soon to be followed by trouble, for the anxiety which Brother William's conduct had been causing was now to come to a head.

In December, 1792, a letter suddenly arrived from Marine Barracks, Portsmouth, from a young naval officer, John B. Savage,[92] which revealed to George the depth of his brother's perfidy.

It appeared that in the previous year William had secretly eloped with Savage's sister, Jane. They were married by license at Lambeth, on July 8th, 1790. Jane had hitherto lived with an aunt near the family seat, Rock Savage, at Portaferry in Co. Down. She came to England at the end of 1789, bringing with her a letter from William Lenox, professing his regard for her, but stating reasons why he could not marry her immediately.

John Savage explained in this letter that Lenox had

> requested that I would receive her as a sister, and he would be over in a few months to make her his wife. In July 1790, Mr. Lenox came to London and said that it was his utmost wish to marry her but impossible to take her to Derry, as he was much involved, and it would cause ruin to himself and to the woman who of all others he wished to see happy, but that, if I could consent to her remaining in England for a year, he would allow her a sufficient sum to support herself. I agreed, and attended the wedding ceremony at St. Mary's Church, Lambeth. He left her in lodgings in London and his remittances were so scanty that she was frequently almost in want of bread.
>
> I was obliged to send for her and her child to Portsmouth, where I have rendered them every assistance since, and have involved myself so much that I was obliged to solicit my Uncle Harry for a supply, when my Commission was at stake. He generously sent me twenty guineas which saved me from destruction. I have not heard from Mr. L. for many months. *His wife*, Mrs. Savage and I have frequently wrote, yet I find from good authority that he is well and at Derry, and has affirmed that he is not married.

Mr. Savage then begged George Conyngham to use his influence with his brother to settle the affair amicably, and hoped that no hasty expressions which might have dropped from his pen would give offence. He asked for William Lenox's address and offered to procure for George the certificate of his brother's marriage.

George Lenox Conyngham kept a much corrected copy of his answer to this disturbing letter.

Sir, 30th Dec. 1792.

This morning I was favoured with your letter, the perusal of which operated on my mind with the strongest sensation of surprise and pain. I feel for your situation in the most lively manner, and heartily excuse any expressions of warmth that might have dropped from your pen ... As to my having any knowledge of an attachment subsisting between your Sister and my Brother, I never heard of any such untill I was informed by common report nothing more than they were married and that your sister lived in England with an uncle. I spoke to my Brother on this subject (I think about two years ago). In reply he said it was an idle story and took its rise from the conjections of foolish people in the County of Down, who were pleased to imagine that he had paid her particular attentions. I pressed him to be candid . . . and, like a man of honour, make it known to me and the world, expressing myself in nearly the following words –

'William, you are your own master ... your own feelings and happiness are engaged, therefore if Miss Savage is your wife avow it, and I will receive her with every mark of brotherly affection. I have no children, nor likely to have living ones, (at that time this was the case) and it will be a great comfort to me that my Estate should not pass away to distant relations, which it must do on failure of male issue of you and myself.' He still positively denied the report and seemed to laugh at it as a matter ridiculous to suppose. From what he asserted and from the following reasons I was led to believe that the whole was without any foundation of truth. Cou'd I suppose that any Lady would submit to have her marriage doubtful who had justice on her side and spirit to defend her reputation ... judge then what surprize your Letter must have occasioned to me.

You tell me one thing in your letter which I did not know before. It is that Mr. Frank and Mr. Henry Savage are uncles to your sister, I have the pleasure of informing you that both these gentlemen and I have lived, ever since I was a Boy, in the most cordial intimacy. I have seen them often within the year past, and neither of them have ever spoken a sentence to me on the subject of this marriage. It seems strange that such a thing cou'd be kept from their knowledge, and stranger still that they did not disclose it to me. One would be naturely induced to be that some enquiry wou'd have been made respecting their niece's long absence from Ireland, also where and with whom she was. It is impossible but that her Aunt cou'd have answered these questions ... and the whole truth must have been developed.

If my Brother has acted dishonourably by your Sister, he is not a man of honour and consequently unworthy of notice or esteem.

I must beg leave to defer for explanation and decision. I cannot possibly interfere in so delicate a case as this appears to be at present, but this I will tell you, that if upon an *éclaircissement* it should appear that your Sister is my Brother's lawful wife and that he acknowledges her as such, she shall be received with every mark of fraternal protection and attention by, Sir,

Your most obedt. and very humble servt.
Geo. L. Conyngham.

This letter throws light on George's character. It would appear that he still cherished a hope that his brother might not be so great a rascal as he feared, and that his former love for this wily William inclined him to try to lay the blame on the Savage family, so as to diminish William's guilt.

There are long letters from Lieut. Savage to his aunt at Rock Savage, Portaferry, in which he recounts his grievances, this faithful brother, having not received one shilling from W. Lenox for over a year, had been supporting his sister and paid £10 per annum for nursing the child.

This was a time of grief and pain for George L. Conyngham, and the climax came when, in April, 1793, his beloved Jenny died in Dublin, after a vain attempt to give birth to another child. At that moment all other sorrows were eclipsed, and at first he had not the heart to answer two letters which he had received from his unhappy sister-in-law.

Jane Lenox's runs thus:

> Portsmouth, April the 12th.
>
> It has at this moment occurred to me, my Dear Sir, that in the hurry and agitation of my spirits, when writing to you yesterday, I omitted a part of your address. ... My mind really is in that state I am totally incapable of doing anything. Let me once more solicit your favour with a few lines by return of Post, if only to say what Mr. Lenox could say in vindication of his conduct. ... This surely is a reasonable request, after which, if it is your *desire*, you never shall be further troubled on this subject by
>
> Your very Humble Servant,
> J. Lenox.

Here is George's reply, and this copy is much corrected:

> S. Hill, 18th April 1793.
>
> Dear Madam,
>
> This morning I was favoured with your letter. You seem surprized at my not having replied to your first very tender and sensible and affecting letter, but when you read what follows your surprize will cease— . A few days after I had re[cd]. that letter I wrote to my Brother, and to convince you that I have done all in my power to relieve you from your present unhappy Situation and also to make him act like a man of honour and a Christian, I have written on this sheet a copy of my letter to him. I got no answer from him whatever untill we met in Dublin at a time when my mind and soul were overwhelmed with agonizing affliction. My Amiable Wife, the Virtuous Partner of my Youth, was lying a corpse in the next room. She died in childbed, a fatal accident put a Period to the existence of the best of women. I need say no more on this subject. I then spoke to my Brother; he confessed his marriage. I urged him with every argument not to forsake you but bring you to his House, but if that was not

convenient at present, he knew mine was ready to receive you and your Child.[93] He wou'd not consent to your coming over for three months, when his affairs wou'd be so arranged as to make your meeting more pleasing to both. He also told me he had written to you on this subject and that you are satisfied; he said he had sent you a remittance. After what I have said and done, I am sure you cannot accuse me of want of attention to you, believe me it wou'd highly gratify me were it in my power to contribute to your happyness, but I cannot force a man to act properly who seems totally carried away by unaccountable misconduct. I therefore request that any letters, either your Brother or any other of your friends may write, in order to compell him to do you justice, may be directed to your Husband and not to

Dr. Madam,

Your affect, and distressed humb. servt.

G. L. C.

This grandiloquent letter has a semblance of kindness, but though George realised that he could not influence his wicked brother, he surely might have sent pecuniary help to the hapless Jane, knowing that William's word could not be trusted. Perhaps he did send money to her, for the correspondence is not complete. It includes letters from Mrs. Savage, of Rock Savage, and one from her to Mrs. Kennedy of Cultra, bewailing the unfortunate affair. We gather from ensuing letters and events that George became totally estranged from his brother after this episode, though there is a long and plausible letter written early in the next century by William from England, mentioning a wife and numerous children, who were probably not those of the luckless Jane.

As a widower, George seems to have continued to take an interest in public affairs, though he does not appear to have been present at the Tyrone Summer Assizes of 1793.

An old Grand Jury list gives the following as having been present: –

High Sheriff – A. Cole-Hamilton.

Thomas Knox, foreman

James Stewart,	William Richardson,
John S. Hamilton,	Jas. Hamilton,
N. Mont. Moor,	Andrew Ferguson,
Daniel Eccles,	Geo. Sinclair,
Robert Lowry,	Chas. Crawford,
Hamilton Stuart,	Thos. Caulfeild,
Charles King,	Saml. Galbraith,
Robert Lindsay,	Wm. Pringle,
Jas. Verner,	Wm. Irvine,
George Perry,	Hugh Auchinleck,

Alex. Richardson.

But George's mind was engrossed in larger issues, for those were anxious times. The French Revolution was at its height and England began to wage war with that Republic.

Affairs in France had made both the Roman Catholics and Presbyterians of Ireland more keenly aware of the unfair disabilities which were imposed on them, and it was in this year that some of the burdens laid on the Catholics were lightened. But the seeds of revolution had been sown already, ere long to grow into the Rebellion of 1798.

The country was becoming turbulent, and as some of the Volunteer Regiments were said to be disaffected, they were all disbanded by the Dublin Government in 1792. To replace them, a Militia of regulars was formed to protect the country from foreign invasion. The raising of this Corps is mentioned in several letters to George Conyngham from General Whyte. The first of these is headed:

> Belfast, March 31st.
>
> Dear Sir,
>
> I have waited with Impatience for Intelligence that must determine the numbers of Troops and the necessity of sending them to different places, where you had been so good to take particular pains and care to accomodate them if sent. I have had constent Information since I saw you, and have sent People I can rely upon into several Parts of the country, who upon their Return all agree that things are taking a very proper Turn, and little Doubt but all will be perfectly quiet, but I shall not remain content till I hear confidentially from you the exact state of your part of the country, and whether you still think Troops are necessary.
>
> The Magistrates, by my advice, particularly Mr. Leslie at Ballymoney, where there were a few companies of Volunteers, wrote to several leaders of them, enjoining obedience to the Proclamation declaring all such bodies illegal, and that in obedience to the law they had an opportunity of laying down their arms with the same Honor they had taken them up. This has had the desired effect, and they have come to the Resolution of no longer parading or meeting. I suppose the attendance of Messrs. Caldwell, Glandy and Reynolds at the Lords' Committee, with the Destination of the last to Kilmainham Gaol for country air, will help to open the eyes of the poor deluded People. We are perfectly quiet here and in all the neighbourhood, nor do we hear the name of Volunteer.
>
> Let me have a line by return of Post and you will much oblige,
>
> Sir,
>
> Your most obed. Servt.
>
> Richd. Whyte.

In May, General Whyte wrote again as follows:

Dublin, May 7th 1793.

My dear Sir,

I received your very obliging letter with those enclosed and return you my most grateful thanks for your Goodness and Kindness, and this I had done by return of Post, but by a mistake of the Servant my letter was not put in the Post Office.

I also recd. one by yesterday's post, directed by the Lord Lieut. to Moneymore. This was dated the 23rd April, and those you enclosed, being of a very old Date. I cannot but think there must be some extraordinary neglect or delay in your Post or some others on that Road, and Ld. Bellamont, Postmaster Genl. who was with me when I re^{cd}. the Lord Lieut's letter, of himself desired the cover, that the Post Office here might inquire into the Delay.

We are waiting with Impatience the arrival of the Packets, four are due, there is little appearance of truth in the Counter Revolution at Paris. Jersey is, I believe, certainly attacked, and I am particularly anxious about its fate, as I long commanded there and raised many of the works for its Defense; there are very few troops there. I saw Mr. Conolly but for five minutes. Everybody is going, or gone, to their counties after their Militia. Sterling desires to join in best wishes for you and my young friend, with, Dear Sir,

Yrs. most sincerely,
Richd. Whyte.

The Londonderry Militia was formed in February, 1793, and its first Colonel was Mr. Thomas Conolly of Castletown, one Robert Stewart of Mount Stewart, in Co. Down, being Lieut. Colonel. The Major was George Lenox-Conyngham, of Springhill, who has preserved a packet of letters to him from Robert Stewart, afterwards the famous Lord Castlereagh.

Many of these deal with the problems of the Militia Regiment.

Both Stewart and Lenox-Conyngham were married in the following year, 1794, George having chosen as his second wife, and successor to Jenny, Olivia Irvine, of Castle Irvine in Co. Fermanagh, and Stewart's bride being the Lady Emily Hobart, daughter of Lord Buckinghamshire,[94] who had been Lord Lieutenant of Ireland from 1776 to 1780.

Some of Castlereagh's letters to George must be copied here:

My Dr. Sir,

This letter will be delivered to you by John Kienan of Kilrea, he informs me that he wishes to serve in the Militia Regt. (in which it gives me great pleasure to learn that you have a Command). May I beg you to enter him upon your roll of Volunteer Substitutes.

I am Dr. Sir,
With great truth,
Your faithful Servt.
Robt. Stewart.

Mountstewart,

18th May 1793.
My dear Major,

We regret your absence excessively. When your business will permit you to leave home, come to us. You will be better with your Corps than in retirement, and they with you. Poor Stark lost his wife in childbirth yesterday; it has proved as severe a blow as it was unexpected after being delivered of a dead child.

Our little Drummer is also dead. We have been obliged to send Whitesides to Lifford to stand his trial, had we not done this, the McCloskey's would have created an unpleasant disturbance in the Regt.

I enclose two letters, which came last post. Considering the weather, this discipline goes on very well. I flatter myself we are considerably steadier than we ever were, even in our best days. We have received your whiting, it will come considerably cheaper to the men than what is sold in town. I hope, my Dr. Major, you will communicate actively to our Deputy Govrs. on the 11th. It is certainly important that the Regt. should be completed to its full numbers. Capt. Gait carries a list of the deserters, also of the men discharg'd as unfit for service, the latter class must be immediately balloted for, the others in 6 months from their absconding. I make all the dirty and unsteady men mount guard, standing sentry these cold nights will soon reform them.

Ever
Dr. Major most
faithfully yours
R. Stewart.

The following is labelled 26th September, 1793.

My Dr. Major,

I have not yet been at Mt. Stewart, therefore have heard no news of you since we separated, but I am sure everything under your inspection must proceed happily. I find our Deputy Governors have done literally nothing. You know that Gait has resigned, he did not enlist a single man. I see by the Act the going Judge of Assize may fine the particular districts deficient in this quota – but the money so levied goes into the Exchequer, not the Stock purse of the Regt. and it is at the disposal of Par^{lt}. However this would rouse them from their inactivity, and if something is not shortly done to complete the Regt. it should be in my mind resorted to. Before I left Ballyshannon, I wrote to the Secty at War to ask leave to have 4 Drummers to our Grenadier Comp., as is usual in the Army. You will see by the enclos'd that it is granted. This will still give us greater facility of having one band of the permanent Corps.

There is a charming boy of 13 here, his name is George Oldham. I will carry him with me to Dublin, when I go to Par^{lt}. and send him down in the Enniskillen stage, the other you will dispose of either to Mr. Goldrick or one of the boys now on private pay, whichever you think most advantageous. I beg to hear from you as often as is convenient, – Everything relating to the Regt. is interesting. Remember me most affectionately to my brother officers

and believe me my dear Major
Most faithfully yours,
R. Stewart.

The next letter is to 'Major Cunningham, Commanding L.D.M., Ballyshannon,' and was written 29th December, 1793.

Dec. 1793.

My dear Major,

I enclose Boyd's Commission and the list of precedence which I brought away by mistake among my papers. Mr. Conolly sends me by to-day's post a grievous account of our soldiers, pray send me the delinquents names. I have a curiosity to know whether they are those whom I refused papers to, – if a strong example is not made, I fear the subordination of our Regt. will be lost. I see they hope to escape, from their numbers, however that trick of sinning by hundreds must be stop'd. I long to hear from you on the subject. I have written two long letters to Mr. Conolly in respect of the deficiencies in the different districts. I hope he will take decided steps to have them completed.

I have this moment your letter, a thousand thanks for it. I hope that even this misfortune will have its good effect and teach the men that they must submit to remain with the Regt. whether they like it or not, when it is their officers' orders. I have only time to send you all my blessing and to assure my dear Major

of my sincere friendship and regard,
R.S.

I send some Militia men's letters which follow'd me and which I now send back – pray have them deliver'd.

Newtownards, Jan. twenty one, 1794.

My dear Major,

However painful it must have been to you, and however distressing to us all, to have recourse to severity, yet I feel very great satisfaction in learning that the insubordination of our soldiers has been met with becoming firmness. I am in great hopes that your feelings will not be again tormented after the present delinquents are dispos'd of. The men must be sensible that the officers administer punishment with extreme reluctance. It surpriz'd me very much to find McKillop turn out so ill. I thought him the most correct faithful Serjeant we had. Cooper I disliked at first, but afterwards thought better of him; however they are evidently both rascals and we are well rid of them. How goes our band? I long excessively to return to you, but as yet I see no possibility. I go to Dublin the day after to-morrow. What sort of a Session we are to have, I cannot guess, write to me at the House of Commons, send me any orders you have, and believe me my dear Major with love to all our officers.

Your most
faithful friend
R. Stewart.

This is addressed to Major Cunningham C. Officer L.D.M. Ballyshannon. The next letter is addressed to 'Major Lenox Cunningham, Drogheda, Ireland.'

My dear friend Cunningham,

it gives me very sincere pleasure indeed to have so interesting an occasion of wishing you joy, as that which our Col. announces in his last letter; permit me also thru' you to offer my congratulations to Mrs. Cunningham (if she yet bears that name.) I trust you may both long live a happiness to each other.

Mr. Conolly has been very indulgent in permitting me to extend my stay here. I have not idly desired it. My venerable friend and father, Ld. Camden, is in so declining a state and his family so agitated, that it would be painful to me to leave them, besides I have other business which makes it of the greatest importance to me to be permitted to stay.[95] Perhaps my absence may impose more attendance upon you than may be either convenient or congenial to a honeymoon, which I trust will not be of short duration, if so, my Dr. Major, I shall feel excessively distress'd. If on the contrary in the full enjoyment of happiness you can carry off the fatigues and troubles of your Military Situation without entrenching on your civil duties, the indulgence will be gratefully acknowledged by me.

I find the Regt. is torn to Rags by detachments; as long as we are in Louth our discipline will not advance. I have got some charming musick for the *band*, which I will send by the first opportunity. All idea of invasion seems past.

Affect. love to all the Corps. I will write to Stark next post.

Ever most sincerely your friend,
R. Stewart,

Hill St.,
Ld. Camdens, Sunday

I beg to hear from you.

Drogheda 14th.

My Dr. Major,

Ly. Emily and I have been settled here since the 1st. The Col. informs me you are to succeed me in my Command. As I should be glad to see you and Mrs. C., if it was only for a day, and to deliver up in person this *mighty fortress* into your hands, I hope nothing will prevent you from being here the 1st of Nov.

I am under the necessity of setting out the 2nd for the purpose of leaving Ly. Emily at Mt. Stewart and proceeding to England to attend the opening of Parlt. in haste

Dr. Major,
Your affect. Servt.
R. Stewart.

Castlereagh was evidently of a cold nature. He was ambitious, and his heart was set on attaining prominence in this country, but still more so in England. His constant absence from the Londonderry Regiment left George Conyngham mostly in command, and it was George who was called upon to master the many difficulties and to shoulder the grave discomforts of Camp life. This duty he performed cheerfully for some years and was most efficient in bringing the Regiment into good order.

The Colonel, Mr. Thomas Conolly, was grand-nephew to the William Conolly who built Castletown, and whose letters, written just after the Siege of Derry, have already been quoted in this history.

Thomas Conolly was Governor of Co. Derry and Speaker in the Irish House of Commons. He had a town house in Merrion Street, Dublin, and married Lady Louisa Lennox, daughter of the Duke of Richmond and sister of Lady Sarah Lennox and of the Duchess of Leinster.

The nickname of this prominent person was 'Squire Conolly,' and his portrait by Sir Joshua Reynolds hangs at Castletown, shewing a handsome, pale face with dark pensive eyes.[96]

George Lenox-Conyngham was greatly attached to his Colonel – (far more so than to Robert Stewart, the Lieut. Colonel) and has left twenty of his letters, which display a genial personality and give a vivid picture of the difficulties encountered in training the Londonderry Militia. In past days Conolly had been corresponding with George's Uncle – William Conyngham – as to his troop of Volunteers in the year 1783.

Ten years later, in a letter from Lissan of April 16th, 1793, he expresses his wish to have George Conyngham as a Deputy Governor of Co. Derry and also as an officer in his Regiment.

> My dear Sir, Lissane,
>
> I should take it as a particular Favour if you would allow me to name you to my Lord Lieutenant as a Deputy Governor for our array, and as it is necessary to send an answer to the Secretary at War by Thursday night post from Derry, I should wish to have your answer deliver'd to my friend Staples. I should likewise be happy to have you in preference to anyone for our Major, which I know will be a troublesome business, but it is necessary to have Gentlemen of Property, Spirit and Activity in that situation, especially as He will frequently have the Command of the Regiment, from the absence of young Mr. Robert Stewart and myself. Our families were always connected together and this will cement that connection.
>
> May I trouble you to give my compliments to Mr. Millar and desire to know if he will act as a Dep. Governor and an officer.
>
> I am Dr. Sir,
>
> Yours most Truly, Thos. Conolly.

Two days later came another letter, from Mr. Conolly, from 'Newtownlimevady.'

Thursday evening April 18th 1793,

My Dr. Sir,

It gives me more pleasure than you are aware of to have you for our Major, and I return you my Thanks for the very flattering manner to me in which you have taken upon you this Troublesome, but necessary, Duty. As you are a Resident County of Derry man you will have mostly the Command, and, when I return to Dublin on Monday night, shall chiefly communicate with you. I do not think we shall have much trouble in the Array on this side of the Mountain, but you will have some at Magherafelt and its neighbourhood.

I beg you would look out for your own Lieutenant and Ensign, and I shall certainly appoint whoever you name.

I am Dr. Sir,
Your much obliged
Humble Servt. Thos. Conolly.

The next letter contains the names of the Captains appointed when the Londonderry Militia was first embodied.

Dublin, May 18, 1793.

Dear Sir,

I shall be very happy indeed if your Subdivisional Meetings go off as well as your first, and I am in great hopes they will do so, if everything is quiet about Magherafelt, The Meath Defenders are up again in great numbers. They give out strange stories to prevent the Array of the Militia there. I have signed your Commission and enclose it, being dated the day after my own. I have not signed any more, except Colonel Stewart's and our seven Captains, and our Adjutant, who you will love and who has been a Lieutenant of Grenadiers for many years. I have made him a Brevet and he will command my Company.

Both Mr. Stark and myself will attend, and so, I am sure, will Lt. Col. Stewart. He wishes to stay some time with his Father at Mt. Stewart, but if you want him, let me know, and I will write to him.

Thos. Conolly.

He appends a list of the Captains.

Captains. Andrew Ferguson, David Ross,
William Ross, Robt. Galt,
James Stevenson, Nathaniel Hunter,
Robt. Smith.

Capt. Brevet – David Stark,
Adjutant – David Stark.

I shall recommend it to our Captains to toss up or draw straws for Rank. Gett them to settle it amicably amongst themselves as I have promised no preeminence to anyone.

In a letter from Dublin, of May 23rd, 1793, Mr. Conolly writes:

> 'We are preparing our cloathing and must begin with Jacketts and Trowsers and Round Hatts, as the cloathiers will not have the full Regimentals ready till September. The Rich ought to pay according to their abilities, which will be put into a stock Purse and by that means ease the poorer men. … I think that in another year Parliament will make some provision (as in England) for the wives and familys of those that go out of their Countys, at least I will endeavour to accomplish it. I do not believe our Parliament will meet before the 5th of June, and in the meantime all the Trouble of the Array lays upon you, and be assured whatever you do will meet with my Approbation. … Now about our Cloathing Accoutrements, I am going to send down all the Captains' Commissions, but Mr. James Stevenson has declined at the C— of his father. Would young Ellis or a Mr. Gage … or John Spotswood be the best man to put in his place? Lett me know your opinion by Return of the Post.

> Dublin, June 22nd.
>
> Dr. Sir,
>
> As I have heard from nobody about the second General Meeting of Deputy Governors. But in the Act now pending in Parliament … we shall be allowed to take Volunteers, as you will see by the enclosed Cause, of which I must beg you to send a copy to all the Captains and Deputy Governors and desire them to act accordingly, otherwise the Derry Regt. instead of being the first, will be the last Raised. The moment I can signify to Government that the men are Ready, that moment we shall be put upon Pay. The Jacketts, Hatts and Trousers will be ready the first week in July and Colonel Stuart, Mr. Stark and I are ready to sett out at a moment's warning after next week, when all Business will be finished in the House that is of Consequence.
>
> I am Dr. Sir,
> Yours most truly,
> Thos. Conolly.
>
> I have appointed Mr. Downing Nesbitt a Captain in the Room of Mr. James Stevenson, who has declined.

In a letter from Castletown, December 24th, 1793, Mr. Conolly tells that Commissions in the Londonderry Regiment were applied for by a Mr. Church and a Mr. Ennis, and that he had recommended Mr. Archibald Hamilton for the Vacant Ensignry, as he had promised Staples.

George Lenox-Conyngham left copies of some of his own letters to his Colonel, Mr. Conolly, which shew his mind with regard to these events. One of them is as follows:

My dear Colonel,

These resignations and alterations in your Regt. I know full well are tormenting you. To relieve you from this disagreeable situation has been an object nearest to my heart and I think I have accomplished it. Sterling is oldest Lieutenant, his father and he have money enough, I have land enough, we understand each other; make him Captain of Grenadiers, and let the envious rascal or vile attorney attack him, if they dare. This comes better from me than anyone else, as I know him to be a gallant young Gentleman, who cannot be prevail'd upon to shrink from his duty when our country is threatened with internal commotion or foreign Invasion. …

'I love you, dear Colonel, and nothing shall be wanting on my part that can contribute to the prosperity of your Regt. and your own peace and happiness.

I am with great truth
Your ever affect, friend and humble Servt.
Geo. Lenox Conyngham.

In a long letter from Castletown on December 26th, 1793, Mr. Conolly deplores the conduct of 45 soldiers who had on former occasions been treated with too much lenity.

They were raised reluctantly. They were treated with Affection and Humanity, and they mutinied. They must be treated with Rigour and every Punishment that Martial Law will admit of. The Ring-Leaders ought to be drummed out of the Regiment. I beg you, in my name, to return Thanks publickly to Messrs. Church, Sterling and Brown for their very Gallant Behaviour.

'I was sorry that this disagreeable but necessary Business falls to your Lott to attend.'

Yours very truly, T. Conolly.

Private Staples will be in Dublin till Parliament meets. Lett me know privately what Religion the different Branches are of, as something may be discovered by that Means. The men depend upon their numbers for their security against Punishment.'

From George Lenox-Conyngham to Mr. Conolly;

Ballyshannon, 1st Jan. 1794

Dear Colonel,

I take the liberty of enclosing you the proceedings of a Court Martial.

He goes on to inveigh against the partiality and want of justice shown in the verdict on this delicate affair. The copy of the letter is much corrected. In these letters the 'Defenders' are mentioned. These were a body of rebellious Roman Catholics, who later on were merged in the United Irishmen.

Soon after this, George's second marriage, with Miss Olivia Irvine of Castle Irvine,[97] took place, and a letter from Mr. Conolly of Co. Fermanagh, May 16th, 1794 begins:

> My Dr. Major,
>
> I hope this will find you and Mrs. Conyngham well and as happy as I wish you.
> (He then comments on the conduct of 'Davy Ross' *who would go to the Assizes* tho' he had been so little with the Regt.)
> While I have the honour to command this Regiment I will not be trifled with. … Love to Mrs. Conyngham and her sister, and believe me
>
> Always yours truly, Thos. C.

> Castletown, July 7, 1794
> My Dr. Major,
>
> Our Review is fix'd by Genl. Craig for the 2nd of August. I am afraid this will break upon your Retirement at Springhill, as it will be necessary for you to be with us at least Ten days before that time, as the General means to send down a plan of a Review that it will be necessary for the *Major* to practise and to be master of. ... We are order'd to send a Captain, two Subalterns and 50 Privates to help, to make up the Garrison of Dublin, the 34th Regt. being *embark'd* to enable Gt. Britain to dictate a Constitution to France which is unjust, Impolitick and Impracticable. But God's Will be done, we Paddys must make the best of it and defend ourselves, and I long much to have our Regt. compleet, but that I fear cannot happen unless we take others than Derrymen, which I should not like to do in any numbers. But I believe I must now take any Handsome young men I can gett.
>
> 'Our love to Mrs. Conyngham, Her Sister and Miss Hamilton.
>
> Believe me,
> Yours very truly,
> Thos. Conolly.

It seems that the bride, Mrs. Olivia Lenox Conyngham, brought her sister to Springhill, and the Miss Hamilton here mentioned was Rebecca, the sister of little Jenny and devoted aunt to the two year old 'Wims.'

A Postscript to a letter dated August 23rd relates:

> Our Grenadiers Return'd to Quarters last Monday. They were sent off at a few Hours Notice to make way for the 95th from England, the greatest Ragamuffins you ever saw.

George's second marriage was evidently engrossing him very much and making him restless at the prospect of being so much with his Regiment, and away from home.

Dublin, Saty. 15 Nov. 1794.

My Dr. Major,

No Rebellion, No Invasion, but my Lord Doneraile and the S. Cork Regt. Being tired of Quarters in the mountains of Leitrim and Sligo, chose (I believe) to liquidate some political promises by being removed to some better Quarters. Who should be removed? Why Conolly and all those Fellows near Dublin, who do not think our system of Government the Best. The Commander in Chief absolutely *Avoided* me this day. But I will see him to-morrow morning to putt him in mind that he told me we should not leave Drogheda, *unless circumstances made it necessary, Till the Spring.*

Yrs. ever,
T. C.

On April 16th, 1795, Mr. Conolly relates that he had just returned from Carrick and hoped that the Deputy Governors of the Co. of Derry would exert themselves and get the six pounds per man, according to the last Act of Parliament.

Almost all the other Counties have got their additional numbers but I have not heard from you or anyone how you are going on in Derry.

He adds:

I have sent Capt. Sterling to superintend the Recruiting, as you will be soon coming up to see Mrs. Conyngham and to go to Carrick. Col. Stuart has sent me word that the Lord Lieut. will order them to Dublin or to an encampment that is to be found near it.

The last of Conolly's letters was from Dublin on May 12th, 1795:

My Dr. Major,

My mother is so ill and dying that I shall be obliged to go over to England at furthest in the course of next week. Col. Stuart, being the Relation and Intimate friend of the Lord Lieut., stays much with him if not employed in Parliament which is still sitting. Our Regt. … will be encamp'd in wooden houses near Loughlinstown … the clothing of the whole Regiment will be ready in July.

I am yours Ever Truly,
Tho. Conolly.

I saw your wife yesterday. She looks well, but must suspend her Impatience for the *Major* for about a fortnight more.

In this correspondence there is a significant undercurrent. It deals ostensibly with the struggle to form an efficient Regiment from rough, unruly material.

But meanwhile the letters throw sidelights on the characters of the three Commanding Officers of the Londonderry Militia – Conolly appearing to be wise, considerate and genial – Stewart coldly courteous but calculating, his aim seemingly to seek for himself political rather than military prowess, and causing him to leave to his Major an undue share of the hardships and problems which fall to the acting Colonel of a Militia Regiment.

It was George who bore the burden of the Command, which was distasteful to his impetuous and domestic character, for his love of home was intense. As time went on, he saw that the danger of invasion was over and the Regiment well trained – largely by his own efforts – and began to think that the hour was nearing when he might return to live in peace with wife and children at Springhill. The home-coming was hastened in an unforeseen manner, and what occurred is clearly described in a long letter to his Chief, in which he gives his own account of the episode:

> 10th Aug. /95.
>
> Dear Sir,
>
> I did not hear of your return to Ireland untill yesterday, or I wou'd have taken the liberty of intruding this letter on your patience sooner. My resigning the post of Major in your Regt. was a matter which probably you expected when you left Ireland, be that as it may, I cannot be longer silent in explaining my reasons for having taken the step in your absence. It will be necessary for the sake of my own recollection hereafter as well as my justification at present, to take a general view of my conduct since I first was induced to accept of a Command in your Regt. the 16th of April 1793. I had the honour of receiving a letter from you requesting that I should be your Major in preference to any one. I comply'd with your wishes, and you in the most flattering manner expressed your thanks for my having done so (to make use of your words 'it was an unpopular, a very troublesome and a very unprofitable business'). I engaged in it, and I cannot charge myself with want of zeal or activity in assisting to overcome the many difficulties that occur'd in a measure at the time so obnoxious to the country. When you came to New-town you found a body of men, the number of which surpriz'd you. I will not repeat the different circumstances that took place previous to the Regiment's being ordered to Ballyshannon. I shall only observe that I exerted myself as far as lay in my power to bring a body of my young Country-men, disposed to mutiny, under military discipline. In this our efforts were, as we thought, crowned with success. I march'd with the Regt. to Ballyshannon … and when I return'd, I found our soldiers had conceiv'd an idea that they might do as they pleased … forty-five of them march'd from quarters without leave. … By the exertions of my Brother Officers most of these runaways were brought back. Severe punishment was inflicted and subordination again restored. To be short, when we met you in Drogheda, I had the satisfaction of delivering to your Command a well disciplined Regt. of soldiers … and you in the kindest manner expressed your approbation of the conduct of all our officers. They deserved it. A change in my situation in Life soon

after took place, and I had your leave to spend some time at Springhill. I attended your Review. Your Regt. meritted every praise so justly bestow'd on it by the General. I returned to my Seat, where my time was not alone dedicated to my Domestick concerns (which, indeed from long absence, had been greatly neglected) but mostly employ'd in recruiting soldiers for the completion of your Regiment, ... My exertions were extended to serve the Regt. in general, and this every Captain in your Regt. will bear witness of. This Duty being done, I left Home with my Family for the purpose of Commanding all Winter at Drogheda, where it was expected the Regt. was to remain in absence of both you and Colonel Stewart, whose duty in Parliament compell'd you to be from it.

We were disappointed in our expectations. The Regt. was ordered to Carrick-on-Shannon. My wife's situation at that time absolutely put it out of my power to accompany them on the march; I went to Dublin, and soon after her recovery from childbirth I went to Quarters, where I stay'd untill my duty as Sheriff of Tyrone compelled me to attend at Omagh Assizes. At that time the Act of augmenting the Militia had passed, and before I returned to my Family (who were still in Town) I attended the first general meeting at Newtown Limevady for the purpose of persuading the Deputy Governors to exert themselves in order to gratify your wishes with respect to the parishes furnishing six pounds per man. In this I was successful, as I informed you by letter from S. hill, and I gave you a hint of what was probable I intended to do – that my situation in life, having a large establishment etc. wou'd oblige me to relinquish a military life, unless I was indulged with liberty to enjoy domestic happiness and not to be a *fag major*.

I received no answer to this letter. I returned to Dublin, and when the accounts came on Thursday of the serious disturbance at Leitrim and Roscommon, the Saturday following I breakfasted at Dromona with flints for our soldiers, whose arms without that supply wou'd have been useless.

I now come to that part of my history which it gives me pain to recollect, yet much more to repeat. You knew full well the situation I had left my young and amiable wife in. You knew that I had brought my only son to Dublin to be inoculated for the smallpox. Thus circumstanced, it will be natural to conclude the feeling of a Father and Husband must have been great, when I was informed my Child had taken that distemper. I had intended to have written to you requesting your leave of absence for a short time, when in the midst of my anxiety, I received a letter from you, desiring that I wou'd remain with the Regt. untill it was ordered to Camp. The country having been subdued, and all quiet about Carrick, I did not hesitate a moment, I confess, about leaving Quarters, when I left most excellent and competent Officers behind me. I returned to Dublin, Colonel Stewart went to take his *turn* of duty. I saw him the morning he went away. The day the Regt. arrived in Dublin I was informed Colonel Stewart did not wish to see me, as he had returned me absent without leave. In consequence I did not join the Regt. but after the Division had been dismissed, I waited on Col. Stewart at your house, when he told me he had it in order to put all Officers under Arrest who were absent without leave, and that it was not in his power to dispense with such an essential part of his Duty. No reciprocal obligations having ever passed between Col. Stewart and me made me look on this strict military *correctness* with frigid indifference. I saw the motive – Had I experienced the same conduct by you, very different indeed wou'd have been my feelings. I shou'd have suffered in the extreme that heart-felt wound which is inflicted by disappointment in friendship. You know I had it next my heart and did everything in my power to remove all matters that had a tendency to create in you a moment's disquietude, and I shou'd have expected a mutual return. You cannot suppose I had any other object in view. Let me now come to the last part of my story. I waited on Mr. Stewart at his house near the Camp. I asked him if he had unlimited power to act in your absence respecting Regimental business. He said in reply that he had. This being the case and his convenience and mine interfering so much in opposition, left me no time to determine what I shou'd do. I therefore addressed myself to him in nearly these words: 'Sir, if the resignation of my Commission at this time will be attended with inconvenience to the Londonderry Regt. I will continue to hold it and do my duty, let the consequence be ever so injurious to me and my Family's domestick comfort, but on the contrary, if it will not, you will oblige me by accepting of it for Colonel Conolly, who I suppose has authorized you to receive it.' He said he wou'd take it on himself, as being Commanding Officer in your absence. I resigned my Commission and with it my sword. But if this country unhappily shou'd be involved in the calamity of war, you shall find me with it drawn in my hand at the head of one hundred *Loyal Protestants* ready to join my brave Regiment to repell foreign Invasion or quell internal insurrection. – Before I conclude this Letter, permit me to observe that you have Officers in your Regt. whose situation in life renders strict attention to the duty of Major no ways inconvenient to them, and whose military qualifications are perhaps superior to mine, but I will not give up to any man the ardent desire I always had to promote the honour, prosperity and respectability of the Londonderry Regiment of Militia.

I am, Dr. Sir,
With great truth,
Your most obedt. and very
humble servant,
Geo. Lenox Conyngham.

Right Hon. Thos. Conolly,
S. Hill, 10th Aug. 1795.

It was thus that George ended his task of commanding the Londonderry Regiment. He acted with what his wise old uncle had termed 'his usual rapidity,' feeling burning indignation at the severity with which Col. Stewart had treated one who had been so useful to him in the past. Perhaps it was this sense of obligation which had embittered Stewart, who must have known that he had often imposed on Conyngham's good nature. However, George himself was in the wrong for letting his warm domestic feelings interfere with a strict sense of military duty. and the cold-blooded Stewart lost no time in taking advantage of this slip. The episode casts a side-light on the character of Castlereagh, which title he afterwards inherited.

From this time onward George Lenox-Conyngham's life was spent at Springhill with his wife Olivia, who gave him five daughters and one son – another George. No portrait of Olivia survives, but it is known that she was a harsh step-mother to Jenny's son – poor little William (nicknamed 'Wims'). She is said to have put him to sleep in a dark closet near the pantry door at Springhill. Other reprehensible actions of Olivia were the burning of a whole set of beautiful old Jacobean chairs, which she found uncomfortable, the selling of some of the Lenox silver, and the inscribing in some of the prayer-books of affected, sentimental prayers, which have an insincere ring.

At the time of which I write, few of the children were born, and little Wims was under the rough wing of his step-mother. There are but few mentions of his childhood. His mother's sister Rebecca, afterwards Lady Galbraith, was fortunately able to be sometimes with him, and there is a letter to her brother-in-law, addressed to Ballyshannon, which expresses her devotion to the child. She wrote:

Jacobean chair

> Bell[98] and I went yesterday to see our dear little William and he really is as well and looks as well as you could wish him. He would scarce speak to us he was so busy painting a *Hobby-Horse* that Tatty has made for him. I think he has grown rather fatter than he was when you left home. Your brother told me that he had let you know of Nurse's husband being at Springhill – he stayed five or six days. However he is now gone, and I am very glad of it. Nurse says he is quite reformed and wishes to get a place in this country. She I am sure is a good woman and so much attached to William that I believe she would not leave him on any account while he required her care. I think, my dear George, that there are few things in this life cd. give me more real pleasure and Happiness than being of use to him. I would do so for his own sake and for the sake of his poor mother, who I shall never cease to regret. It was the last words she said to me to take care of him.
>
> Yr. ever affect.
> Rebecca Hamilton.

'Wims' high nursery-chair is still in the Springhill night nursery and has been used by his great grandsons and by his great great grandson, Marcus Henry Clements.

It appears that the warm-hearted George L. Conyngham gave a home at Springhill to his brother Clotworthy ('Tatty'), who eventually died there.

Though now no longer in the Derry Militia, George continued to exert himself on behalf of the Province, for dark clouds were again gathering over Ulster.

The Protestant 'Peep of Day boys' had been continually sparring with the Catholic 'Defenders,' and now the formidable society of 'United Irishmen' was daily gaining strength and enrolling both the persecuted Roman Catholics and aggrieved Presbyterians, whose wrongs gave them a fellow feeling.

The United Irishmen received both inspiration and help from the Revolutionists in France. One of the leaders was the ill-fated Lord Edward Fitzgerald, who was strongly influenced by his wife, Pamela's, parents – Mme. de Genlis and Philippe Égalité, Duc d'Orléans. Madame de Genlis posed as a model of circumspection and a prim trainer of youth, but her private life was far from virtuous, and her association with the dangerous foreign secret society – the *Illuminati* – caused her to be instrumental in fanning the French Revolution and in turning her lover, *Égalité*, against his cousin, the King. It is easy to conceive how this clever, determined woman swayed the opinions of her simple-hearted and excitable son-in-law, whose rebellious activities in Ireland led him to a tragic death.

In the year 1796 alarming rumours were current in Northern Ireland. A body of Yeomanry had been formed for its protection, and in the July of that year Mr. Thomas Knox of Dungannon [99] wrote to George Lenox-Conyngham as follows;

> My dear Sir,
>
> I enclose some copies of the Dungannon Association – a measure actually of self-preservation and which, if it becomes general, may be the means of saving the country and extinguishing the treasonable conspiracies that we know have been formed in this part of the Province. If you approve of it, and that the people of your neighbourhood come to similar resolutions, be so good as to send them to me and I will have them printed in the Newspapers with ours.
>
> Very truly yours,
> Thos, Knox.
> Dungannon, 16 July 1796.

Other letters followed. In the following October Mr. Knox wrote:

> My dear Sir,
> Two persons calling themselves Taylor and McCullagh have been very busy of late in the country propagating the Belfast Doctrines. They are said to be inhabitants of Coagh. Are there such personages in that town? and of suspicious character?
>
> Very faithfully,
> Thos. Knox.

Dungannon, Nov. 18th 1796.

My dear Sir,

May I beg the favour of you to inform me in a post or two whether a House sufficient to accomodate forty soldiers can be had in the town of Coagh. I have stated to Lord Corhampton the necessity of sending troops hither, provided temporary barracks can be had. It certainly would not be prudent to billet soldiers upon the inhabitants, many of whom are suspected of disaffection.

I am my Dr. Sir,
Yours very faithfully,
Thos. Knox.

George apparently responded with zest, and not long after, a paper was drawn up as follows:

We the undersigned Inhabitants of Ballindrum and Ballydawly do associate and unite together as yeoman for the Protection of our Lives and properties and the support of the Laws and Constitutions of this Kingdom against all foreign invaders and internal insurgents.

Geo. L. Conyngham.

(and in a different handwriting)

We the inhabitants of B. drum & B. dawly can only add, in adition (*sic*) to what we formerly purposed, that we will chearfully swear that we will protect the person & property of our worthy and well-beloved Landlord Geo. L. Conyngham Esq. against either foreign or Domestic *Enemies* at the risk of our lives.

The following paper is at Springhill:

Nov. 1796.				
Down	15,556	£27	2	3
Derry	8,000	16	16	10
Tyrone	6,500	21	12	3
Louth				
Armagh	2,500	15	15	11
Donegall	3,000	2	2	4
Monaghan	2,500	0	0	0
Cavan	800	0	0	0
Meath	1,776	0	0	0
Antrim	20,000	50	4	4
Fermanagh	1,500	0	0	0
	63,332	report £133	15	1½

We recommend the different Societies to have their arms in requisition and secretly conceal'd, as it is the intention of administration to disarm the North part of this Kingdom. We recommend it also to the Societys that they will be patient under their oppressions, as things are not in entire readyness, but they may depend that everything that can be done is doing, and to prevent the dangers attending large bodies of Delegates, be it res. that only one delegate be received for every 12 Societies in the next county meeting. It was moved and carry'd that the now existing Ex Coms are dissolved from their next monthly meeting and that we now appoint new members for the same. Resolved that Ex. Com. be responsible to us for measures and expenditures of money and 2 of its members regularly attend our meeting, report that 8000 maps are to be printed in Belfast and 3000 in Strabane. Resolved that we are of opinion to abstain from spirituous Liquors as from their consumption gain arrizes our most inveterate Enemies.

Pat Quin H. Hamil
Ph Devlin G. Orr
Pat Henry Wm. Orr [100]
Jas. Devlin John Keenan
Michael Meares.

Conyngham must have acquired this paper by stealth. It clearly refers to the secret organization of 'United Irishmen' and was a useful discovery to those who were trying to maintain law and order. Coagh was evidently a centre of conspiracy.

Mr. Knox wrote again from Dungannon:

My dear Sir,

I have but a moment to acknowledge your letter and information – very useful – can you get others to corroborate Taylor's belief? Will you dine and take a bed with me on Saturday. You'll meet Genl. Lake[101] and my brother Genl. Knox. The latter is to reside at Dungannon. Troops certainly at Coagh.

Faithfully yrs.
Thos. Knox.

Conyngham's friend and neighbour, Lord Castlestewart, was also busying himself in aiding the precautionary measures in case of rebellion. He wrote from Stuart Hall on the 20th of March 1797 saying:

General Knox called here this morning and suggested a measure which, if you approve of, you will please to subscribe. It is to be printed and dispersed by Handbills, and it is conceived will be less irritating to the people than taking their arms from them, which some of the County of Armagh Yeomanry had this morning commenced in this vicinity. Lady Castlestewart unites with me in best wishes for you Mrs. Conyngham and all the little ones. I shall be very happy to hear you are all well. I am my Dear Sir,

Most faithfully and affectionately yours
Castlestewart.

Dungannon, March 21, 97.

Dear Sir,

I have this morning received your letter, and return you many thanks for the trouble you have taken respecting the Fencible Corps. I expected that everything would have been settled long before this. The letters of Service issued Terms – explained, but it does not appear that Government has yet come to any Resolution on the subject, or if they have they have laid it on the shelf till they have money to go through with the Business.

The United are taking up Arms about Carrenteel. I think that as soon as the Registry Business is settled we shall recover most of the Arms in the Barony.

I am Dear Sir,
Yours very truly, J. Knox.

Two days later General Knox wrote to Conyngham the following:

Dungannon, March 23rd 1797

Sir,

Notice having been dispersed through the County for all persons, who had registered their arms to come to the Justices of the Peace to deliver an inventory of the Arms in their possession, to be verified by their Affidavits, I submit to you the following points:

First that the Justices of the Peace should not leave in the possession of one person more arms than he thinks it necessary for that person to have.

Second that the Justices of the Peace shall withdraw *all* the Arms from persons of known disloyal character and from those in whose keeping they would not be safe from the attempts of the United Irishmen to seize them.

Third that the Justices of Peace shall give a certificate to those persons who he thinks may with safety be entrusted with arms,

Fourth that the Justices of Peace shall return the affidavits to the Clerk of the Peace and state what arms are permitted to remain with, and what taken from each person that they may be noted in the Registry Book.

Fifth that the Justices of Peace shall put interrogatories upon oath to those persons who declare that they have lost their arms or that their arms have been taken by force.

In all cases where the Justices of Peace call in Arms they must give Receipts for them, as pointed out by the Act, have them labelled with the owner's name, and sent under escort to the Fort of Charlemont.

I have the Honour to be Sir,
Your very obedient servant, J. Knox.

A later letter of May 6th from the General states that the state of the Country required that the Dragoons should be taken out of billets and securely lodged with their horses, either in barracks or in the outhouses and stables of gentlemen who could accommodate them and were willing to receive them. He therefore begged to know whether Conyngham could spare room for an Officer and twenty Dragoons of the 24th Regiment at Springhill.

The fortified barn in the upper yard

This was probably done, as Springhill possesses a plethora of outbuildings which doubtless proved very useful, as they did in recent history.

Pelham, the Chief Secretary for Ireland, also wrote to George Conyngham at this time, on thick gilt-edged notepaper, as follows:

Dublin Castle,

Sir,

I received the Honour of your letter enclosing examinations respecting Mr. Ledlie, and am to acquaint you that he is entitled to pardon under the proclamation, if he has surrendered to a Magistrate of the Quorum and given recognizance for his good behaviour. I am afraid therefore that he cannot suffer for his past crimes. In a letter, written by you some time since, you mentioned having received information against Capt. Thomas Russell, now in custody for his conduct as Leader of the United Irishmen. I wish therefore particularly to know whether the person from whom you received it can be induced to come forward, and I should be obliged by your transmitting to me as soon as possible the particulars of the information.

I have the Honour to be Sir,
Your most obedient and humble servant,
A. Pelham.

It must be remembered that the French had tried to land in Southern Ireland in the previous year, and that revolutionary France was actively aiding the rebellious element in Ireland, and Dutch ships were preparing to sail against England.

The Yeomanry in Northern Ireland were busy searching for arms, and troops had been brought from England to assist.

In the May of this year the wise and patriotic Henry Grattan, assisted by his friend Ponsonby, had tried to reform the laws against Catholics and to bring them on to the same footing as Protestants so as to have a just and representative Parliament.

This fair measure would have allayed hostility and helped to quell rebellion, but Grattan was defeated in the Irish House of Commons and thenceforward ceased to attend Parliament.

There is no doubt that the efforts of George L. Conyngham and his friends did much to break the rebellious formations in N. Ireland, where outbreaks were few, in spite of Belfast having been one of the main centres of the conspiracy.

In October General Lake's Yeomanry seized seventy-two cannon, fifty thousand muskets and thirty thousand pikes.

Before the outbreak, the capture and death of Wolfe Tone, Fitzgerald, and some of the principal leaders, stemmed the tide of revolution, but in the south, and especially in Co. Wexford, the struggle was fierce, and alas it cannot be said that the warfare waged by British troops against the rebels was merciful. Many innocent had to suffer with the guilty, and horrible atrocities were perpetrated by both sides.

Histories of the Irish Rebellion of 1798 have been written by Maxwell and by Sir Richard Musgrave, which are painful to read, and Cruickshank's illustrations do much to emphasise the horror.

Sir Richard Musgrave consulted George Lenox-Conyngham before writing his history, and on April 27th, 1799, wrote to him as follows:

> Sir.
>
> As your loyalty and activity as a Magistrate are well known to me, though I have not the honour of your acquaintance, I take the liberty of addressing you on the following occasion. I have undertaken to write a history of the Rebellion, and have got very copious information of what passed in Leinster and Munster, but I have little or no knowledge of what occurred in Ulster. May I request then the favour of your assistance as to what happened in the County of Derry.
>
> For the sake of perspicuity I submit the following queries to you.
> 1st when did the Defenders first appear there?
> 2nd were they not exclusively of the Papist religion?
> 3rd what seemed to have been their design?
> 4th when did they joyn with and become subservient to the United Irishmen?
> 5th Did the Papists and Presbyterians ever cordially unite and at what time in the Rebellion?
> 6th From the great antipathy which ever existed between these sects I am much at a loss to know how they could ever be made to unite. I have been assured that the Presbyterians quitted the Papists as soon as they discovered that they were impelled by that sanguinary spirit which was ever peculiar to their religion. Any anecdotes of atrocities committed by the United Irishmen will be very acceptable (!) I don't mention the names of any gentlemen who are so good as to favour me with their assistance.
>
> I have the Honour to be Sir,

Your most obedient humble servant,
Richd. Musgrave.

Dublin April 27th 1799.
'I send you the speech of Mr. Addington.
G. L. Conyngham, Esq.

George Conyngham kept the rough notes of his reply:

> In the year 1793 the first insurgents appeared in this neighbourhood – They did not stile themselves defenders, but were distinguished by the name of Green-Cockade-men, from their wearing such in their hats. They paraded and exercised in the different villages publickly. I informed Government of their proceedings and General White was directed to this Country – He accordingly came to my House and an immediate stop was put to their public meetings – from that time a more secret plan of proceeding was adopted by persons styling themselves United Irishmen.
>
> In your second query – the Conspirators were composed of Presbyterians and Papists and some of the Established Church.
>
> To your third – their object was to overturn the present Government, both Church and State, and introduce a Republick on the very same plan as that now exists in France.
>
> To your fourth – I have already sayd that they were never called Defenders in this Country but from the very first of their secret proceedings they were styled United Irishmen.
>
> To your 5th – I am confident that the Presbyterians and the Papists never did cordially unite and that from the first they were jealous of one another, this I know from certain information and my own observation – for instance, when the Rebellion broke in the County of Antrim and Derry few or none of the Papists appeared in arms. About three hundred men arose in arms in and around Maghera, but they were soon discomfited, and of all the prisoners that were taken and tryed only one of them was a Papist – all Presbyterians, except one Church of England man. With respect to your wonder why the Papists and Presbyterians shou'd ever unite, I am clearly of opinion that the Protestant traitors never intended that the papists should derive any benefit from a Revolution; they only wanted their assistance to bring such a measure about and afterwards crush and trample on them. The Papists saw through their design, but carefully concealed their knowledge, depending on their superior numbers for absolute power and control in the end. Thus, for the purpose of making tools of each other, they apparently drew together, but you may be assured that the rooted antipathy, which ever existed between them, did and still does remain.

In the year 1800 the Union of the Governments of England and Ireland took place. Pitt, the English Prime Minister, was resolved to carry out this measure, his chief agent in Ireland being the aforementioned Robert Stewart, now Viscount Castlereagh.

The vast majority of the Irish people was opposed to the Act of Union, but opposition was overcome by promises to the Catholics alleging that they would be admitted to office, and by the shameful bribery which Castlereagh used to force the measure through the Irish Parliament, thus inducing it to vote for its own extinction.

Twenty-eight new peerages were created, and there were many promotions. Eighty boroughs were bought from their owners for vast sums.

It is pleasant to record that many Irish gentlemen were too honourable to accept bribery. Chief Justice Bushe [102] refused to sell his principles for £30,000 and a peerage, and others were equally scrupulous.

It has been said that George Lenox-Conyngham refused a title, which was offered on condition that he would use his influence on behalf of the Union, and we must hope that this tale is true.

This was a very critical time in Irish History, and some of the letters, which have been preserved at Springhill, give a glimpse into the opinions which were then rife.

A packet of letters – *circa* 1798–1803 remains which were written to a forebear of the Conynghams, The Right Hon. John Staples of Lissan, by his friend, Colonel Napier. This man was the distinguished father of famous sons – Sir Charles Napier and his brothers. He had married Lady Sarah Lennox, the Duke of Richmond's daughter, and aunt to the unhappy Lord Edward Fitzgerald, and they lived at Celbridge in Co. Kildare.

This correspondence throws so much light on the events of these days that some of the letters must be given.

Napier usually addresses his friend by the nom-de-plume 'Cornelius Tacitus.'

> Jan.5th,
>
> My dear Cornelius,
>
> I have received yours containing an account of Orange violence which shocks without surprising me, as I am not new to learn the deadly effects of religious fury when combined with political prejudice and party zeal; we too have had our horrors, but in my opinion they are not quite so detestable and certainly not such barefaced breaking of Law and good Government as those which have been perpetrated in your vicinity; ours are indiscriminate outrages, which attach to no particular Sect or Party; in fact the Catholics have been the principal sufferers, and the culprits were the outcasts of the Rebel Army, miscreants proscribed by Aylmer himself. For the recent murder of 'Cooly' and his mother we have taken up numbers of suspected persons, but without being able to attach guilt to anyone as yet, tho' I trust time and activity will at last detect the villains. I showed your account of the murder and rescue mentioned in yours to our friend Conolly, who agreed with me in thinking it was right to transcribe the passage without mentioning your name and sent it to my friend General Hewitt, that such abandoned outrages may not accumulate from impunity; and as I know your feelings on these subjects, I trust I have not done wrong.

My appointment is not yet completed, every underhand attempt to impede it by throwing mortifications in the way have been tried, and in its present form much odium, much labour and (without infamous breach of trust) little pecuniary profit can be derived from it. I have therefore from the very beginning considered its value arising solely from the very handsome friendly manner in which Lord Cornwallis[103] conferred it, unsolicited on my part and without the recommendation or suggestion of any one Friend, as I have his own authority for saying; he told me I owed it to his long friendship for me and his confidence in my 'firmness' and 'integrity,' and this he repeated oftener than once. However having all the good of it already, which I conceive consists in the esteem of such a man, I am perfectly indifferent about the office. Lord Cornwallis is as much abused in Dublin as he can possibly be in the North, how, my dear friend, can it be otherwise? he is a man of unsullied honour, incorruptible integrity and unbounded humanity; are not these sufficient titles to the abuse of cowards, knaves and cut-throats?

You desire my opinion respecting the impending question of 'Union.' I have not yet decided; I see so much self interest and little public spirit, so much rage and so little reason; in fine so many political Rogues for it and so many against it, that an honest man must suspend his judgment till the measure appears in a 'questionable shape.' I cannot help considering the number of Publications on this subject (above 30 I hear) before the proposal terms are promulgated, as a strong symptom of national insanity regarding the 20,000 tight jackets which Billy's[104] liberality has bestowed on the country to keep *Paddy Quiet!* The sturdy 'Anti Unionists' boldly assert that no possible arrangement can render a legislative Union beneficial to Ireland. This may be 'proud patriotism,' but it is unfortunately 'political nonsence.'

On the other side the obsequious Unionists modestly insinuate that a Kingdom derives consequence from having its legislative powers transferred to another country and accumulates wealth from 130 of its richest subjects with their long sequel of Pimps and Parasites, transporting themselves to pursue the trade of Parliament in a distant capital. In my opinion no light can be derived from analogical reasoning on this difficult subject, for though there are examples of other countries having tried this important experiment, yet manners, Religion, national prejudice, local position, soil and even climate, all combine to prevent a prudent Politican from depending on such precedents as sufficient … a sound and correct judgement; from all these considerations I draw the following conclusions that it would be prudent to form a 'provisional Union,' susceptible to being altered, confirmed or dissolved after a specified time, this might reconcile many to the measure who are now honestly hostile; and the knaves who are interestedly inimical would be compelled to silence if a reasonable experience had proved that 'Union' was beneficial to both countries.

Ever my Dear Cornelius,
Yours,
G. N.

A recent photograph of the Gun Room showing hand-painted wallpaper previously covered by the panelling.

July 18th

My dear Tacitus,

I am much obliged to you for the two shillings worth of horrors which I have just received, evil as I do think of our ministers, I cannot believe them of encouraging such wanton enormities, tho' their supineness in not bringing the perpetrators to justice is a very warrantable ground for accusing them of being accomplices in the guilt.

The conduct of one 'Executioner' do's not surprise me, when I recollect the general tendency of his disposition, and the circumstance of his juvenile amusement, which I hear was giving money at school to the Butcher to let him supply his place; what happened to him when a Subn. at Gibraltar did equal honour to his Honesty and his Courage, and his behaviour in Flanders entitled him to a severe reprimand from H.M.H. The Duke of York, whose honourable attention to the Army will I hope soon purge it from the infamy which such miscreants cast upon the profession; the cruel and undeserved reflections he threw out on his own Dunghill against the unfortunate gentleman whom his Sovereign had honoured with Commissions in the Irish Brigades was a specimen of his liberality as a man, and his respect as an officer and a subject.

People talk of Peace with much anxiety and much hope, and the opinion begins to prevail in England that Billy must march in either case; if both these events should fortunately take place we may yet be saved from Revolution and Republicanism, for tho' I am certain he will endeavour to become a Demagogue, yet I have no apprehensions either of his abilities or his popularity, when he loses support of the Sovereign and the means of corrupting the Senate.

Lord Moira was to set out for Dublin yesterday. Mr. Conolly is gone to the North. I trust you have seen his excellent address to his constituents at Derry. Lady Sarah joins me in affect. love to Mrs. Staples, Grace, Bess and Fan as do's Louisa. Tom Packenham arrived yesterday. ... I have seen William Staples[105] and his wife. She seems to be an unaffected, pleasant girl; the poor fellow, I am sorry to say looks excessively ill. Tom is well.

Remember me to your Br. and believe me,

Ever yours tho' in great haste,

(addressed to Colonel Staples, Ballycastle). G. N.

The following letter is dated February 2.

My dear Cornelius,

I have executed the Bond according to your directions, and I have paid your two subscriptions. Your letter is dated from Madden, but where that place is I know not. … The name I think would suit Dr. Willis' Acadmy. … To-morrow I set out for that Hot House of every rascality – Dublin – to assume my office with as heavy a heart as others feel at dismission? There have been many impediments thrown in my way during the progress of this Business by Enemies, who were little aware of how sincerely I wished them success; but this kind and persevering friendship of Lord Cornwallis removed every obstacle, even to my own repugnance; in fact nothing short of Foreign Service could justify a longer resistance, and even for that I have apply'd, but as yet without success. The papers will give you as much intelligence as I can respecting the grand question, which at present divides the Demons of Corsica; as these evil spirits are nearly equal on both sides I anticipate gratification at the disappointment of some of them which must be the certain result of the contest, let it end how it may. I most sincerely hope the consequences of Pitt's insanity or rather his ambitious knavery may not terminate in Democracy (which I always hold to be the worst species of Tyranny) and its blasted concomitant French alliance! It would make you laugh, were it not accompanied by ideas and recollections too horrible for mirth, could you hear some of those who during the late Rebellion wielded the whip, the torch and the Halter now exclaiming against the cruelties of Camden's administration in which they themselves acted the parts of Executioners; but shame and remorse are the indelible Brands with which a merciful God has stigmatised Cruelty, even when its horror has been masked by the pretence of retaliation – Adieu, my dear Cornelius, believe me

most affectionately yours,

Geo. Napier.

Sept. 10th.

My dear Cornelius,

I have received yours and am very glad to hear you are all in the Land of the Living, which I can scarcely say, having had a severe relapse of my complaint which absolutely tortures me

'In answer to your enquiries respecting Fees of Commissions, they are still paid by the officers but they are now applied in aid of the expenses of the War Office Establishment, the Secty. and Clerks receiving an additional salary in lieu of their perquisites; this arrangement took place long subsequent to Burke's Bill, to which it had no reference. Remember me to all at Ballycastle, particularly the Syrens of the Coast, not forgetting the simple Grace. As for the mermaids, they have long been under you, and I have not sufficient temerity to interfere with such a vigorous staff 'Non sum qualis eram,' but I still remain,

Your affect Friend,
Geo. Napier.

The following letter refers to the passing of the Union:

Thursday 6th,
My dear Cornelius,

I have received yours and accepted your draft, but I deferred answering you till it was in my power to tell you the result of yesterday's commencement; the Debate terminated at a Quarter past 12 to-day, so that the House sat longer than it ever did before. The question was for committing the Bill, I believe, however the Division was as follows:

Govt. 160. Oppn. 117.

Much gross abuse and threats of Impeachment, which nobody minds because nobody is in earnest. The populace very numerous but perfectly quiet, neither hissing nor huzzaing – I don't know what you may think, but I confess myself glad to see a probable termination of an Assembly that advised sustained and indemnified Free Quarters, Conflagration and Torture. Many thanks for your congratulations on my Brevet. If you knew how I am overwhelmed with Business you would receive this as a mark of sincere friendship, with which I am, my Dr. Cornelius

Yours,
G.N.

Remember me to all with you.

On the recent messages
Why Bonaparte pants for Quiet,
And Billy to prolong the riot
Requires no deep reflection
Without a *Peace* at his command
The Gallic Consul cannot stand
Nor Britain's mentor with one!
Plenipo.

Napier was a wise counsellor to the careless and extravagant John Staples. On, February 12th he wrote:

My dear Cornelius

I congratulate you most sincerely on your niece's marriage to a very sensible, pleasant young fellow, whom I like much as far as I have seen him – It is impossible for me to express in a letter how sincerely I feel for the other part of yours, having had the strongest hopes of country air in your inveterate complaint. It is absolutely out of my power to do anything before the middle of next month, as I have been disappointed by a Br. Field Officer, whose note I have for a considerable sum, payable the 1st of Jany. past, but which is not yet paid, tho' he is as rich as a Jew – I have therefore sent it to Greenwood, with orders to insist on the payment, and I shall then do my best to get enough to discharge your Bond – and yet I shall do so reluctantly.

I well know it is only so much gone to *Daly's Sharks* – I cant help writing to you thus freely because I see feel and Lament with the sincerity of real friendship a propensity which must eventually ruin a man whom I love and esteem.

I am my dear Cornelius,
Yours most affectionately,
Geo. Napier

Sept, 28th.

My dear Cornelius,

Immediately on reading your last I went to the Kildare Street Club and wrote in the Book desiring that the note in question s'd be sent to me whenever it appeared, but I have hitherto heard nothing about it.

Your friend, Genl. Medows, when I dined with him spoke very warmly about you, and I think if he had it in his power would act up to his professions, for he seems in my judgement to be a man of practical friendship and honourable principles. It would be well for Ireland if we had a few more great men cast in this mold but—

I am more confined and more hurried than ever; and having no news to relate I shall not apologize for hastily assuring you (with Kindest love from all with you).

Yours faithfully,
Dear Cornelius,
Geo. Napier.

Jan. 6.

My dear Cornelius,

I have just received yours, but I have not yet seen either of the Drafts which I shall endeavour to discharge; tho' it certainly do's distress me very much, as nobody pays me and I cant even obtain an answer from my agents on the subject of money which is due me; In short this respectable minister of ours ruins both friend and foe, I mean one of his Sovereign's Subjects only, for, as to the King's foreign enemies, they seem perfectly safe. The Duke of York I hear, is fighting the Battles of the unattached Officers most nobly, for which I feelingly applaud him. Adieu,

Ever yours,
Geo Napier.

As this did not go yesterday I have opened it to say that my poor old acquaintance Williamson is found guilty of being *brave* and *loyal*, and is therefore put at the Bottom of the List. Packenham says the sentence is the damnedest nonsense that ever issued from a Court—

I believe it is in contemplation to move in the House of Commons a censure of Lord Moira's conduct in his English speech, as if his character was not far above their censure and beyond their praise – You must mark on the back of your Bond that 200 of it is paid because a humane fury may produce you as a Pendant to us.

Sir George Hill is appointed Clerk of the Commons, and Ferguson, the Mayor, contests the election with Lecky, Conolly gives his interest to the latter; by this I have had an opportunity of showing them what I think of their infamous cowardly lying attack on Lord Moira. I believe the rascally Corporation wont be at the expense of printing my Letters.

My dear Cornelius, Nov. 8. 1801.

If instead of the Kildare St. Club you had informed me that your draft was to be presented at your Br's House I would have saved you just £2. 9. 1 which with the note, I have just paid to an ill looking attorney. It is reported that Parliament will be dissolved before Xmas, Mr. Sheridan opposes the Peace. Lord Granville has written to inform Addington that he also is hostile. The Duke of Richmond and Lord Westmoreland are to oppose it likewise, if they vote – Billy is believed to be at the bottom and top of everything which has been recently transacted. The Catholic Emancipation is now admitted on all hands to have been one of his rascally Juggles, he has been a blasted Juggler throughout his whole political life, without having once shewn himself a conjuror.

'I have no time to say more than that I am, my dear Cornelius,

Yours faithfully
Geo Napier
Give me love to all at Lissan and very especially to Grace.[106]

P.S. I cant devine what members of the Board of Works could tell you they were acquitted, I did not even know they had been tried, as our Commission went only to examine the mode in which business was transacted in that Department and to suggest such improvements as we conceived might ameliorate their formation. Of this no Report has *yet* been made to Govt. altho' my share of writing in notes, minutes statements and Examinations &c. amounts to 126 Folio pages!

This is addressed to 'Cornelius Tacitus'
'Erector.'

Army Account Office

Feb. 8th. 1803
My dear Cornelius

I have delayed answering your kind letter till I saw your Draft for 20£, which only made its appearance yesterday and shall be duly honoured. I unite most cordially with you in wishing that you had £5000 to lend me for both our sakes, for though my income is considerably increased, my expences have so far outstripped it that I never was poorer – As I am winding up all my affairs lest the grim Tyrant, who has so often threatened me, should make good his caption suddenly, which seems of late to be a favourable manoeuvre of his in Dublin; I wish you to inclose my Bond with a Receipt on the back of it to Sir E.B. Littlehales – News are more in expectation than possession, tho' it is strongly rumoured that alterations are on the eve of taking place in Engld. General Fox succeeds Sir Wm. as Commandant of the Forces, which I am glad of, since we are to lose the former, for whom I have the most sincere regard and esteem, as an honourable gallant, warm-hearted, pleasant, sociable veteran, in short I could employ all the adjectives of praise with strict truth when describing his character—

Report also states that all Commissions are to go through the Line by general seniority – The disturbances in the South, I understand, are neither tinctured with religious prejudice nor tainted by constitutional disaffection, but derive entirely from the ferocious avarice of Landlords or their Agents, operating upon their turbulent and unindustrious (because oppressed) tenantry.

Neither Ly. Sarah nor myself have been in a good state of health for some time past, but we unite in best wishes to you and all at Lissan.

Conolly is tolerably well, though he is worried with Lawyers etc.
Lady Louisa is very well, as are all our other friends, except Tom Packenham, who has got a very sore leg owing to an accident –

God bless you my dear Cornelius
believe me ever sincerely yours
Geo Napier

Poor old Col. Blaquiere died last night from a spasm in his stomach in three or four minutes' illness.

The last two letters are written in the year 1803 and run as follows;

My dear Cornelius

Anxiety, disappointment and excess of business precludes all communication with my friends that does not relate to matters of more consequence than idle topics, which usually compose what is termed familiar correspondence; this I trust will sufficiently account for my long silence, what you have to offer in extenuation of your taciturnity besides indolence and inveterate habit, I cannot devise, but to avoid shocking your Pythagorean principles I shall at once enter into business.

Field officers *retired* from the Service are anxiously sought after in Britain as Inspectors of Volunteers of Yeomanry. They are allowed Lt Colonel's pay, and I believe izal of Forage, they have the temporary rank of Lt Colonels during the war, and I rather believe that a memorial from the *quondam* Lt Colonels of the Black Horse addressed to His Royal Highness, the Commander in Chief, and transmitted through his Secty, Colonel Clinton, Horse Guards, London, would obtain you one of these appointments. I am at present labouring under the deepest anxiety about my dearest wife, who I fear will lose her right eye by a *gutta serena* of which there exists strong symptoms at present. She unites with all my Family in affectionate remembrances to you and all at Lissan.

I believe the Corsican is humbugging us and that his attack is directed more against our Purses than our Persons, if so, he has taken his measures too judiciously for our prosperity; you remember I admired him as a Hero, I venerated him as a Pacificator, but I now abominate his tyranny & detest him as the Perturber of Europe. I wish he had a *live* British Shell in his pocket and be damned to him – or what would do as well, I wish he had our Medical Ministry to guide his Councils and *purge* his Treasury. Adieu my dear Cornelius. Yours affectionately

Geo. Napier.

The last letter runs thus:

Dec: 1803

My dear Cornelius

I think your letter a very proper one and have consequently put it in the post – Deep or shallow, I rejoice at the approaching nuptials of your Niece, I am confident she will make B—ks happy; and even should it be shallow, I am sure that was his Benefice an Archbishoprick, he would not find the bottom. I fear the Apothecary is but a scurvy Quack, and as we are infected with a damned Corsican nervous intermittent, I doubt whether he is equal to our case. I never believed the first Consul was so foolhardy as to invade either country, I always thought the vulnerable point he arrived at was our gold and not our Valour, if so he has succeeded but too well, thanks to the Doctor and his Loblolly Boys.

As a steady monarchist, I regret the publication of the Royal Correspondence. To see this crisis unite everybody but the Branches of the Royal House is vexatious to all true Britons and matter of exultation to their Enemies.

Adieu, my dear Cornelius, I write in much pain, but that cannot prevent my being with Compts. & congratulations to all

Yours ever

Geo. Napier

The Right Hon. John Staples, the recipient of these letters, has already figured in these pages, and he and his charming lame wife were among George's nearest neighbours.[107]

* * * * * * *

The early years of the nineteenth century passed without much incident, and few letters remain to shew how George and Olivia spent their time, though doubtless their children occupied most of their thoughts.

The old house once again rang with the voices of laughing children, and the great trees in the Beech Walk looked down upon their games and races.

As is usual in large families, illness came occasionally to cloud the skies, but though they were victims of the dreaded small-pox, all recovered from this disorder.

Mrs. Olivia recorded this fact in the Family Bible. After writing a list of her children, Sophia, George, Olivia, Harriett, Anna and Eliza, she penned these words underneath; 'All the above children have had the smallpox.'

When a hundred years later (in 1908) the night-nursery was re-floored, the mother of more recent children, remembering the smallpox, felt glad that the old boards had been removed. Underneath these a George the First penny was found, poked there, no doubt, by little bygone fingers.

The youngest girl, Eliza – or 'Liney' was a child of independent character. She made for herself a little garden, or 'bower,' on the brow of the hill above the high road – just below the present tennis court, and every winter the snowdrops in 'Miss Eliza's bower' still break through the soil in increasing multitude, as a flowery memorial of the little maiden of long ago.

The lesson and story books of some of these children still remain in out of the way bookshelves. There is an early edition of Defoe's *Robinson Crusoe*, given to his 'dear little friend Harriet Conyngham' by Baron McClelland, whom we know to have been the builder of Anaverna in Co. Louth – a house now possessed by a younger branch of the Lenox-Conynghams.

How quaint are some of these bygone books for children! They inculcate correct and priggish behaviour, and are devoid of all imagination and charm. One of these is before me now, and I cannot resist copying a few pages which cannot fail to provoke a smile.

> In the County of Salop lived the Earl of Fairfame, remarkable for his generosity to the poor and his affability and good nature to the rich. In a village not distant lived Mr. Gracemore, a tradesman of indifferent circumstances. He had a son whom he named John. When Master Jackey grew to be about eight years old his papa, who was excessively fond of him, sent for his cousin to be a companion for him, and after school hours they would play at marbles. Master Jackey was so constant in his good behaviour that everybody in the village talked of nothing else, which at last reached the ears of the Earl of Fairfame. There was an old woman who used to come to my Lord's house with butter.

> My Lord one days says to her:
>
> 'Well, Goodey Creamer, what news? Who is the best boy in the town now?' to which the old woman, making a low courtesy, answered, 'An't please you, my Lord, Jackey Gracemore. I never saw him behave rudely and I hear he is a fine scholar.' 'Ah indeed,' says my Lord, 'then I must make him a present,' when putting his hand into his fob, he pulled out his fine watch and bid her give it to Master Jackey and tell his Papa he would call at his house tomorrow.
>
> The next day my lord came, dressed very grand in his star and garter, his sword by his side and his gold-headed cane, and was received with great respect. Jackey made a very low bow and entered. My lord asked him questions, all which he answered so prettily that his lordship was charmed with him and begged the favour to have Jackey home with him for a month, saying he had a young lady about his age at his house who would serve him for a playmate – her papa was a grocer at Shrewsbury, and my lord brought her home to live with him on account of her good behaviour. The young folks lived very happily together. One day my Lord was very ill and in a few hours resigned his breath. The next day my Lady shewed the will, in which he had left them five hundred pounds each.
>
> Eight years after, she dying likewise, left them joint heirs to her vast estate. After the time of mourning was over, Jackey and Hariot agreed to be married. Accordingly the happy day being arrived, they went to Church, where they were married by the Reverend Mr. Trueman, who had formerly been Chaplain to Lord Fairfame. Thus Jackey and Hariot were now the richest as they were before the best people in the County of Salop and lived many years beloved by all the country round. … This little history will I hope be a sufficient inducement to make all girls and boys behave themselves in a proper manner to everybody. If they hope to be rich and happy, let them take care to follow the example of Jackey and Hariot.

Another didactic romance for older children relates the tale of the Misses Woodville – Diana and Ellen – who disobeyed their parents and sat in the ice-house on a hot summer's day, afterwards going to sleep in their mother's dressing-room with doors and windows open. They became very ill, and

> after being bled till they fainted, they were kept in darkness and quietness with a plentiful supply of barley water. But on the fourth morning these two sweet girls lay lifeless before the eyes of their heart-broken parents. The loss of her two children gave the simple and affectionate heart of Mrs. Woodville a shock that it never recovered and occasioned a lingering illness, which caused her death within a year of the melancholy event she so bitterly deplored. Mr. Woodville did not long survive the loss of his beloved companion, but lived long enough to be aware of the grand error he had committed in allowing the immature judgments of his children to be exercised in opposition to his own, an error which brought four amiable people to a premature grave.

On reading further we learn that Matilda, the obedient and virtuous member of this family, went to visit an improving lady friend: –

> While she was there a young nobleman became charmed with her person, and his attachment was rivetted by acquaintance with her virtues. He was a fine-looking, amiable young man with a large unincumbered fortune. Despising the eternal and senseless round of town amusements and seeking the delights of domestic society with a rational and amiable wife, Matilda realized his fairest reveries. He saw her elegant but not expensive, with manners simple and quiet, but not insipid, no reformer in petticoats of Church and State, but possessed of a quick discernment and taste to appreciate the merits of the works she perused, and she being precisely the sort of wife Lord Valence desired, he offered her his hand. Her sister Caroline (who had survived the ice-house episode) took up her residence with Lady Valence and soon greatly profited by the misfortunes of the family. She acquired the habits of a perfect gentlewoman and attained a proficiency in several accomplishments. Several years afterwards she became the happy wife of a worthy baronet belonging to the same County.

We can imagine the interest which this edifying book aroused in the young Sophia, Harriett and Anna Lenox-Conyngham, who shared an oak-floored bedroom in the top story of Springhill mansion, each sleeping in an alcove hollowed out of the wall and designed to exclude the dangerous night air.

Mrs. Olivia was evidently a pattern of maternal solicitude and possessed a character in which worldly prudence blended comfortably with conventional piety. Her girls were probably brought up with the ideals of the romances which they perused, and later on each of the elder daughters made a suitable marriage – Sophia espousing The Hon. Andrew Stuart, younger brother of the Earl of Castlestewart, Harriett wedding a distinguished officer of the Royal Engineers – Colonel Portlock,[108] and Anna jilting a charming Colonel Kennedy to become the second wife of the rich Mr. Nicholson of Balrath in Co. Meath. As for poor little Olivia, she died young, to the intense grief of her father, whose pathetic entry in the Family Bible shews his deep sorrow for her loss.

Eliza – or 'Liney' – had a strong personality, but, though handsome and attractive, she never married. Several anecdotes of this young lady are still remembered. An Eastern potentate was so charmed by her wit and beauty that he offered to buy her for a large sum!

On one occasion, when Liney was trying to help a young man of her acquaintance to join the Army, she boldly asked King George the Third to grant him a Commission, as a favour to herself. The old king's answer was that he would willingly grant the request if Miss Lenox-Conyngham would bestow a kiss upon him, and the strong-minded young lady promptly kissed the monarch and obtained her wish.

George Conyngham never followed his Uncle's example of entering Parliament, but doubtless shared in the excitement of the parliamentary elections of those days.

In 1806 a heated contest took place for the representation of the county, and a collection of electioneering squibs and lampoons, preserved in the 'Oak box' at Springhill, shews what scurrilous methods were used long ago during such contests.

It appears that Colonel W. Ponsonby and a Mr. Samuel Lyle were chosen as candidates to oppose Lord George Beresford and General Stewart,[109] and feeling ran riot and pens were dipped in venom. In these papers we notice that in those days much stress was laid on family and lineage. The opponents of the latter gentlemen alleged that these had tried to gain support on account of their high birth and titled superiority.

In a fictitious letter purporting to have been sent to Lt. Colonel Ponsonby, the following passage occurs:

> Let us ask what was the first origin of their (the Beresfords') boasted lineage. Why verily an INKLEWEAVER! who settled in the town of Colerain, the site of whose dwelling is remembered to this day! By acquiring agencies in succeeding generations he became tolerably rich, and that when King James 1st. was disposing of an honour then newly created for sale on occasion of planting the Province of Ulster, Mr. T—m Beresford in common with another adventurer, purchas'd for the sum of two or three hundred pounds the dignity of a Baronet! by sinister intrigue they chicaned the unfortunate borough of Colerain.

Another vituperative, and probably untrue letter runs thus:

> CONFESSION & DYING DECLARATION OF S. L—e Nov. 22
>
> I was born of poor but honest parents at Coleraine in this County who took pains to have me bred a Presbyterian & to have taught me the catechism of that Church, for which purpose they paid for my education at a night's school. … I became a Rag man &c.

The statement also alleges:

> The only rational grounds on which any body of men can offer their support for a Parliamentary Candidate are family Connections, popular principles and tried Fidelity.

An adversary of Colonel Ponsonby penned this ditty:

Have you read the address of the great Ponsonby
Promising vaunting Pon
If you have, does it strike you as wondrous to see
A pup boast so much of his Grand Family!
Chorus: With R—ss of Claudy
Cleland Me—y
Dungiven ugly Boy
A—n L—e and Fry

All kissing the hand of Pon.
All Loyalists do this grand Family hate
Galloping runaway Pon,
When they think how they skulked in the year 98
And abandoned their Country, their King and the State
They gave up their Honour
Swore hard for O'Connor
Through fire, water, brimstone
They cheered him at Maidstone. …

At this time the County of Derry was divided into twelve Freehold estates, and, of these, six supported Ponsonby. These were:

Drapers Proportion	..	..	Sir Wm. Rowley
Merchant Taylors		..	Capt. Richardson
Cloth workers		..	T. K. Hannyngton, Esq.
Grocers	..	..	David Babington, Esq.
Skinners	..	..	Robert Ogilby, Esq.
Goldsmiths	..	..	Col. Wm. Ponsonby.

Of the remaining six, the Vintners, Ironmongers, under Heirs of Rt. Hon. Thos. Conolly and Jas. Dupre respectively supported Stewart.

The Salters, under Lord Londonderry and Sir Thomas Bateson, contained no votes. The Mercers (Alexr. Stewart, Esq.) belonged to the Stewart family, and the Haberdashers and Fishmongers were owned by the Beresfords.

The Linen Trade supported Ponsonby and Lyle. One song runs thus: –

Rejoice ye jolly weavers for Ponsonby and Lyle
Support the linen trade, the riches of our isle
Sam Lyle you know him well, a good fellow is he
Tho' he sticks to his trade, yet he'll set the country free
Then speed to the shuttle, the shuttle and the flail
Success to our trade boys, and may its friends prevail.

A verse alluding to Stewart and Beresford runs:

Themselves alone they loved who sold their country's State,
They hanged and burned and slaughtered our friends,
They raised a Rebellion to serve their own ends,
But now we'll endeavour to make them amends
By kicking them out of the Country, my friends.

* * * * * * *

Our oppressors and tyrants will soon look blue
For Berry and Stewart, we abominate you.

Other songs are entitled 'The Bellaghy Garland,' by Dawson Downing, which begins; 'Huzza for Moneymore, Castledawson is the town,': 'Oh fie ye Castledawson Men,' 'The Moneymore Lad.'

'The Moneymore Lad' begins:

> Ye Moneymore lads with your lasses
> For Ponsonby fill up your glasses
> Here's Freedom, then boast, rejoice and be glad,
> For the lad of all lads is the Moneymore Lad.
> *Chorus*: No jailors, no conscripts, no Bribe, no Bastille
> But each hearty voter to vote with his will
> Here's the Moneymore boys and the Ponsonby Lad.

In these papers there are many unflattering allusions to County personages:

> Colonel Co—gham intends to command a very strong Regt. when he can raise, cloathe, equip and discipline them. They are all to be armed with very Long Bows, a weapon at which the Colonel particularly excels.

A list is given of the cloth merchants who have not subscribed to Sam Lyle's electioneering Committee list:

> They are of the first propriety and respectability, and are resident Freeholders. They have not been dupes of Sam Lyle's manoevre:
>
> Kennedy Henderson – John do.: J. Bennett, Wm. Bond, Alex. Boyle, John Given, C. Galt, T. Rice, A. Orr, J. Orr, William Clarke, Alex^r^. Clarke, J. Knox, J. Courteney, G. Clinton, J. Bryan, R. & W. Dysart, James Stevenson, Fortwilliam, J. Stevenson. Knockan, Wm. do. J. Ross, N. Irvine, Kat Hunter, Fred McCausland, Dan McLoughlin, S. Glen Schoales, M. Connell, E. Davenport, R. Hamilton.

Result of the Election.

Close of the Poll, 16th Day.

For Colonel Ponsonby	979
For Mr. Lyle	601
For General Stewart	1,397
For Lord George Beresford	1,123

The election aroused vivid interest. These carefully preserved papers testify to that and give sidelights on the current opinions and prejudices of those turbulent times.

In those days the landlord was wont to instruct his tenants as to how they should vote, and few dared to disobey.

In a letter written to George Lenox-Conyngham by his neighbour Colonel

James Stewart, of Killymoon, a parliamentary candidate, pleads for the votes of his friend's tenantry. It is as follows:

> My dear Major
>
> If I could with safety go from home, I should certainly have the pleasure of paying my respects to Mrs. Conyngham and you at Springhill, but my lameness is now so bad that I am obliged to keep my leg quiet and to submit to confinement. The approach of the General Election obliges me to be troublesome to my friends, though your constant and uniform goodness to me leaves me no doubt of your kind intentions to me at present. Yet allow me to request your protection and your Recommendation to your very respectable Freeholders in Tyrone, and I would beg of you to make my apology for not waiting upon them in Person, which, under your direction, I should certainly wish to do, but my present situation makes it nearly impossible.
>
> Mrs. Stewart and my daughters unite in best Compliments to you and Mrs. Conyngham, allow me to add mine. We hope to have the pleasure of hearing that you are both well and all the Children.
>
> Believe me my dear Sir
> Most faithfully yours
>
> Cookstown. 11th day of 1797. Jas Stewart.[110]

The Donegal property, which had been shared by George Lenox-Conyngham's first wife, Jane Hamilton, and her three sisters? ('Bess' Colthurst, 'Beck' Galbraith and 'Bell' Fox), continued to be under George's supervision, and various letters regarding its management survive. Rebecca Galbraith's husband, Sir James Galbraith, who has already figured in these pages, was a genial and excellent personage, and on November 20th, 1812, he wrote a long letter to his brother-in-law and great friend, acknowledging congratulations on having been made a baronet – an honour which he hesitated to accept, though

> the Marquis of Abercorn was so kind as to send his servant to me to say that there was to be a creation of baronets and that he had the power to have me included, if I wished.
>
> I have heard with sincere Regret from Baron McClelland of Mrs. Henderson's death. Bell would not have him before, perhaps worse for both, I doubt much if it would not be better for both to repair the fault & marry yet. … Beck writes that she had a very affectionate letter from William.[111] No word yet of a governess. If we cant go and see you, you and Mrs. Conyngham and Sophia must come to us. Remember me affectly to both and to all the rest & Believe me
>
> Ever truly yours
> J. Galbraith.

This letters reveals traces of a bygone romance. Evidently Mr (Kennedy?) Henderson had wished to marry Isabella Hamilton. What a pity the marriage did not take place to prevent her from espousing the 'villain' Fox!

Two years after Sir J. Galbraith's letter was received, a great sorrow came to the fatherly George in the death of his little daughter, Olivia, who died on January 17th, 1814. His entry in the Family Bible runs:

> On the 17th Jan 1814 the Almighty God was pleased to take to Himself my beloved child Olivia Conyngham. She died at Drogheda and was buried at Lissane. She was aged sixteen years. This was written by her afflicted father
>
> Geo. L. Conyngham

Always devoted to his family, this event must have increased the melancholy which was beginning to envelope George. We wonder if his wife made him happy. Her voluble expressions of grief and the effusions which she wrote on the fly-leaves of Olivia's Prayer Book are in sharp contrast with the few heart-wrung words penned in the large Bible by the sorrowing father.

Mrs. Olivia is said to have 'had an eye to the main chance' and to have sold some of the old Lenox silver. We cannot be sure that a list of the Springhill silver, made at about this time, is in her handwriting, but it may be of interest to scan the list:

A LIST OF PLATE.

1 Large cup – *crest, a Lion Rampant*[112]
1 do. – *crest, a Turk's head*
1 Large Salver – *crest, a lion rampant*
1 do. – *no crest*
1 do. – *crest, a Unicorn*[113]
2 Small Salvers – *crest, a crane's neck and scale*
Coffee pot and Stand – *crest, a Unicorn*
2 Coasters – *crest, a Unicorn*
2 do. – *crest, a man*
6 Open Sale cellars – *crest, a Unicorn*
4 Butter boats *do.*
2 small cups *do.*
1 Tun dish & Stand *do.*
1 Saucepan *do.*
1 Cruet stand in full *do.*
1 Sugar bowl & tongs – *no crest*
2 Gravy spoons „
2 soup ladles – *crest, a Unicorn*
2 butter spoons „ „
6 dessert spoons – *Crest, a Unicorn*
11 do. *no crest*
6 do. O.L.C.
22 large spoons – *crest, a Unicorn*

3 do. – *crest, a rampant lion*
18 4 pronged forks – *Crest, a Unicorn*
12 3 pronged do. – *Crest, a lion rampant*
3 do. – *Crest, a tree & a coronet*
12 silver-hafted knives – *Crest, a lion rampant*
3 do. – *Crest, a tree & a coronet*
24 silver-handled knives – *Crest, a Unicorn*
24 do. do. forks – „ „
4 round Salt cellars – *Crest, a Crane's neck*
1 Fish Trowel – *No Crest*
1 Marrow spoon – *Crest, a Unicorn*
1 Bread basket – *Crest, a Unicorn*
4 Chased Candlesticks „ „
4 Fluted do. – „ „
4 Silver do. – *Conyngham Arms*
1 Snuff stand – *do. do.*
2 pr. snuffers & stands – *no crest*
4 Card table Candlesticks „
2 Old do. „ „
2 Bedchamber do. „ „
1 Toastrack „ „
1 egg stand marked H.H.
1 Tea Urn – *crest, a Unicorn*
4 dishes & covers, *crest, a Unicorn*
1 Epergne in full but no cruet, *no crest*
1 Cream spoon marked J.L.
1 Silver Skewer „ „
4 Salt spoons – *Crest, a Unicorn*
2 do. *no crest*
9 Tea spoons
9 do. – *Crest, a Unicorn*
1 Teapot – *no crest*
18 Ivory handled knives – *crest, a Unicorn*
18 Dessert knives & 18 forks – *no crest.*

S. Hill.

Much of this silver still survives at Springhill.

Of great interest to this devoted father was the young William (or 'Wims' as he was called by his family) son of George's first wife, Jenny.

On the 27th of December, 1814, George wrote to him the following letter in his clear rounded handwriting. It is addressed to Glasgow.

> My dear William
>
> As I know you got safe to London, I thought answering your letter from Birmingham was unnecessary. I have little to tell you of but such Rain Snow and *Tempest* as has been here this winter never was known in the memory of man. ... A sad misfortune happened to poor Mr. Carter, the uncommon flood in the river of Coagh tore away forty yards of the Mill race, and had it not been for the great kindness and assistance of the Country, he must have been inevitably ruined. One hundred men, without pay or reward, assembled every day for five days, and at least sixty Horses, to repair the breach, & have succeeded to a wonder. Cassoons made of Wattles were sunk & filled with stones in twenty feet of watter, and who do you think was the acting engineer, why truly a son of old Hugh Mallan & nephew to Billy, the children's maid. His contrivances were astonishing, you see what Patt can do when he is employed and encouraged!
>
> Nine or ten trees have been broke or blown down, but I am sorry to tell you that the greatest Branch of the fine Cedar[114] was twisted off like a gad. However Field says that he will manage the stump so that the defect will not be perceivable. Let me know when you intend being in Ireland, I have a great deal to say to you, far beyond the bounds of a letter.
>
> Your truly affectionate Father
> Geo. L. Conyngham

But the gloom of old George's spirit did not lighten, and at length, on a dreary day in November, 1816, when we can imagine the wind and rain sweeping round the old house of Springhill the climax came. George Lenox-Conyngham met with the same fate as his one-time comrade, Viscount Castlereagh. His wife Olivia's entry in the Family Bible gives the particulars without reserve:

> George Lenox-Conyngham being in a very melancholy state of mind for many months prior, put an end to his existence by a pistol shot. He lingered from the 20th of Nov. 1816 to the 22nd, and died, thanks to the Almighty God, a truly penitent Christian. He was in the 64th year of his age. Buried at Lissan.

So ended the life of this warm-hearted and impulsive man, who was so unable to control his feelings of joy or sorrow: and those who have never endured the depths of depression which engulfed his ardent spirit must refrain from condemnation of this rash act.

Though not certain, it seems probable that this tragedy took place in an upstairs bed-chamber at Springhill. During George's first marriage he and Jenny would probably have occupied his late Uncle's and Aunt's rooms on the lower floor, and to it, with all its memories, he would have been unlikely to bring his second wife. Moreover that upstairs room has been the centre in after years of some curious experiences (could they be called 'after effects'?) which seem to confirm the theory that any strong outburst of anguish lingers for a long period in the place where it led to a tragic happening, and under special conditions, causes some persons to see a vision of the event and of those who took part in it. There are strange stories of this room, some of which must be recounted. The Hon. Andrew Stuart, husband of George's eldest daughter, when sleeping here used to find that his belongings were mysteriously moved in the night. Two small great-great grandsons of George, who were in the large four post bed, were heard by their governess, who occupied the adjoining dressing room, to be talking of a strange lady whom they saw standing by the fireplace. 'She must be a ghost' ! said one of the children calmly, and without fear.

A recent photograph of the 'supposedly haunted' pink bedroom.

A Miss Wilson, who was staying at Springhill in the 'Eighties,' had a vivid experience. She and the eldest daughter of the house had been sitting up very late one night in the Cedar-room. After Milly Conyngham had finally said goodnight and gone to her room in the top story, Miss Wilson found her friend's private diary had been accidentally left behind. She at once resolved to restore it immediately, and, on opening her door, paused to feast her artistic eyes on the sight of the moonlight streaming down on to the broad oak staircase. At that moment the tall figure of a lady appeared at the head of the stairs and passed rapidly to the door of the X room, where she stopped, and flinging her hands up, as though in despair, she vanished.

Miss Wilson was filled with acute terror, and went back into her room. And it was afterwards ascertained that all the rest of the house had been in bed and asleep at that hour, so no occupant of the house had been astir.

Some years later an even more remarkable occurrence happened, when a Miss Hamilton came for the first time to stay in the old house, and was given the X room. On the following morning she came downstairs looking rather shaken, and related to Charlotte Lenox-Conyngham the following experience; I give it in her own words.

> I had gone to bed in the great Four-poster and the fire had died down and I had begun to grow drowsy, when it suddenly seemed as if the room was filled with excited people – servants, I thought – who were pushing, and wrangling in whispers. I felt overcome by fear, but just then I heard a clicking sound behind me, as though a door had been opened, and then a light shone at my back, and someone seemed to come out through this light and stilled the commotion, so that all fear left me, and after a while I fell asleep. It was strange that I fancied a door had opened behind me, as the head of the bed is against the wall where there is no door.
>
> 'But there is a door behind the bed' said Charlotte, 'though quite hidden by the tester of the bed, and it has been papered over for quite a long time.'

In more recent days, when the present chatelaine of Springhill ordered the bed to be moved and the paper cut, so as to open the door, she found a powder-closet, in which there is a built-up window and a built-up fireplace, the ceiling being higher than that of the bedroom which it adjoins. This closet was empty, save for a pair of ancient gloves and a small bag which contained a few bullets. Readers may interpret these mysterious tales as they choose.

As an ending to this long chapter, which recounts the life of George Lenox-Conyngham, a page is copied from the Family Bible, giving a list of the children born to him and his second wife, Olivia Irvine, whom he married on the fifth of April, 1794.

1. Sophia Isabella, born Jan., 1795.
   godfather, Right Hon. Thomas Conolly.
   married the Hon. A.G. Stuart.
2. George William Lenox-Conyngham,
   born April 13, 1796, married Elizabeth only daughter
   of Robert Holmes, Esq.
3. Olivia Frances, born July, 1797. Godmothers, Lady Tynte
   & the Hon. Mrs. Rochfort, died 17 Jan., 1814.
4. Anna Jane Florence, born Jan. 31, 1799.
   married C.A. Nicholson, Esq.
5. Harriet Letitia Conyngham, born May, 1801.
   Godmothers, The Countess of Rosse and Countess Castlestewart.
   married Capt. J.E. Portlock, Royal Engineers.
6. Eliza St. George, born June 24, 1803.
   Godmothers, Mrs. St. George Irvine and Miss Tynte.
   Godfather, her brother William.

All the above children have had the smallpox.

X

The fourth William

1792–1858

The fourth William – 'Wims'

The owner of Springhill was now William – or 'Wims' – George Lenox-Conyngham's elder son and only child of his first wife, Jane Hamilton. William's childhood must have been shadowed by his having lost his mother in infancy, and Olivia is said to have been a harsh step-mother to the poor little boy, and treated him differently from her own youngsters.

'Wims' was educated at Glasgow College and called to the English Bar on February 16th, 1816, at the age of twenty-four.[115]

No doubt the sudden death of his father was a great shock to the youth, but he shouldered his burdens manfully, and instead of shewing resentment at his step-mother's former treatment, he was exceptionally generous to her and her family. This characteristic of 'forgivingness' has also been shewn by his grandson and great-grandson.

In person William was tall and massively built, with good features, dark curly hair and an expression of frankness and good humour. As far as can be ascertained, he kept no diary, but his account-books are so detailed that they reveal a character which was kind and generous, though perhaps rather thoughtless.

The estate was bringing in a goodly income, and its owner seemed to spend money freely.

Olivia must have felt confident that her stepson would treat her well. Here is a letter which she wrote to him two years after her husband's death.

> Dec. 9th. 1818
>
> My dear William
>
> Having written your opinion to Mr. Newton, and he giving me his return, urges me to trouble you with this letter. ... He is certain your opinion is from the kindest motives with the fullest wish to serve me. ... His opinion is that he thinks the safest, surest and most honourable way to divide the question for me, your tenants and agent, is to direct him to receive the arrears from those of your tenants that are still due ... and he thinks in this case I should speedily be paid. ... The sum of arrears can be but of a trifling nature to you, but I assure you, my dear William, 'tis of considerable moment to me & my family, wishing as I do to live respectably & also do wonderfully so on our income in little or no debt. I am particularly pressed hard just now, tho' hope next month my mind will be at ease ... for Debt I abhor. I am sure Mr. George did not know your agreement with the Baron.
> I am sure you will settle the matter between your Tenants & me at once.
> May we hope to see you & George ye l6th May, do, my dear William, if you can.
> With the united love of the girls & myself believe me
>
> Your affect. & attached
> O. L. Conyngham.

This letter was written from Belfast and shews that Olivia did not hesitate to make 'a poor mouth' so as to induce her stepson to attend to her interests, which no doubt his kind heart prompted him to do.

A letter from Cheltenham from Olivia's third daughter, Anna, points to a generous action on the part of the young owner of Springhill towards his step-brother and sisters.

> Cheltenham
>
> June 31st /25
> My dear William
>
> I should have sooner answered your kind letter, but waited till I could at the same time acknowledge the receipt of the money, which we now do. ... Pray, my dear William, accept the united thanks of Harriet, Eliza and myself for your very kind, generous offer. We accept it as such & beg you to believe how

sincerely obliged we shall always feel. It certainly adds considerably to our income. We leave for London on Monday next and have got a very nice house in Bolton St Piccadilly. We shall remain only one month in town –

How beautiful your young plantations must be looking! Mama & the girls unite with me in affect, love. …

Yours most affectionately
Anna Lenox-Conyngham.

This letter evidently alludes to William's generous action in selling his own mother's Donegal property to provide for his step-brother and sisters.

He had abandoned his idea of adopting Law as his profession, and was well content to settle down in his old home; and, as already mentioned, his account-books give much information as to his purse and his habits. The younger brother, George, received £200 a year from the estate and soon after their father's death, Dr. Sinclair of Dungannon was paid £5 10s. 9*d.* and Dr. Potter of Cookstown £20 – no doubt for their attendance on the unfortunate old man.

Charlotte Melosina Lenox-Conyngham, daughter of the Rt. Hon. John and Henrietta Staples, *née* Molesworth.

'Mr. George' was at this time agent for Springhill and must have been son of the faithful agent, Matthew George. Mr. Newton of Coagh also received money for William, and Andy Field worked at Springhill – one of a long line of Fields who were in the Conynghams' employment and lived in the hamlet of 'Irishtown' – About £78 15s. 0*d.* per quarter was paid to six labourers. The women servants' wages came to £12 10s. 0*d.*, for in those days labour was cheap.

In these old account-books we find that taxes came to £83 2s. 6d. One, Billy Shaw, received £13 14s. 11d. for killing crows. William was charitable and gave substantial sums to the poor of Coagh and Moneymore and to the Bible Society. Forty pounds was spent at the Omagh Assizes.

These must have been busy days for the young owner of Springhill, but three years after his father's death, when at the age of twenty-seven, he chose a very charming bride.

Charlotte Melosina Staples was the third daughter of the Right Hon. John Staples – the 'Cornelius' of Colonel Napier's letters – who, with his interesting wife, Harriett Molesworth, has already figured in these pages, and a hint was given of the anguish she experienced in the tragic death of her mother, Viscountess Molesworth.

It may be remembered that the latter lovely lady was the widow of one of the

Duke of Marlborough's generals, Richard, 3rd Viscount Molesworth.

In May, 1763, the Molesworths' London house in Brook Street caught fire, and the terrified crowd saw the heroic dame assisting her young daughters to jump for their lives. Henrietta, Elizabeth and Louisa leaped from the burning pile, just before their mother fell back to perish in the flames with two younger daughters, Mary and Melosina. The London world was aghast! Kind King George III took a house and furnished it for the motherless girls and also assisted them by doubling their mother's pension. As for the young Henrietta (or 'Harriett') she had fallen on railings and so injured one of her legs that it had to be taken off at once. Horace Walpole refers to this tragedy in a letter to George Canning dated

> May 6th. Very late. 1763.
>
> I meant to tell you of the most dismal calamity that ever happened. Lady Molesworth's house in Upper Brook Street was burned to the ground between four and five this morning. She herself, two of her daughters, her brother and six servants perished. Two other of the young ladies jumped out of the two pair of stairs and garret window. One broke her thigh – the other – the eldest of all,[116] broke hers too and has had it cut off. The fifth daughter is much burnt. The French governess leapt from the garret and was dashed to pieces. … The catastrophe is shocking beyond what one ever heard, and poor Lady Molesworth, whose character and conduct were the most amiable in the world, is universally lamented.

Mary, Viscountess Molesworth, née Ussher. Mary died when her London house burnt in 1763.

William Hoare of Bath

A detailed account of the Molesworth family, which gives yet another description of this tragedy, occurs in Francis Gerard's *Celebrated Beauties of the 18th Century*, and I will quote it here:

> Robert Molesworth of Pencarrow in Cornwall, having done good service in assisting the English to subdue the Celt, was rewarded with 3,500 acres in Meath. … He became very wealthy, built for himself a fine house in the corner of Fishamble St., called Molesworth Court. There his son, Robert, was born in 1656. Robert was more distinguished than his father. He was ambassador to the Court of Denmark, the friend and associate of Locke, Shaftesbury and Molyneux. He wrote a book on the political situation of Denmark, which, according to Horace Walpole, overturned the constitution of that country, and he was before his death raised to the rank of Viscount. Richard, grandson of the Ambassador, succeeded ultimately as 3rd Viscount. Richard followed the fortunes of Churchill, Duke of Marlborough, and was his A.D.C. at the battle of

> Ramillies, where he with great gallantry saved the General's life. For this and for his good military service he received rapid promotion – was master of Ordnance, Field Marshal, and Commander-in-Chief of the Army in Ireland. He married first a Miss Lucas, mother of Mary, Countess of Belvidere. Secondly Miss Ussher (an absolute beauty). Mary Jenny Ussher was daughter of the Venble. William Ussher, Archdeacon of Clonfert. As a widow she resided in London, where in 1763 she met with a tragic death. Her house in Brook Street taking fire, she and nine of her household perished in the flames. This lamentable event is mentioned in all the letters and papers of the day. … The three remaining daughters, who jumped from the windows, were terribly injured. One was caught on the railings and tore her leg so that it had to be cut off. Horace Walpole is full of pity for these young creatures. Lady Grosvenor has taken them into her house. The one whose leg is cut off has been kept for days intoxicated with laudunum, she knows nothing of what has happened to her.

As mentioned earlier in this history, this poor girl was adopted by Elinor, Countess Blessinton,[117] and came to Ireland, where she became the second wife of the Right Hon. John Staples of Lissan, and mother of Charlotte Melosina Lenox-Conyngham, her third daughter. Charlotte's birth is recorded in her mother's little diary of 1786, which is still at Springhill, and gives a short account of daily life at Lissan, the children's ailments, the drives which were taken, the visitors[118] who came to stay and the weekly accounts kept by this capable and charming woman.

Charlotte's dress

Young Charlotte's elder sisters were married before she herself became a wife – Grace to the 1st Marquis of Ormonde and Frances ('Fly') to her first cousin, the Hon. and Revd. Richard Ponsonby, Bishop of Derry – and 'Cha' was thirty-three years old when she espoused William Conyngham of Springhill. In a collection of letters of that day she is always alluded to as 'dear beauty Cha' and her marriage took place on June 7th, 1819.

Charlotte was not tall: one of her dresses – a cream-coloured *moiré antique*, which remains at Springhill, bears this out – and her portrait shows a comely face, surmounted by the fashionable turban of the day. We also know from her letters and from hearsay that she was bright, witty and full of *espiéglerie*.

This marriage was a very happy one and was followed by years of devoted companionship.

As well as having a happy abode of her own, 'Cha' Lenox-Conyngham had the joy of living only four miles from her old home at Lissan, which after her father's death passed to her brother Sir Thomas Staples, who lived there with his wife, often alluded to as 'Aunt Kitty'. Her own aunt – Elizabeth Stewart – one of the girls rescued from the fire in Brook Street – lived at Killymoon, six miles away, and Cha's elder sister, Frances Ponsonby, the wife of her cousin, the Bishop – 'handsome Dick Ponsonby' – was domiciled for years in the Bishop's palace in Derry. She was always known as 'Aunt Fly.' This prelate was evidently nothing loth to having his portrait painted. At Springhill his likeness is to be seen in oils, in an engraving, in a silhouette and in a water-colour profile by the famous Dighton.

Uncle Dick's children will long be remembered at Springhill, for while staying there as young creatures, in 1826, they carved their names and initials on one of the great trees in the 'Beech Walk,' and this inscription is still plainly visible;

1826
H.P.
W. Ponsonby
L.P.
P.P.

Charlotte's dress

I wonder what punishment was meted out for this act of vandalism?

But by now other children were beginning to toddle about under the trees of the Beech Walk, for to William and Charlotte Lenox-Conyngham were born three sons and three daughters. The eldest boy, George Richard Thomas, died in infancy in Dublin in 1823, having been preceded by a girl, Harriet Rebecca, born 1820, and then, to the parent's joy, another son was born in 1824 and named William Fitzwilliam, the second name being that of his grand-uncle and god-father, Earl Fitzwilliam.

Two other daughters followed – Jane, born 1825, and Charlotte Melosina (1827) and a son, John Staples Molesworth. Now the little circle was complete, and many were the tales of childhood related in after years by 'Aunt Hazzie'[119] who lived to be eighty-one.

John Hall reigned as a sort of house steward. This faithful and trusted servant for many years kept his master's household accounts, and his brother Tom, who was the butler, acted as mentor to the children of the house. These upper servants dined in the Housekeeper's Room and included 'Nin' (Mrs. Grant), the nurse, and her daughter, 'Cree,' who was lady's maid.

The Conynghams liked going abroad and had several sojourns in Brussels, where they brought their family and servants – often accompanied by a party of relations – and enjoyed foreign society. In the year 1823, when little Hazzy was a baby, a pleasant time was spent in the Netherlands. A few old letters discovered in a Killymoon cabinet at Ashfield Lodge, give an account of this visit, which was shared by two of Cha's sisters – Grace, Lady Ormonde and Harriett, Lady Clancarty and their husbands, as well as by other relatives.

These letters were written to Cha's aunt, the Hon. Mrs. Stewart of Killymoon, by one of the Staples' uncles, Colonel Thomas Staples who was nicknamed 'The Scram.'

One of these runs as follows:

Brussels. Aug. 25, 1823.

I am sure 'tis with pleasure that dear Aunt Bess will hear of all her friends being perfectly well at this place, particularly Grace and her infant who is nameless. The two boys, Walter and James, lately set out for school in England, so that, with Thurles, but eight of the young family remain at this hotel.

I hope at length your weather is as fine and even as hot as here. We have had various *orages* and such violent thunder as frightened Jane Lindesay out of her wits, but she soon recovered and is in such high bloom and looks so well that I expect she will soon be carried off by some Burgomaster to Holland.

The Conynghams and little Hazzy as well as can be. Charlotte's matron adds to her charms. I had the pleasure to be one of the party and to accompany them, Willm. & Cha, .with Jane Lindesay & A. Montgomery, on a Grand Tour excursion from hence this day sennight. We returned back here last Friday after visiting Nantes, Liege, Maestricht. What a delightful fertile and beautiful country *partout*! I never ceased admiring the *propriété* of the Hotels, houses and places.

Yesterday was the King of the Netherlands' Birthday; he gave a dinner on the occasion. L. O.[120] and Conyngham dined there – with Ld Clancarty: Perhaps I should have had that honor also had I gone to Court & been presented, which want of uniform and dress cloathes prevented.

The Duke of Wellington arrived yesterday eve with M. & M^{chess} Salisbury. His Grace visited Clancarty, where we were in the evg. Harrie Clancarty & family all well, whose past kindness I am sensible of to me. The Duke and Clancarty dined with the King at his country place about 2 miles 1/2 to-day. His Majesty always dines at four o'clock. The Queen everyone says most amiable & also his little nice Princess. The Pr. & Princess of Orange, who is reckoned very pleasant, & Princess Frederick were at the dinner – sixty-four, L. O. says, at table & amongst them two priests – Bishops. William Conyngham remarked their having fine Orange ribbons. The King, being a Prot: prefers going to the Dutch Service, but sometimes to the French Protestant Church, where I have gone, & after to the English in the same Church. There are 2 English ones, very handsome ... organs, singing & congregation. The Clancartys are to give a *très grand* party here next Wednesday. Their house very spacious for the occasion. If William were here he might have great cricketting. L. O. & Thurles were at the match. Tis horrible hot; *on attend un orage bientot.*

We passed Waterloo on our late tour. The Church full of monuments & inscriptions of officers who fell in the Battle, & also the garden, where Uxbridge's leg is buried under a beautiful weeping willow. King George IV visited there & traversed the extensive field & plain, now overgrown with wheat. The Chateau, where so many fell, is the most interesting ruin imaginable. The little Chapel only remained pretty safe. The Belgian obelisk & Sir Alex Gordon's are conspicuous. I'm surprised Sir W. Ponsonby was not noticed, we were shewn where he & many others fell. The town was most brilliantly illuminated last night. We drove round the Boulevards in carriages – the weather most intensely hot.

I fancy Killimoon, Lissan & ye vicinity flourishing & delightful & hope my numerous friends are all in the happy prospect I wish them.

A little *petit diable* of a fly has bit or stung J. Lindsay's leg above her Ancle, 'twas very painful last night. This is Tuesday, when the post goes out – this day & Friday only. The Marq. of Salisbury went with the Dk. of Wellington to Waterloo this morning & proceeds on to visit the fortress & return here next Sunday.

I beg my love to William & Mary.[121]
from Dr. Mrs. S.
Most affect.
Scram.

The allusions in this letter to the Conynghams give a glimpse of what was perhaps their first visit to Brussels – possibly planned to distract their minds from the sorrow of losing their first-born baby son.

It is interesting to know that William L. Conyngham must have been acquainted with the great Duke of Wellington and that he was invited to Court by the King of the Netherlands – we can well imagine his humorous remarks on seeing at the dinner-party Catholic priests decked with 'Orange ribbons'!

There is another surviving letter from 'the Scram' to Mrs. Stewart, written in the following November from The Hague. By this time the Conynghams had returned home, but Charlotte's sisters and their husbands were still in the Netherlands, and the Scram enjoyed a pleasant tour with them to Delft and Rotterdam. Grace Ormonde travelled with five girls and two boys and their nurses, etc.! The Scram recounts that the whole party met with a pleasing reception indeed:

We have feasted there ever since (at Delft), Grace has been wondrous busy in fitting up so small a house for so numerous a family, which is to be increased before Christmas, not as usual – but by Thurles & the two boys, Walter & James' arrival – *multum in parvo*. Lords Clancarty & Ormonde dined with the King to-day also the P. & P[css] of Orange & the young Princess & P. Frederica. The Queen is to give a grand dinner & a most splendid ball on her birthday, the end of this month. They are all residing at present in this town wh. is full of palaces much handsomer than at Brussels, where we dined twice & most sumptuously at Ly. Northland's & were at grand party's. Here are the finest walks with trees, oak & beech, large as at Killimoon. The Musée here is much resorted to – always open till 3 o'cl. The ladies, Louisa & Harriet, copy pictures – 'tis full of finest tableaux – one beautiful one that the glorious King William used to take with him to England. We are all Orange from top to toe.

I beg my love to your Willm & Mary – & to Richard,[122] who I believe could scarce be happier were he even a Bishop. I wish him a good wife, not forgetting all my numerous friends in Cookstown & Loy.

I hear the Caulfeilds are returned to Moy & hope are well.

George Crofton has lived several months near Waterloo. I saw him often at

> Brussels. He enjoys a fine shooting, has excellent rooms breakfast & dinner for only three Franks per jour.
>
> I hope little Hassy is very well & all at Spring H, as well as the vicinity of Derryloran, Loughry, & Frederick's beautiful Bride &c.
>
> Lord Athlone died of an apoplexy the day of our arrival – his widow has 37 thousand a year. I wish to God William was married to her. Excuse my long scrawl from – dear Aunt Bess –
>
> Most affect Scram.
>
> We all regret much Ld Clancarty's resignation. Lord Granville is to be his successor after Xmas.

This lively fellow, Colonel Thomas Staples, died in 1825, not long after this letter was written. His handsome face is to be seen in a miniature now in the possession of Mr. and Mrs. Thomas Staples at Blackrock.

As soon as William's children could sit on a horse, they learned to ride, and often made their mother anxious, especially after Hazzie had a fall from her horse which caused a small scar near her mouth, but which did not greatly detract from her decided good looks. Charlotte, the youngest girl, grew up to be very plain, but with lovely hands, and was witty and extravagant.

There were seven years difference in age between the sons, William and Jack, and while William was interested in outdoor sports, musical and sociable, Jack was very clever and studious and was at Rugby School in Dr. Tait's time – a headmaster who formed a high opinion of his character and ability.

William (or 'Billy') was sent to the Royal School, Dungannon,[123] as at this time the sons of Irish landowners were usually educated at Irish schools. One of his school-fellows was the celebrated John Nicholson, of Indian fame, and another was Armar Lowry, one of the fourteen children of James Lowry of Rockdale. Another friend of William's boyhood, who often spent his holidays at Springhill, was Robert Lowry of Drumreagh, afterwards a General. Each of these two friends had seven sons.

William F. Lenox-Conyngham was destined for the Army, and John for the Diplomatic Service, perhaps because of his Uncle George's position at the Foreign Office, of which he became 'Chief Clerk,' which was equivalent to the present office of Under Secretary for Foreign Affairs.

This notable man wrote sparkling letters from London to his elder sister, Sophia Stuart of Lisdhu. An early one of these is worth copying, though the first sheet is missing.

> ... believe that she would rather stay in the house all day improving her already too well polished appearance than mix in the busy bustle of what has been called unenlightened Society. I shall say no more upon this subject at present and will conclude domestic affairs with a few words:
>
> 'I detest them as I do the gates of Hell
> Who one thing think, another tell.'

William Fitzwilliam Lenox-Conyngham in the uniform of the Royal School, Dungannon, *c.*1834

I went to the theatre last night with a party from Mrs. Cooper's to see an actor who has attracted general notice, his name is Kean – rather low for acting what nature has suited to him – that delight of mine, a noble Tragedy. The play was the 'Merchant of Venice,' which I don't think much of for moral reasons, but … only fixing your eyes on Shylock … was feasting them, when performed by a Kean, drew forth such bursts of applause like a violent burst of thunder … leaving everyone in astonishment looking & gazing upon each other. … You could have heard a pin drop … I was charmed to a degree, so much so that I forgot, when I was asked by a pert minx the name of the play, and answered that it was, think! the 'School for Scandal.' I wished her at the Deuce for intruding upon my well occupied time. I was surrounded with Rank, Fashion and Beauty, but they had no attraction for me equal to Shylock, Shylock, Shylock.

… Perhaps, Mrs. Stuart, you think I can read of nothing else than that which belongs to diplomacy, and though I like it very much, yet when I am occupied in some more innocent amusement than studying the physiogonomy and minds of men, I feel more inclined to tackle to the business. I must conclude with most affectionate regards to Andrew. In this letter you will find the sentiments which have always been nearest my heart & which I shall always cherish. … Truth, sincerity and a conscience free from restraint, guilt &c.

Your for ever attached and affectionate Brother
Geo. Lenox-Conyngham.

George was eighteen at this time and his sister Sophia only nineteen and the wife of the Hon. Andrew Stuart. George wrote on June 22, 1814, to this sister as follows:

Foreign Office.

My dearest Sophia

At last I have the pleasure of informing you that we are in hopes that things will run in their right channel, as the Royal visitors set off tomorrow. The King of Prussia, I hear, is gone. Joy be with them. I never was more tired of anything in my life than looking at most wonderful sights. We have had nothing for these three weeks past but reviews and fêtes, fireworks and fooleries of every kind – in short everything capable of leading men's minds away and giving you the sensation of perambulating the streets without a Boot or Shoe on your foot. I am sorry to see in a newspaper that the country in Ireland, and Dublin especially, is not what it should be ... in a state of fervent Liberty or death. Pray write me a cool, sedate letter upon this subject and tell me some news of your own country & not moralise on the Pss. of Wales, Politics or Diplomacy.

Lord Cochrane & the whole party have received the sentence & a tight one too – how very degrading for a Gentleman – a nobleman – to be put in the Pillory, it will be a warning to all Stock-jobbing rascals.

William has just come into my room & says as he will soon be on his way to the land of his forefathers that it will be useless for him to write any more. The Cumberland Place people are to give their first fashionable party tomorrow. I heard from my mother yesterday.

With best wishes that you and Andrew may enjoy 'Heaven's choicest Blessing' ... we subscribe ourselves

Yr. affectionate Brothers
Geo Lenox-Conyngham
W. Lenox-Conyngham.

Early in 1827 'George of the Foreign Office' married Elizabeth Holmes, the only child of a Dublin lawyer and niece of the patriot, Robert Emmet.

The following letter, on thick gilt-edged paper, written to his elder brother at Springhill, alludes to the impending marriage.

F. O. Nov. 30.1826.

My dear William

I have recd. yours inclosing the interest. Tell Charlotte she must keep the account between us ... a big Bank note would be more convenient to me than Magill's infernal longsighted bill. Eliza will no doubt have shewn you Mr. Holmes' last letter to me; besides the consent which it conveys, it is in other respects very satisfactory to me personally, although I felt not the least apprehensive on the score of my character, still it is very gratifying to me to know that others know me as well as I know myself. All I feel I want is something to start upon, but I expect he will (the father) give us a little gratuity to begin with, over and above the settled thing – the rent of the house is what I fear most.

I have seen the Galbraiths twice – the last time I saw Sir James I was told he was worse, and indeed he looked very ill. Remember me kindly to Charlotte and 'all at home.'

Ever affectly yours
G. Lenox C.

Tell me how my dear little Billy gets on.
I *only* wish that I may have such another.

George's wish was soon fulfilled. A son was born to him and named George – 'Gino' for short – and he was also father to a daughter 'May' – (Mary Ann Grace Louisa) who afterwards married Hayes, Viscount Doneraile – who died of hydrophobia from the bite of a mad, pet fox.

'Gino' wished to marry Mary, the beautiful daughter of Lever, the novelist, who was a dispensary doctor at Portstewart: but his parents would not consent to what they considered a *mésalliance*, whereupon the grief-stricken youth fled to the Argentine and is said to have died unmarried. May Doneraile had an only child, 'Clare,' who espoused the 2nd Lord Castletown and died, leaving no children. So 'George of the F.O.' left no descendants. He and his brother kept in close touch throughout their lives and have left many letters, some of which refer to the old bête-noir of the family – their Uncle, William Lenox. This reprobate, having for years pursued his course of guile and impecuniosity, had considerately changed his name to 'Edwards' and wrote many begging letters to his nephews. In one he observes ' The day may perhaps come when Mr. E. shall be no more, that Mr. C. will have reason to believe that he has been a very different character in life to what Mr. C. had been taught to believe!!'

George begged his brother 'not to destroy the Edwardian correspondence' – and expressed fear lest under certain eventualities Edwards might one day claim the Springhill property.

F.O. May 26/29.

My dear William

Enclosed is another application from Mr. Edwards. I fully expect he will give me trouble. …

I would not have done Ben Mauls[124] work on the 20th for the Loughry estate. Four horses indeed! The Lord help us! God bless you all.

G. Lenox C

Have you ever thought of a chance (which God in His Mercy forbid) of you and your generation being all cut off, and this very Lenox-Edwards or his descendants being placed in possession of Springhill Estates. For should such

> ever be the case, G. Lenox-C (nor his descendants) will ever be entitled to take possession of the lands of his Forefathers.

George goes on to point out that on his brother's death without issue Springhill would either escheat to the Crown or follow the will of the Testator, who bequeathed them to his father in trust, and he begged his brother to settle the matter, suggesting that Mr. Holmes, George's father-in-law, could give a legal opinion.

William's reply to this recognised that he thought Edwards 'a great rogue', wished that the Bishop of Meath could be consulted about Edwards, as he could tell much about him, and adds

> My property is settled on my issue male and female. To make your mind easy, if Mr. Holmes could draft a will by which I could, failing my own issue, entail my property on you, I would be glad – but mind I will not give him a fee for his trouble![125]

* * * * * * *

The life which William and Charlotte spent at Springhill was happy, prosperous and rather uneventful, their children, demesne and property forming their chief interests. William, of course, took his natural place in the Counties of Derry and Tyrone, of both of which he was Deputy Lieutenant and High Sheriff.

No Conyngham of Springhill had ever stood aloof from military matters, and we find that William took part in the Londonderry militia, which his father had commanded. The following letter shews this:

> August 1839 Ilery Lodge
> Castlederg.
>
> My dear Conyngham
>
> I have great pleasure in enclosing the Commission for the Majority of the Londonderry Militia which reached me so late that I feared there would be no use in sending it to Urney Park[126] to you.
>
> Wishing you many happy years to enjoy your honours.
>
> I remain Sincerely yours
> W. W. Ferguson.

In this year, 1839, the family went to stay for a while at Cheltenham, then a fashionable resort, William and his elder son, Billy, escorting them there and then returning home together. After her husband's departure. Mistress Charlotte wrote to him as follows:

To Wm. Lenox-Conyngham.

Monday July 29th

My Dearest W^{m}

We are charmed to hear of your prosperous journey, by your letter from Dublin, which I received yesterday, you reached home as soon as by Belfast.

We are, thank God, all well, but felt very sad and quiet after you and Billy. I am now beginning my housekeeping and expect to make a fortune by my savings.

We are to dine with the Kennedys to-day. On Saturday evening, we went to Mrs. Whitishes, where we met a Mr. and Mrs. Noel, brother to the good Noel, & Lord Barham, very nice people. Captain Talbot came in on Thursday for the Conservative dinner, where Col. Blacker covered himself with glory. You will see all the speeches in the paper. The Dr. insisted on taking a family ticket for the concert tomorrow, which takes Haz and me & Eliza with him. He is very well and was charmed by Dr. Hook's preaching yesterday. Poor Mr. Montgomery never even shewed his face – he is quite outpreached. I did not go near him, I have not heard if the Baronet came on Saturday.

Such a day of rain never was. Mrs. Rowe just gone. She has made them begin water-colours to-day, with which they are greatly taken.

Tell Billy I received his pattern letter yesterday. I am very sorry for the loss of my namesake.

I have not yet heard when Grace[127] comes. Louisa and Bessy are both gone to Leamington & I hope Grace will soon move. My poor Brownie is very low. I don't think she is making much progress. Lady Dillon is still with her, and she expects another sister – Lady Foulkes – to-day. Old Nick[128] set out at twelve o'clock, he had a neck of venison in the evg. for him and his son to guttle together, tho' Anna would not give 3/9 for a gown for the housemaid. I told you I would send gowns home & I *did*, & I am sure you are not angry. I am going out & may gather something to tell you. Not a step did we get out since 1/2 after one, it has rained in torrents & is getting worse every minute & I must go dress for dinner, but will send this that you may know of our state

God bless you both dearests
Yours ever C M L-C

Aug 5th

My dearest W^{m}

I shall not be able to write you much just now, as we have been all day at Appleby Court, where the Dr. took us, but you will expect a line & I will write you some more gossip tomorrow or next day. We are all D.G. well. My whole week's bills including coals, were not £11. I went to the Bank and only took £30, I met with a great loss in dropping my Specs in the street, and my new ones cost a guinea. I hope you have had the same fine weather we have, but the whole flat ground around Appleby is like a lake, with rows of trees in it. … Miss Strickland has 40 acres of Hay under water & lost.

We took sandwiches & we got bread & butter & nice fresh small beer. … I have heard nothing from Grace, but one from Burleigh Stuart[129] on Saturday tells me she was to go to Leamington on Friday, from whence she comes here & then returns to London for Walter's marriage. *Perhaps if she asks us*, Haz and I will go there with her, and you can meet us there via rail road – What say you? I think you are very well conducted to write so often, and I will now give my best blessing to you both and God bless you.

Ever dearest, most affectly
C M L-C.

This letter is addressed to Boom Hall, Derry, Ireland.

As these letters give insight to the character of Mrs. Lenox-Conyngham and of the terms on which the family stood to each other, they are worth copying. They also give a faint sketch of Cheltenham society and the *beau-monde* which gathered there over a hundred years ago.

Monday Aug 12th

My dearest W^m^

Not having heard from you, I scarcely know where to direct this. I think I will to Boom Hall, and another home. We are all D.G. well. Haz wrote to Billy a long history which leaves me little to tell in the way of gossip. The Bishop of Meath has made a wonderful recovery. Jos. Alexander is also alarmingly ill of inflammation. Henry A. is to be married the day after tomorrow. I have not had a line from Grace, but am told she is at Leamington. I had a long letter from Mrs. Hewitt telling me all they mean to do – viz. to set out from Belfast to Havres & proceed to Hiers for the winter. The Drs. do not think Alicia's lungs are yet affected. Mrs. H. is to be confined in Oct. and Dr. Ryan goes and stays with her till she has finished. Old Lady L comes to Astley. I am going to dine with the Blackers to-day. We have got Lord & Lady Warwick at No. 18 … What think you of Lord Brooham's speech? It is now said that parliament is to go on sitting the whole Summer. My house bills to-day were £9 14. 0. They would not have been £9, but I had a *Soirée*, which cost me 12, and Mary got some things for me in her book–lining and tape &c. Angelo attends Jack twice a week, between him & Mr. Hart I hope the heads will be well up. I paid Chank in full of music. … I find Haz did not tell you of my *Swarry*. I had Miss Walker to sing for my old friend Louisa Smith, Miss Synge to play and Lady Ricketts to listen & the Gibbs ditto, which with the Clement's[130] and … was all and I gave them some ice and fruit and tea and coffee & I did very well. On Thursday we went to the Fireworks … all cost 18/-. There were jugglers and Rope dancing. … We dined with the Kennedys and all went together. The children came after dinner to call for us, when the Majorca[131] took them into the dining room we had just left. Tell Billy the blue-nosed lady, who he says cheated at Commerce, is going to be married. Nin[132] is come away from Mrs. Toby, having finished her. They gave her £10 for her five weeks care and were charmed with her.

God keep you both.
Your ever affect.
C. M. L-C.

The 'long history,' which Hazzie wrote to her brother. Billy, is fortunately still extant and gives a picture of this lively girl of sixteen, who was having her first experience of 'Society' and possessed her mother's lively and vivid style of letter-writing.

Cheltenham
Thursday August 8th

My dearest Billy

Mamma got Wim's letter this morning. I am charmed to hear such pleasant news of you all, but tell him he is very forgetful not to tell me of *Rattler*. You have not once mentioned him on any of the days. We are very anxious to know how the gowns pleased. I am sure Mrs. Wright's eyes did not shut for a whole week. Today is the grand Centenary Fête – there is to be a public breakfast at the Rotunda to which none of us would be bothered to go to, but I think, indeed I am sure, we are going to see the fireworks in the gardens. There is a bridge made across the road from the Pump Room to the gate. ... I hope no necks may be broken. Jack is in a mortal fright that it should break. We dine with the Majorca to-day – his brother Hugh is here now, he must have been very handsome. ... We took a drive to Apperly on Monday – the Dr. came with us, & Louisa Dillon. She is very little older than Jenny, tho' she looks so tall. She is a gay, merry girl & she amused us very much. We had a very pleasant day there. Old Lawson was not there, but we got bread & butter, cheese and some of the home-brewed beer. There are 200 acres under water there. We went after the Promenade to Lady Coghill's the same evening. It was pleasanter than the evening you were there. One young lady executed some pieces of music in a most wonderful manner – the poor piano-forte suffered a great deal, I am afraid. Edmund Walker is come back from Wales, he looks more comical than ever. Mamma bids me tell you to bring *La Fontaine's Fables* when you come. They are in one of the little bookcases in the large drawingroom, bound, like Madam de Sevigne, in 2 Vols. I don't know what you will do having missed taking Jane L. through the crowd tonight. Just think the loss you had! We went to hear Mrs. Stockhauser sing the other morning. ... Pio was there in all his glory and *beauty*. I am still reading *La Villagiatura* – some of it is very amusing. Giovanni[133] makes many enquiries for *Elmucio*. There are a great many people come to this town, among them the Dean of Ossory, Lady Louisa Bourke's brother. Mamma went to see Mrs. Burke yesterday, she kissed her three times and seemed charmed to see her. Lord Decies is here also, he made us laugh so yesterday evening at the odd people in the baths. We dine at *four* every day. I don't admire it particularly, but *we be till do it*.

... I know you hate crossing, so I will tell Jenny I have written you so long a letter I will not write to her for a little while. With many loves from us all

Believe me your most affect, sister
Harriet R. F. Lenox-Conyngham.

Tell us what Aunt Kitty's[134] studs are like. I was nearly forgetting to say we heard from Uncle John[136] yesterday of the Bp. of Meath's illness. Mamma's Brownie has removed to Sir Charles Morgan's house in Suffolk-Square, so Mamma will have a longer way to go, which I am glad of, as it may prevent her going so often – the poor woman is sometimes better, sometimes, worse.

Shortly after this, Hazzy's mother wrote again to her husband, describing a visit to Lord Ellenborough's 'with the Blackers and Lady Jane and Mary.' She adds:

I wish you were both back again, but don't hurry as long as you find it pleasant, though I know it cannot be so much so as if I was with you. … I am going to see George Dawson's two old sisters, who have arrived from Bath. Liney is, I think, more thin than ever. Her head has been a *shade* less frequently bad. Lady Dillon sent me a venison pasty, but alas, the buck had been killed rather too long for my nose, and when the pie was opened we all ran away. Lord de Vesci's son is to be married to Lord Pembroke's sister – youth, beauty, accomplishments AND £25000, everything like me but the last item. Ormonde is gone to Kilkenny at last. Grace tells me he was to leave town this day; Harriet Fowler is better. Mrs. Blacker tells me Sir R.F. is left trustee to Mr. Ogilby's will and that the property is to accumulate for the son of his now surviving son. The eldest son only left a daughter. She has an immense fortune from her mother. I leave you to speculate on Miss Ogilby for Billy – and say God bless you both, dearest and dearest.

Yours ever most affectly
C M L C

Aug 21.

My dearest Wm., you horrible old monster, I have not had a line since the Monday you went to Derry. I wrote both there & to home & to Mrs. Hewitt. I hope I may hear from you tomorrow & that Billy had some good shooting & will send me some grouse. Grace came to me on Saturday with Louisa and Mary. … She and Lou[136] are very well but Mary is delicate and is now under the Canon who Grace likes very much. She was uneasy about her lungs. We can scarcely get into the hall for cards pitching at the Marchioness.

I am as economical as possible and hope you will think so. We are DG well, and Grace wakes me much earlier of a morning, which I tell her you will worship her for. The town is much more full, but not many I know. Henry Clements is, I know, expected on Monday. This you probably know. Ormonde does not leave London for at least a fortnight. No Conservative peer is to leave till the end of the Session. I have not heard from Dr. Magill since he left this. The Butlers arrived in the nick of time. If you chuse you may bring me a garter-blue satin Tusk from Wier's, and if Kitty has a very pale pink feather you may get it for Haz, but I don't *much* care, if you don't find it convenient. Walter is to be married in London, and then Grace goes abroad for the Winter. Grace then goes to Ireland. We are just going to see Old Nick's pictures – the day very fine. Last Sunday a body of Chartists came to the Parish Church. They had noticed Mr. Close they would. We all went, quite unconscious of anything unnatural till we reached the Church. I never heard a more beautiful sermon and such a dressing given in such good feeling and still telling them he hoped that tho' it was their first appearance it would not be their last. … All was quiet. … I trust I may hear of you tomorrow – Goodbye dearest. God bless you both.

Ever your own
C M L C.

The delay in William's letter may be accounted for by his movements in Ulster at this time, for many friends were writing to beg him and Billy to visit them.

Judge Torrens of Derrynoyd wrote thus, addressing to William at the Bishop of Derry's, Londonderry:

Derrynoyd Lodge
Tobermore Aug 10: 39.

My dear Conyngham

I heard yesterday from our friend R. Miller that you and your son are at Derry to remain for a week. I now write in the hope that I shall prevail on you & him to take this place on your way home & stay with us as long as it may be your convenience to do. … William's friend *Samuel* is at home & most anxious to see his young friend. ... If any friend should be returning with you we have ample accommodation.

Believe me dear Conyngham
Very truly yours Robert Torrens.

P.S. The Feeny road very good if no intervening flood carries away the bridges.

A fortnight later Judge Torrens wrote again to congratulate William on his little boy Billy's *début* in shooting, and asking him to bring his gun, so that he might try his skill on 'our hills' – and asking to be remembered to 'A. Stuart and lady.'

Another invitation received at this time was from J. Stanhope, from Urney Park – the home of her parents, Sir James and Lady Galbraith – who were, as we know, Aunt and Uncle to 'Wims.'

Urney, Monday night

My dear William

We shall be delighted to see you & Billy on Wednesday. I cannot tell how delighted I shall be to see you again. … Mama said she was sure you would not leave the country without coming to see her.

Yr. affect J. Stanhope.[137]

We trust that William did not disappoint his kind 'Aunt Beck,' who had befriended him after his own Mother died – and we can understand what pleasure it gave him to present to her his promising boy of fifteen.

On August 21st Charlotte wrote again from Cheltenham to her husband and son:

My dearests, old & young,

I received your Sunday's letter, which gave great consolation as to the effects of the storm and, except the ash-tree which fell on the coach-house stable, I don't think any great favorite is down. Until yesterday we lived under a waterspout.... Bess Cooper, Anna and *all* the Wades sailed for Antwerp on Monday. ... I heard of H. Clancarty[138] being much better of her maladies.

No sign of Grace yet. Mr. Hart gave the children their first dancing lesson yesterday – he gives nearly two hours to the *three* for seven shillings. Yesterday we dined with old Mrs. Caulfeild. ... Sir James Stuart is *alive*, but that is all. Henry Alexander and his bride are to be at Ardbraccan[139] the middle of this month. Anna Maria Nicholson is very ill there. Old Nick still at his son's. I suppose Billy is in high delight. Make John send white currants to Mrs. Wills. I hope there is a firkin of butter on the road. The Dr. leaves for Paris next week to amuse himself among the hospitals there. I don't despair of his meeting us at Brussels. There is no news of a public nature. ... I hope to hear very often from you. You have done pretty well so far.

Yrs. Ever dearest
C M L-C   Sir Robert never came.

Young Hazzie again put pen to paper and wrote to her brother as follows:

Cheltenham Aug 24.

My dearest Billy

Thank you for your very long letter from Derry ... as you may imagine seriously, we were all charmed by Wims' long letter. I am sure you were half mad at your first day's shooting. You are not shot yourself yet, I suppose, or the exhilarating tidings would have reached us ere this. Aunt Grace, Louisa and Mary came to us this day week. Aunt Grace is looking very well and Lou too. Mary is looking delicate and is very like Emmy. Bessy staid with Harriet, who is a good deal better. Lou is not breaking her heart for Mr. Freke, by all accounts she has had a good escape from a goose. I dont think any *wise* body would have put on *weeds* as he did when he found the match was ended.

'We are going to Gloucester to-day – except Jack and Baby, who are going with the Majorca to Toddington. I wish you would try at Brown's if he has any Coagh pearls, & if so, dont you think it would be a *bella cosa* for you & I to give rings of them to the Minorca and Ivica,[140] the prettiest way is just a *single* pearl set *quite plain*, as the one Wims gave to Fan. I hope you will have time to get them, but I know you were wandering on the face of the '*arth*,' so it was useless to tell you before. Mamma begs you to get the rose geranium. Ask Aunt Kitty to shew it to you also the primroses, yellow red and white. … Mamma wants a cutting or a plant of the common white heath. Now dont forget all this, *triccone che tu sinoche tu Sarei*. I do hope you have not forgot all your Italian, Lou, Liny, Mary and I went to take a drive yesterday in a phaeton with a postillion, & after a very pleasant drive round Charlton, just at the top of Lansdowne, off came one of the wheels. … I did laugh so – We were so fine driving about, and then to come to such a finale was rather too bad. We went to hear some Alpine singers last night; they were very pretty. They danced such a comical dance, very like Dick Stewart. There is such a talk in the room I can hardly write. Giovanni desires his best respects to you & begs you w[d] bring him some *aqua vita Irlandaisi*. I said I was afraid you would not. I have many more things to tell you, but I have not time. Miss Emmeline Coghill is to be married on Tuesday. I saw some magnetising the other day, & it is to me a frightful thing. Little Florence Coghill was the victim, & she seemed quite convulsed. I must have done. With many loves from all. I am dearest Billy

Your most affecte Harriett R. F. Lenox-Conyngham.

Charlotte's next letter is dated 3rd September.

Carissimo Vechio

I had a scold written yesterday which with people coming in prevented me sending. I hope this will find you preparing to turn your steps this way. … I think it would be a good plan of you to arrange some way at Belfast & Liverpool for getting over sacks of potatoes, they are now 1/6 per peck & half a peck is the least we can use – bread is expected to be very dear & I think the carriage would be much less than what we pay here. You might bring *with* you a hamper of fowls of *sorts*, tho' not Michaelmas. Geese are very good, and young turkeys, as well as fowls. … John may despatch butter to be sure of no interregnum, the last is so good we eat it as fresh butter. Lou and Mary Butler were quite charmed with it. Grace is still at Leamington waiting for Nanny Wynne. Ormonde has been waiting for them all in London, but, in a letter I had from him today, he says his patience is exhausted, John is in London & will probably be here to-morrow, as he only waited for Grace. We were last night at Lady Coghill's, she signs herself to me 'Yours *affectly*,' a regular Cheltenham party – *c'est tout dire*. Sir Osborne Gibbs wants me & Haz. to take the two vacant places in his carriage *gratis* & go to the Worcester Musical Meeting on Friday – the highest tickets 15/- the rest 7/-. This is a secret. I have not told Haz of the offer, & he promises to keep his toe in his pump too. It is as cold as Nov. last night I could not sleep for cold.

If it was John Lindesay, Robert L. did not visit, he was not at home at the time. Was it John Staples? Has Andrew set out yet? Bobby Mauleverer & his Aunt are here.

The last letter relates that

Grace left us yesterday & returned to Leamington where Nanny Wynne is to meet her. She does not know the day Walter is to be married. She will go for the Winter to Torquay if Broadstairs does not remove Mary's delicacy. Of course you have heard of Jos. Alexander's death. The Blackers go tomorrow – the young ladies have not had a very gay time. … Emmeline Coghill was married yesterday to Lady C's brother – we saw them coming out of Church and got plum cake. The Clements still here, but Henry has consented to Louisa going to Leamington. Harriett Fowler is to remain till Robert F. joins her there. I long to find if you think I have done well in money matters.

Grace has made us all presents – the 3 girls gowns, and she brought one for me, but the remnant was not enough, but I will not tell her. She gave me besides 3 Indian plates, & as she stepped into the coach she put a sovereign in my hand to get *something pretty* for the young ones, not of clothes kind.

On Saturday we – that is Grace & her 2, Me, Hazzy & Jenny & the Majorca. … We dined at 4. Lady Jane came with us. My fly there was my own expedition. Haz will write next.

Harriett to her father

Cheltenham August 31.

My dearest Wims

I am writing this by way of the newsletter you bid me write, but I am afraid it will be a failure as there is not much to tell. We are all quite well & frisky, though we felt very lonely after Aunt Grace &c left us. We heard twice from her since. Harriett is very much improved. She remains at Leamington, but Aunt Grace's stay is uncertain. How did Billy get on at Derrynoyd? I hope he did not waste as much powder as *usual*. We heard of Old Nick & Aunt Anna from Ipswich, where they were sadly disappointed as it is a wretched place & they got no fish, which was his great consolation for whatever else he might lose. They are now at Mr Newcome's in Norfolk. … Of course you have heard of Jos. Alexander's death. … The Majorca & Minorca went on Tuesday to her father's near Hereford, for 10 days. Jack and Baby went with them one day to Toddington & Sudely Castle, to their great delight. The Majorca's brothers, Hugh & Longford, were there. I think the former is a *wee* thought cracked & the latter just a quiet old bachelor. Last night we went to a ball at the Widder's. She has changed her house again to Aban Court, opposite Lydia Dixon's. I danced five quadrilles, one with a great friend of Billy's, at least he says so – a Mr. Smith of Annesbrook – or some brooke. There was an old Portugese Count there – the Count Condeixa, he chose to be introduced to Mamma and me, & he talked English in such an extraordinary way that I left him to mamma – & he could not speak French. I am sure I have seen him going about with an organ and monkey. I never saw such a tribe of *ourang outangs*, the Zoological Gardens must have been scoured for the collection of animals who were there. We left at *one*, so we were not *very* late. Col Clements[141] was to have come last night, & has just sent to know if we did. They are going to Leamington soon. Mrs.

> Clements is greatly pleased, as she has a fancy for trying Dr Jephson. The grouse have not yet made their appearance. ... My work is going on beautifully – all the ground part is finished. Tell Billy, Giovanni has brought Silvio Pellico for us to read. I have begun water-colours with Mrs Rowe & like it very well. How does my dear magpie Rattler seem, & the old cloak woman? Billy did not mention her, so I suppose she is still alive. Liney hopes Billy has not forgotten her beads, if he *has* forgotten them, he is to get 2 plain necklaces & crosses from Portglenone. Have you read Lady Blessington's 'Idler' we have only just got it – it seems amusing. We heard from Hazzy Wakefield[142] yesterday. Mamma's poor Brownie has been very ill. Lord Oranmore was here last week, he is nearly as wise as his sister, Mary Anne. Will you ask Aunt Kitty if she can spare me the old strawberry blossom pattern I left with her. I have written a fine long letter & you dont like crossing for your *old eyes*.
>
> With many and best of loves to you both
> Ever dearest Wims
> Your very affect. child
> Harriett R. F. Lenox-Conyngham.

It is to be noticed that William's children were on intimate terms with him – addressing him by his pet name 'Wims,' and the family seems to have been a united one, sharing their interests and little jokes, and living in great harmony and affection.

Life at Springhill passed on happily and usefully. The girls organized a sewing class for cottage girls, which was held every day in the upper room of the Eastern side-building, and was no doubt encouraged by Mrs. Charlotte, who was ever ready to help her poorer neighbours.

Much of the young ladies' own leisure was engaged in needlework, and Hazzie in her old age used to recollect the hours which she once spent embroidering tapestry pictures on a frame placed near the middle window of the large drawingroom. She also remembered sitting, as a little child, on a small chair at the far end of the black marble chimney-piece, listening to the old people talking of long ago episodes.

In the long summer days it was the custom to engage in making preserves and cordials, and we can imagine these charming girls, in their thin muslin gowns and sandalled shoes, fluttering from garden to still-room, like bees depositing their loads of sweets. There still remain jars of pot-pourri and a few bottles of elder-flower-water over a hundred years old, and the story lingers that once, after the making of black-currant whiskey, the squeezed currants were thrown out to be eaten by the fowl, which promptly became intoxicated and reeled unsteadily about the yards.

Another old custom was the yearly filling of the Turf-house in the laundry yard, which also contained the slaughter house and brew-house. This was achieved by a number of the tenants, who every year each supplied a cart of turf and a day's free work, and after piling up the turf in the long shed, they were given dinner on long tables set out on the grass-plot in the middle of the yard.

Beggars were numerous in those days, and were sometimes possessed of a ready wit, as was the old man who, when he received silver instead of the expected copper, uttered this quaint benediction; 'May your Honour never die but that every hair of your head may turn into a 'mould' candle to light you to glory'! I have also heard of the pleasure experienced by the young Conynghams by the periodic visits of a pedlar, who used to display his wares – packs containing brooches of coloured glass, Jew's harps and other treasures. In the afternoon, riding was the principal occupation, and we feel sure that many of the neighbours were visited on horse back the large family of Hewitts at the Rectory, and the Stuart and Alexander relations at Lisdhu and Portglenone, the Stewart cousins at Killymoon, and old friends at Loughry, not to forget 'Uncle Tom' and 'Aunt Kitty' at Lissan, only four miles away. This uncle and aunt – Sir Thomas Staples and his wife – had no children, but John, the younger Staples uncle, brought up a large family at Lissan Rectory, which he had employed the famous architect, Nash, to build. He had married Elizabeth Alexander, daughter of Nathaniel, Bishop of Meath. Many of these friends and relations came to stay at Springhill, bringing grooms and servants, who were housed in the large chamber over the coachman's room in the west side building. In those days many of the leading families drove four-in-hand, the Conyngham's equipage being driven by servants arrayed in the grey-blue family livery with crested silver buttons.

The present châtelaine was reminded of this soon after she went to live at the old house, for on bicycling to visit Robert Knipe – a man of ninety years – who lived at Irishtown, the old man remarked in the course of conversation that; 'Sir William's Mother never went out except in a coach with four grey horses.' This was said with a covert glance at the bicycle which leant against the cottage wall, though he was far too deferential to allude to the changed times, though doubtless sighing inwardly for the 'vanished pomps of yesterday.'

* * * * * * *

The Conynghams paid other visits to Brussels in after years. We know that their little daughter, Jenny, died there at the age of eighteen, to the sorrow of her parents. The wooden bed in the night-nursery, formerly hung with red damask, must have caused them many a heartache in after years, for it had been hers, and 'Jenny' is still marked on one of its boards.

Though no other letters written at Brussels remain, allusions to these sojourns are found in a bundle of old letters which returned to Springhill after a lapse of ninety years. These were penned in the years 1841–46 by Mrs. Charlotte Lenox-Conyngham to a Mrs. Hughes, and were lying at Tulip Hill – an old house in Pennsylvania – where they were found after 1930 by Mrs. Hughes' granddaughter. When discarding old family papers this lady considered Mrs. Conyngham's letters too charming to be destroyed and returned them to the writer's family through a mutual friend in Northern Ireland.[143]

It appears that the recipient had been the daughter of a Mr. Virgil Maxey, at one time American Chargé d'affaires at Brussels, where a fast friendship sprang , up between his family and the Conynghams, Mrs. Charlotte being especially devoted to their young girl, whom she playfully calls her 'American child,' and who in later life inherited Tulip Hill.

Some of these letters are of much interest. The first is written from No.10 Mountjoy Square, Dublin.

Oct. 30. 1841.

I trust this will find you, my dear child, and all with you as well as it leaves me and mine. I am, thank God, greatly improved in health and got over my long journey wonderfully for an ailing old woman.[144] Twenty-five hours from Antwerp to London, where we remained till Saturday ... when we railway'd to Liverpool and reached this place after a twelve hours' passage. I have had some difficulty in getting a house. ... The run on houses here is very great, owing to the popularity of the new Government, which seems to please *all* parties, *so far*. I found a number of my people here and expect more, the Ponsonbys among others, Captain Portlock, the geological brother-in-law Mr. Hughes was to have known had he come here, regrets he was prevented coming and perfectly knows him by sight... & described him very amiably. I hope my ' grandson' is growing more impudent every day, he will lead you all a merry dance when he gets on his legs, or I am much mistaken. I expect a long history of all your party in return for this rather bothered production, but I am still so unsettled I scarcely know what to say. ... Please God we will all meet at Cheltenham in the Spring.

William and the young ones unite with me in kind love to you, Mr. & Mrs. Maxey and quantities of kisses to the 'President.'

'God bless & be with you, my dear child
Always most affectionately yours
C M Lenox-Conyngham

This letter is addressed to care of 'The Honble Virgil Maxey, American Chargé d'Affaires, Rue de Musée, Bruxelles.'

The next is a long letter, written on May 10th. 1842, and only extracts are given here:

Your long wished for letter reached me on the 8th, my dearest child, and it is a sad disappointment to us all that we are not to have the happiness of meeting you before you recross the Atlantic.

We are at length settled at home once more, & all well except Jenny, who is still delicate, tho' improving. The weather is harsh, which prevents her getting into the open air, and that never suited her, but I hope the new moon, which began this morning, will be propitious both for land and sea. I hope Mr. & Mrs. Maxey do not suppose they are to be relieved of their promise to come to us. I know treaty making is a most indefinite work, but it must end at last. ...

My little Cheltenham expedition will not take place this year ... it is not absolutely necessary for me, and I am unwilling to move if it can be avoided. I cannot think where our mutual letters have gone to. Lady Ranfurly complains of our silence too, tho' Harriett had written as usual. We heard from her yesterday, she speaks of coming home the second week in June. I will not impose on you any more of my gossip. ... God bless you & yours, my very dear child, & grant you may find all you love well & happy in America – after a prosperous voyage.

Our united love and best wishes are with you
Ever yours very affectly
C. M. Lenox-Conyngham.

The next letter contains observations on the Ranfurly family.

None of the young ladies married. Julianna is going out and is very pretty. Stewart, the second son, is in the Army & is a fine-looking youth, very tall & more like his mother than any of the rest. The married one, Louisa, has just had a third daughter. Mrs. Stewart, had a dangerous attack of inflammation of the lungs but is *quite* recoverd, tho' in her 82nd year.

I have not seen Lady Bellew since we parted, and her *Pat*, but once. As to our Belgian & French acquaintance, I can tell but little.' (Here she mentions the de Rumignys – Juliette, very beautiful – Dietrichstein, the Austrian Minister. ... The 'poor little Duc de Beaufort.' Princess Louise Blomberg to take the veil because not allowed to marry Handel, the German Jew. – Sir H. Floyde, the Countess Outremont and others.)

Pakenham is to send the parcel to the care of my brother-in-law, George Lenox-Conyngham, who is the Chief in the Foreign Office. I fear I have not given you much amusement, but I am not an amusing person now, tho' very well in health & many many blessings ... but I never can be the happy creature I was when I ...

God bless and preserve you, dearest, is the constant prayer of
Your most truly affectionate
old Mother C. M. L-C.

Springhill April 30. 1845.

I have just managed to send a small parcel through the Foreign Office to my nephew, Richard Pakenham, it contains a cap and robe for my expected 'grandchild.' Your splendid parcel of apples arrived in March, but alas had suffered much on the way, but enough were safe to make us deeply lament those which were spoiled ... their jelly is superlative. ... The Tulip Hill productions must always be most highly valued here – I mean at Springhill. ... We are all, thank God, well. Billy quite a soldier, he has been quartered in Scotland since he got his Commission; he is now at Aberdeen. I am truly thankful the rumours of War are subsiding – remember no American swords are to be pointed towards the 88th – otherwise Connaught Rangers. ...

> Jack still with a clergyman reading busily, but we contemplate taking him to Foreign parts to perfect him for his intended profession of a Diplomatist; more unlikely things have happened than his going to Washington as an attaché to Dick Pakenham … & he will soon be at Tulip Hill should that ever be the case. The Ranfurlys are rebuilding their house at Dungannon.

The last letter of this correspondence is headed Springhill, August 20th, 1846.

> It appears a long time since I have heard from you, my dear Western child. … I confess my idleness. It is such a pleasure that we are allowed to be at peace – no jars so disagreeable as *family* ones, & I feel any disagreement with America as such.
>
> I hope my nephew, Dick, is liked among you. … I have watched the Mexican War accounts closely – & happy not to see the name of Hughes among the U.S. officers, though I doubt if a certain Captain of that name is as pleased as you or I at being out of what Billy calls 'the fun.' As to us, we have never gone more than 30 miles from home for nearly 4 years, but as Jack is going to school at Rugby, one of the great schools in England, Wm. & I mean to take the girls somewhere in the Autumn, probably to Paris. The Ranfurlys were in Ireland for 3 weeks, looking after their buildings – Lady Ranfurly in very low spirits since her affliction. … We were staying with my sister Ponsonby at the time we were from home. My dear Brother Bishop has been ill, but is now well & on a tour through Scotland with his family.'
>
> God bless and keep you all in every blessing this world can afford, with the blessed hope of everlasting joy in that to come.
>
> Ever your truly affectionate
> Old mother, C.M. L-C.

The above letters give a vivid impression of the personality of this charming Mrs. Lenox-Conyngham – a loving wife and mother and a devoted friend.

It was almost exactly a year after the last of these letters was penned that Charlotte was taken into 'the everlasting joy of the world to come.'

Her husband recorded in the family Bible:

> My dearest, best beloved wife, Charlotte Melosina, died at Springhill Sept. 1st. 1847 aged 61. Altho' she had been in delicate health her death was very sudden and unexpected. God only knows the very great loss I have sustained.
>
> W.L.C.
>
> Buried at Lissan.[145]

In these days, 1946 – not one of the old people remain in the neighbourhood of Springhill who can remember Mrs. Charlotte Lenox-Conyngham, but thirty-five years ago her cherished memory still remained with some of the older cottagers. A bedridden old woman – Mrs. Margaret Thompson – used to recall the lady's kindness to her, and that she had pitied her little bare feet, when standing on the stone flags in the kitchen, and I think had provided shoes for those feet. She also remembered the lovely face which she last saw pale in death, when taken into the room where the mistress' body was lying in the four-post bed after her spirit had left this world. Sorrow had indeed come to William, the bereaved husband, and four years later another crushing blow fell, when his brilliant younger son, John Staples Molesworth (Jack), died very suddenly. After a distinguished course at Rugby School, he had entered Trinity College, Dublin. He was destined for the Diplomatic Service, and high hopes were centred on his coming career. But these earthly hopes were vain, for he was to exemplify the saying, 'Whom the Gods love die young.'

An old cottager – Robert Knipe – has already been mentioned in these pages, and, as a nonagenarian he recounted this sad memory to the writer:

> I was working in the Flower-garden when Master Jack came and talked to me. After a while he said: 'I'm not feeling very well, Robert, I think I'll go indoors.' He went into the house and never came out of it again. In four days' time he died of typhus fever, which had been caught in a crowd which was present at a funeral at the Rectory, typhus being prevalent after the potato famine.

Jack's bedroom was in the top storey of Springhill overlooking the Beechwalk, and Robert Knipe remembered helping to carry the coffin down the winding 'Newel' staircase, and the difficulty in doing so because of its great length, 'for Mr. John was a tall young gentleman.'

Sad words were written in the family Bible by his heart-broken father:

> My dear son John died at Springhill of malignant typhus fever, February the I7th. 1851. He was a fellow commoner at Trinity College Dublin – a noble youth, full of talent and of great promise. He was only four days ill. Buried at Lissan.
>
> W. L. C.

Jack was remembered as handsome and attractive, being both studious and athletic: and perhaps he is fulfilling the promise of his youth in a better world.

Many years after his death it was pathetic to find a MS. book, in which he had written down disconnected jottings, which shew the varied interests of a youth of seventeen years old; – German declensions – some lines on Farriery – the management of greyhounds – receipes for making boots waterproof and for removing grease spots from silk – how to prevent a horse's feet balling in the snow – a greek exercise – a list of masters at Rugby Schoolhouse, Fellows of T.C.D. – a record of fishing expeditions from Springhill, and the numbers caught by the little band of fishers:

> Hunter's Lough May 10th 49 Thos. Hall, J. Conyngham, B. Stuart, J. Greer (18 large) day windy and rainy, water muddy. Lissan river May 19th. Thos. Hall, W. & J. Conyngham, B. Stuart, J. Greer.

And with these assorted subjects there are many poems – some being original. Jack had composed an 'Ode to Evening' and an 'Ode to Peace.' Some of the copied poems are 'Blücher's Lied' (in German), 'Oberon in Fairyland,' 'The night before Larry was stretched,' etc.

A short diary of only three days is found in this little volume:

> Thursday 23rd Nov/48.
>
> Rose at 8 o'clock – breakfast at 1/4 past 9 H.K.R. prayers – read newspaper. Wims went to Stewartstown for Poor-house day. Wheat stack taken in – one rat killed. Got wet through and lay with Billy at the G. room fire, who went in Evg. to Killymoon until Saturday, to meet Lieut. Lindesay. Very wet day – stormy night.
>
> 24th. Got up very late. Had a Headache and very sore bones from wetting the day before. Breakfasted late. Wims in bed. Letters from Mrs. Wills, Aunt Sophia & Izzy Delap.
>
> Nov. 25. Got up at 1/2 10 quite well and rested after the rat hunt & wetting the day before yesterday. A very wet day – had much better remained the whole day in bed –

John Staples-Molesworth Lenox-Conyngham 1831–1851

A very indifferent oil portrait of Jack shews a rather handsome, pale face with long dark eyes. He holds a gun, and a dog crouches beside him.

We now come to the last seven years of the life of William ('Wims'), which he spent at Springhill, living at first with his two devoted daughters, Hazzy and Charlotte, and often visited by his remaining son, William (Billy), who was a Captain in the Connaught Rangers. Old inhabitants of the district remembered old Mr. Conyngham as very tall and stout, with a stentorian voice – walking down the hill with his hands clasped behind his back, and his cheerful kindness impressed all who knew him. He was interested in County affairs, and, like his great-great-grand-uncle 'Good Will,' had much love and knowledge of trees, carefully preserving those in the Beech Walk and filling the hollows with cement. He also improved the old house, adding to it three rooms – the Diningroom, the 'little parlour,' and the Cedar room – which he built over the pantry.

The first of his children to marry was the sprightly Harriett. There had been a mutual attachment between her and a son of the Honble. John Hewitt, Rector of the parish: but Hazzy's mother considered that the cultivated and interesting James Hewitt was no adequate match for her daughter, and the young people had to submit to fate. Some years after her mother's death another suitor appeared, in the person of Marcus Gage of Streevehill, and Harriett long years afterwards remembered the proposal – her lover standing by the black marble chimney-piece in the library and proferring his suit, which was accepted.

A far less striking man than James Hewitt, Mark Gage was genial, foolish and very extravagant, but his wife loved him devotedly and quite forgave him for dissipating his fortune in ostentatious living.

The marriage took place in 1854, when a family party assembled, Aunt Grace Ormonde being one of its number. The bridesmaids, one of whom was Augusta Richardson-Brady[146] of Drum Manor, were attired hideously in crinolines, bonnets and Paisley shawls, and the drawing-room curtains (only recently discarded, after 1930) were dyed olive-green for the occasion.

Springhill's châtelaine was now the second daughter, Charlotte, or 'Glory,' who managed the housekeeping extravagantly, but cheered her surroundings by her lively humour and wit. A constant visitor was her first cousin and great friend Bessie Butler,[147] who spent many weeks every year in the old house. Some of her sketches still remain on its walls, and there are quaint old daguerreotypes of the two cousins in huge crinolines, seated together in sentimental attitudes.

The reign of this younger daughter of 'Wims' was not a long one, for, two years after Hazzy's marriage, William, her brother, made an exceptionally happy union which was to last for over fifty years. His bride was Laura Arbuthnot, daughter of George Arbuthnot of Elderslie, in Surrey, who came of an old Scottish family, and had acquired a large fortune by founding banking companies in India. A book has been written about the Arbuthnot family, of whom Queen Anne's doctor – John Arbuthnot, the friend of Swift and Pope – was a member.

Laura was a woman of great charm, piety and stability. Her brother-in-law, Sir John Gough, held the North of Ireland Command at that time, and the young people first met at a ball given in Belfast. She had come there on a visit from Co. Tipperary, where she and her younger sister, Eleanor, as orphans, had made a home with their elder sister, Jane, wife of the only son of Field Marshal Viscount Gough, of Indian fame.

The Goughs' home, Rathronan, near Fethard, had been the scene of a famous romance, of which Eleanor Arbuthnot was heroine, but as this has been described in great detail in several books, it is only necessary here to give a short outline of the affair.

The two Miss Arbuthnots, being young, charming, and considerable heiresses, were much sought after in Tipperary society and had many suitors.

Among these, Mr. Carden of Barnane – a cultured man of good family and large property – sought the hand of the younger sister – Eleanor, who promptly refused him. He was a man of forty and she but eighteen years old. Instead of accepting his dismissal, the disappointed lover formed the outrageous plan of carrying off the lady by force, his only excuse being that he thought the opposition came from Eleanor's family and not from herself.

John Carden laid his plans with infinite thoroughness and regardless of expense. He bought a yacht, which he fitted up with every luxury, even providing a swinging berth, as a precaution against seasickness, to which he heard Eleanor was liable. Relays of his tenants were posted all along the way to the Galway Coast, so that fresh horses should be available to bring the pair to the sea-port, whence he meant to bring the lady to his friend, Lord Hill's house – 'Hawkstone' in Skye – where she was to be received till her consent to the marriage should be obtained.

Then came the fateful Sunday when the ladies from Rathronan attended Morning Service, and were annoyed to find 'the enemy' (as they called Mr. Carden) amongst the congregation. Jane – then Mrs. Gough – Laura and Eleanor and the governess, Miss Lyndon, comprised the party. They had driven to Church on an outside car, and stayed for the Communion Service, during which a shower of rain fell, causing Dwyer, the coachman, to hurry back to the house to exchange the open vehicle for a closed carriage – a 'covered car' (a providential change, as it happened).

On the return drive, nearing Rathronan, Laura cried out 'Mr. Carden is coming!' and they saw him riding close behind. Suddenly the car stopped, as three hired ruffians sprang out from the hedge, cutting the traces and seizing the horses' heads, as Mr. Carden wildly strove to capture Eleanor and force her into a

The daughters of George Arbuthnot of Elderslie by Andrew Geddes A.R.A. From left: kneeling, Ann; sitting, Jane; head on Jane's knee, 'Leila'; basket on head, Laura (later Lady Lenox-Conyngham); rose in hand, Eleanor; standing, Catharine, who died about this time. Another daughter Mary, is not in the picture.

Lady Lenox-Conyngham sitting in the Beech Walk with her eldest son, William Arbuthnot Lenox-Conyngham.

brougham which he had in waiting. The opening of a covered car is at the back, and a violent scuffle took place, the ladies steadfastly resisting. Miss Lyndon tearing out handfuls of the 'enemy's' hair, as she herself was nearly seized by the hired men, who mistook her for the required prize.

But help came in time. Some of Lord Gough's employés came on the scene to join the fray, and, seeing that his attempt had failed, Mr. Carden put spurs to his horse and galloped from the place, being ere long captured and lodged in the county jail.

A trial followed, and the miscreant was sentenced to a year's imprisonment – a heavy penalty for a man of Carden's standing. However, the punishment did not cure him of his infatuation, for until his death, which occurred some years later, Mr. Carden haunted Eleanor, following her from place to place in hope of an interview. On one occasion, when she had just arrived at Springhill, Sir William Lenox-Conyngham, looking out of his window early next morning, saw a stranger lurking among the trees of the Beech Walk, and, on going to investigate, he found the luckless Carden, who had followed his magnet to Northern Ireland. Sternly indignant words sent the delinquent away at once on his homeward journey, but a letter is still extant in which Mr. Carden humbly apologised for his intrusion, but explained that he could not resist following the lodestar of his life.

After her first indifference to this determined suitor, Eleanor had feared and detested Mr. Carden, and it was not on his account that she never married.

In after years she was much loved by her many nephews and nieces, spending much time at Springhill, which her romantic heart dearly loved, and using the 'Cedar room' as her bedroom. The writer well remembers 'Aunt Eleanor's' gentle fascination as an old lady, her hair still worn in the old-fashioned ringlets. Her life ended at Lough Cutra Castle, in Co. Galway, where she had gone to cheer the latter days of her widower brother-in-law, Lord Gough, with the selflessness which was one of the traits of her beautiful character.

But it is with Eleanor's elder sister that this history is more concerned, for Laura, as Mrs. – and afterwards Lady – Lenox-Conyngham was an ideal wife and mother and also Lady Bountiful of the poor of the district. She leaves a charming memory at Springhill which was her home for over fifty years.

William Fitzwilliam Lenox-Conyngham and Laura Calvert Arbuthnot were married on the 5th of August, 1856, at Rathronan in Co. Tipperary, and the pink muslin dress, which the bride wore before donning her bridal gown, is preserved among ancient dresses in a chest at Springhill.

A number of Arbuthnots, Goughs and Conynghams were assembled for the wedding, and the favourite cousin, Lady Bessie Butler; William's first cousin, Burleigh Stuart, was best man. After a bridal tour of three months on the Continent, the young pair came to live with William's father and sister at Springhill. They were met at Dungannon by a mounted escort of the tenantry, who rode two and two behind the carriage to Moneymore, where the horses were removed, and a cheering crowd of retainers dragged the landau up the hill to the house, which Laura had never yet seen, but in which she was to spend so many peaceful and happy years.

The family party consisted of William's father 'Wims,' Hazzie Gage, his married, and Charlotte, his unmarried, daughter, Mark Gage, the husband of Hazzie, and 'Gino,' the son of old Uncle George of the Foreign Office.

The Blue Room had been prepared for the young couple, the four-post bed furnished with new chintz hangings, which it still possesses, in 1946.

We can picture this shy and reserved young bride coming for the first time among her warm-hearted and effusive new relations, and feeling overwhelmed by their demonstrative ways, which, though so kindly meant, drove her into her shell. But the romantic old house charmed her, with its dignified rooms, fine stair-case and oak panelling, and her affection for it never waned.

She took a daily stroll with her kind old father-in-law – up the Beech Walk, down some steps (now gone) and back along the wooded road, where she probably found new beetles to add to her collection of those insects. The long and formal dinners every night were a trial to her, and during the lengthy pause afterwards in the drawingroom, waiting to be joined by the men of the party, she used to slip away to her room and bed, directing her maid to awaken her the moment her father-in-law left the dining-room, so that she might come down again.

Thirteen children were born to William and Laura, one of each of the two sets of twins dying at birth, and eleven growing up strong, tall and healthy.

The eldest – William Arbuthnot Lenox-Conyngham – was born on September 8th, 1857, in the Blue Room, and his grandfather rejoiced at the arrival of an heir to the estate. Aunt Hazzie remembered being taken by her father to look at the occupant of the cot in the right hand corner of the room, and his proud remark to her; 'There! isn't that a nice little gentleman?'

The child was strong and very beautiful, not only as an infant, but throughout his life. It was during his babyhood that his grandfather died – in May, 1858 – and his mother related that she stood at a window in the Blue Room on the day of the funeral, with the baby in her arms, looking down on to the Court, which was thronged with tenants on horseback. They had come to pay a last respect to the dear ould master, who was buried at Lissan Churchyard, where so many of his forefathers slept in the walled tomb up against the back of the Church.

His son records in the Family Bible:

> William Lenox-Conyngham of Springhill died on the 29th of May 1858 after a long and painful illness. He is buried at Lissan. He was the best and kindest of fathers. None can tell how great his loss is but those who knew him as we did.

The ancient 'wrought' bed hangings, embroidered by a bygone châtelaine, were after the old master's death taken off his bed, washed by his daughter-in-law's maid, and laid by as relics.

XI

Sir William

1824–1906

William Fitzwilliam Lenox-Conyngham

And now the younger William became owner of the property and of the old family home, where he and his wife were to live for fifty long years, beloved by all their friends and dependants. He was a most indulgent landlord, and when tenants were bringing their claims into Court to have rents reduced, he voluntarily reduced them to a figure lower than that to which the Land Commissioners would have reduced them.

Six brothers and four sisters followed the birth of young 'William Arbuthnot,' and a merry party occupied the nurseries under the charge of 'Nannie' (or Mrs. Meighan), the nurse who for many a year was an inmate of Springhill. She took the eldest boy into her charge after his first nurse left, and many were her tales of the children's sayings and doings. Of a Sunday evening they were sent off with her in an open carriage to Service at the little new Church of Ballyeglish: and there is a story of Willy, the first-born, stepping boldly to the lectern to read the Lesson on an occasion when Mr. Jones, the parson became faint and beckoned to the child for help.

The father of this large family took part in the affairs of Counties Derry and Tyrone, as his ancestors had done. His chief pastime was coursing, and he owned several well known greyhounds. In his day no new rooms were added to the house, but he seemed to have a dislike of ponds and wells and filled in a pond which used to be in the kitchen garden, and also one near some large oaks near the stackyard.[148] As for his wife, she was busy in bringing up her many children, giving them excellent care and abundant Bible teaching, as is shewn by books of texts neatly copied in round babyish handwriting.

Mrs Meighan, the family nanny

Her unmarried sister-in-law, Charlotte, though often at Springhill, lived chiefly with her sister, Mrs. Gage, at Ballinacree, a large house near Ballymoney which the extravagant Mark Gage had built. But in the year 1868, Charlotte married Major James David Beresford – a grandson of the well known Irish politician, the Right Hon. John Beresford. Beresford's father – Henry Barré Beresford – lived at Learmount Park, Co. Derry, and James was called the 'handsomest member of the British Army.' As contrasts are supposed to attract each other, he married the plain but witty Charlotte Lenox-Conyngham, who was at that time forty-two-years old. There is a tale that an old country-woman, when congratulating her on her engagement, observed 'You were wise, Miss Charlotte, before marrying you took a good long 'forenoon.'

The couple lived later on in the Circular Road, Moneymore, their marriage lasting for ten years before the death of Major Beresford, whose wife did not long survive him. Hazzie, her elder sister, lived till 1900, and after her husband's death dwelt in comparative poverty in Coleraine. Her Marcus had left her scantily provided for, but she cherished his memory and was an unfailingly loyal wife to a careless, improvident husband. Neither of the sisters had any children.

Mention has already been made of this Beresford family. Through the three marriages with Uptons, they were connected with the Conynghams, who descend from Dorothy, daughter of Michael Beresford of Coleraine.

A letter written to William Conyngham (Sir William's great granduncle) in 1767 by Rev. William Beresford, shows that friendship existed between these kinsmen.

> Dr Conyngham
>
> I am sure it will give you real pleasure to hear that I have been more successful in seling my tythes than I (or I believe any person in the country) expected. I have been here these three weeks and have got over every difficulty, there still

remains about fifty pounds unset, which I think Galbraith can manage without my assistance. I therefore set out this morning for Dublin and propose to call on Mr. Corry to return him thanks for his kindness to me.

My brother comes to Dublin a day or two before I left it and insisted on a promise that I would see him at Curraghmore as soon as my affairs were settled. I pleaded a prior engagement to you, but he insisted on a positive promise, and I was obliged to comply. I am sure that you will excuse me till next Summer, when if we do not meet at Curraghmore, I hope we shall at Springhill. I beg that you will present my thanks to Mr. Stewart, whose influence with his tenants has been of use to me and also to Mr. Lowry.

I am Dear Conyngham
Yours very sincerely

Cooly, September ye 29: 1767 Wm. Beresford.

The writer of this letter was a brother of the first Marquis of Waterford and of The Right Hon. John Beresford, who in Grattan's Parliament was so powerful a personality that he was sometimes termed 'King of Ireland.' These three sons of Marcus Beresford, Lord Tyrone, were all fortunate. William, who at the age of twenty-four, was Rector of Cooly, a Tyrone parish (now named Sixmilecross) afterwards became Archbishop of Tuam and first Baron Decies. He had married, when only twenty years old, a sister of Fitzgibbon, Lord Clare, and had a large family.

The grandparents of this distinguished trio of brothers are famous in ghostly lore – as they were hero and heroine of the famous 'Beresford Ghost Story.' This well known story has often been related during the two past centuries and firmly believed in by all scions of the Beresford family. As a very old copy of this tale, written in faded ink in a note book, is still at Springhill, it may not be inappropriate to repeat it in these pages – in abridged form – giving quotations from the original.

THE BERESFORD GHOST STORY.

Sophie Nichola Hamilton was a daughter of Lord Glenawley, who is said to have lived at Walworth, in Co. Derry. In early life, though not related, she was much associated with the young Lord Tyrone,[149] and, both being orphans, they were under the care of 'persons who educated them in the principles of Deism.' In consequence, the faith of these young creatures was unsettled, and they made a compact that 'whichever should die first, he or she would, if possible, appear after death to the other and declare what religion was most approved of by the Supreme Being.'

In later days, after Sophia's marriage with Sir Tristram Beresford, and Lord Tyrone's union with a Miss Rickards, 'no change of circumstance or condition diminished in the least their former friendship. Their families often visited each other, spending usually upwards of a fortnight together each time.'

A few months before the birth of the Beresfords' son, they were on a visit at Gill Hall, near Dromore in Co. Down, when a strange episode occurred. Lady Beresford awoke one night to find Lord Tyrone sitting by her bedside. She screamed and endeavoured in vain to awaken Sir Tristram, (whose potations, we infer, must have been deep). Then the phantom spoke; 'Have you forgotten your promise? I died last Tuesday at four o'clock and have been permitted by the Supreme Being to appear to you to assure you that the Revealed Religion is the only true one by which we can be saved. I am also permitted to inform you that ere long you will have a son, which it is decreed shall marry my daughter. Not long after this child's birth Sir Tristram will die, and you will marry again a man whose ill-treatment will render you miserable – and you will die in the 47th year of your age.' Lady Beresford asked if Lord Tyrone were happy; 'Had I been otherwise,' said he, 'I should not have been permitted to appear to you.' She then asked him if she might have some proof which next morning would convince her that this happening had not been a dream, 'He therefore waved his hands, and the bed curtains, which were of crimson velvet, were instantly drawn through a large iron hoop by which the tester of the oval bed was suspended.' He also wrote in her pocket-book in his old familiar handwriting. But as she persisted that these actions might have been performed by herself in sleep, he touched her wrist. 'His hand was cold as marble, and in a moment the sinews of hers shrunk up.' 'Now,' said he, 'while you live let no mortal eye behold this wrist. To see it would be sacrilege.'

At this point the lady evidently swooned (an idiosyncrasy of the ladies of that day). In the morning, perceiving that her husband had already arisen, she 'fetched a long broom from the Gallery adjoining the apartment, and with its aid replaced the curtains. She also locked up the pocket-book and bound a black ribbon round her charred wrist.

On rejoining her husband, she 'conjured him' never to enquire why she wore the black ribbon, and told him that they would shortly hear of the death of Lord Tyrone. At this moment a servant entered, bringing a letter sealed with black from Lord Tyrone's steward, announcing the sad event.

Time went on, and each of the phantom's prophecies was realised, though Lady Beresford never disclosed her strange experience until the day of her death. After Sir Tristram's death, in 1701, she went but little into company, associating with only one family, in dread of forming a miserable second marriage. But her doom was not to be escaped, for the son of this family – Richard Gorges by name – proved to be 'the person destined by Fate to be her undoing.' Though many years her junior, this youth persuaded her to accept him as her husband, and they were married in the year 1704 – with all the unhappy consequences predicted by Lord Tyrone.

As his prophecies had each been in turn fulfilled, Sophia naturally dreaded her forty-seventh birthday, on which she believed she was fated to die. But, to her relief, it passed without any disaster: and during that year she did not feel as if she would be safe until she reached the age of forty-eight. When that anniversary of her birthday arrived, great was her comfort. 'She sent for Lady —, of whose friendship she had long been possessed, and a few friends and requested them to spend that day with her.' About the noon of that day, the clergyman by whom she had been baptized came, 'an uninvited guest,' to enquire after her health – and congratulated her on being a whole year younger than she had supposed. 'Your mother and I,' said he, 'have had many disputes concerning your age, and I have at length discovered that I am right. Happening to go last week to the village where you were born, I consulted the Parish Register and find that you are but 47 this day.'

'You have signed my death warrant,' said she, 'I have not much longer to live, therefore I entreat you to leave me as I have something of importance to settle before I die!'

Then Lady Beresford put off her company and requested her son and Lady— to come to her, relating to them all the aforementioned occurrences and requesting that after her death they would unbind her wrist, take from it the black ribbon and behold it. She also observed 'armed with the sacred precepts of Christianity I can meet the King of Terrors without dismay and bid adieu to the regions of mortality for ever.'

They left her, and half an hour later a bell rang violently and hurrying to her chamber, they found that she had died. Ordering the servants to quit the room Lady—[150] and Marcus Beresford unbound the wrist – and found it just as Lady Beresford had described it: 'every nerve withered – every sinew shrunk.'

* * * * *

Brothers Jack, William and Gerald Lenox-Conyngham, taken in India.

The fifty years of Sir William's marriage were chiefly spent at Springhill and in Edinburgh, where the children had the greater part of their education. Summer holidays were usually spent at the old home, riding, fishing and lawn tennis being the chief amusements. There were good horses in the stables, and another J. Greer escorted the young fishermen, probably a son of the man who helped their father and uncle to whip the neighbouring streams.

This was a very united family. But the eldest son, Willy – or 'Bill' – was of a sensitive and reserved nature and stood rather aloof from the others, though an excellent brother to them. After a course at Sandhurst, he joined the Worcestershire Regiment in 1876 and was strongly attached to his corps, spending many years in India, where steeple-chasing and polo appealed to his horse-loving nature.

The second brother – George – went from Fettes College in Edinburgh to Cambridge and became a house master at Fettes. After his marriage to Barbara Turton[151] of Upsall Castle in Yorks, he took holy orders and became Rector of Lavenham in the county of Suffolk, where he did much to restore the beautiful old church.

The third son, Jack (another John Staples Molesworth Lenox-Conyngham), joined the Connaught Rangers, his father's old Regiment. Tall, athletic, forceful and daring, he was idolized by his men and – as will be shewn later – was of the stuff of which heroes are made. He married a Miss Donaldson – an Australian, whom he met in Malta, an accomplished pianist, whose performances were rather lost on her unmusical husband.

Arthur, the fourth son – tall, dark and humorous – entered his maternal grandfather's firm of Arbuthnot, and went to South Africa, where he married Emmeline Dowsett, who proved a devoted wife.

The clever fifth son, Gerald, after passing into Woolwich first on the list, went as a Royal Engineer to India, where at the age of twenty-four he married Elsie, daughter of Surgeon General Sir Frederick Bradshaw, K.C.B. He had an interesting career, was in the Trigonometrical Survey of India. In 1918 he was elected a Fellow of the Royal Society and Reader in Geodesy and a Fellow of Trinity

Lady Lenox-Conyngham (*née* Laura Arbuthnot) with her ten surviving children taken at her home in Dartmouth Square, Dublin.

Standing from left: Gerald, Charlotte, Hubert, Alice, Jack and Edward. Seated: Millie Clark, William, Lady L-C, George and Laura Duff. Another brother Arthur died in 1905.

College, Cambridge. His next brother – Edward – went to grow oranges in Florida and later became a very successful tea-planter in Ceylon. In the interval he married the beautiful Madeline Gunning, whose family belonged to Cookstown – a very happy marriage – the earlier part being spent in Ceylon.

Hubert, the youngest of the seven brothers, was in the Army Veterinary Corps, a very popular young man, full of charm and attractive to old and young. In 1909 he married Eva, the only daughter of Mr. and Mrs. Darley of Fernhill, Co. Dublin. Later in this narrative more will be said of his distinguished service and early death.

As for the daughters, Mary or 'Milly,' the handsome and witty eldest daughter, married, in 1883, Colonel James Clark of Largantogher in Co. Derry, a prominent magnate and H.M.L. for the county. Laura, the third, became the wife of Mr. J.D. Duff of Trinity College, Cambridge, and is mother of three brilliant sons: while Charlotte, the second daughter, and Alice the youngest did not marry, but made a happy little centre for their brothers and nephews and their wives, in later days living at the Manor House in Moneymore village and extending help to their poorer neighbours.

But all this is anticipating. We must go back in thought to the days when the father of this family was busily engaged in County affairs, and in launching his seven tall sons in their professions. Like some of his ancestors he took an active part in the Militia of Co. Derry, which he commanded for thirty-five years – a record – and was rewarded by being made a K.C.B. During each year the training of the Militia occupied several weeks, and in 1876 he arranged to have it at Springhill, where the eighty-acre field at the foot of the wood was studded with tents, and a photograph was taken of the heavily-bearded officers standing by the wall opposite the steward's house. This event created much excitement in the neighbourhood.

The Manor House, Moneymore. Rebuilt by Arthur L-C and later lived in by his unmarried sisters, Charlotte and Alice.

In the year 1875, a trip to Belgium was made by the parents and several of their children, but most of these years were spent in the Edinburgh house while the young people were being educated.

The education of so large a flock naturally involved much expense, and, in 1882, Sir William (as he had become) accepted the Agency of the Draper's Company and managed the property of that great London establishment. This necessitated residence in the Manor House, Moneymore, as was obligatory for the acting agent. So for some years this spacious mansion became a second home for the family, and the house and garden of Springhill, which stands three hundred feet above the village, was temporarily let to the charming young R.M. and his wife – Mr. and Mrs. Garret Nagle, who became fast friends of the Conynghams.

It was at this epoch that Springhill was first seen by the writer, then a shy and impressionable girl. She and her elder sister had once or twice driven from their home in Co. Tyrone with their German governess to the Manor House, once to spend a musical afternoon and play duets with trembling red fingers: but after the long drive of eleven miles no further point had been reached. It was not till just after schoolroom days were over that she had her first sight of the venerable house, Springhill, where so much of her after life was to be spent.

How well she remembers the occasion! Christmas theatricals were on foot, and she was to act the small part of Julia in Sheridan's 'Rivals.' A dress rehearsal was about to begin as she entered the large, dignified drawingroom and saw its occupants standing about in 18th century dress; knee-breeches, cut-away coats and wigs, large silken hoops and powdered heads. There stood the whimsical Sir Anthony Absolute and his gay and gallant son, Mrs. Malaprop, stately in black velvet, and all the others, whose garments were exactly suited to the antique Jacobean furniture and to the atmosphere of long ago which pervades Springhill. It was like going back into another world! or could fancy picture it as a vision of bygone occupants of the old house – 'Good Will' in his large wig, the surly first George, Mistress Anne in silken draperies, 'the beautiful Jean' and the rest, who seemed to have stepped out of their portraits to greet the first arrival of the 'slip of a girl,' who one day was to use her pen in trying to bring them back, as it were, to life again! But this is only a freak of fancy!

At this dress rehearsal there was an amusing episode, when Captain Absolute was beginning to invoke his beautiful lady-love's miniature and to extol her 'heavenly enchanting smile' and rosy lips. He suddenly collapsed, shaking with irrepressible laughter, and unable to speak for some minutes. For, to serve as a miniature, he had been given the daguerreotype of an ugly old woman in a white cap, with wrinkled face and toothless grin.

At the following Christmas, theatricals were again attempted at Springhill. Goldsmith's 'She Stoops to Conquer' having been chosen by the young actors, and the younger sister from Rockdale this time personating Constance Neville. She remembers being again arrayed in one of the old Springhill dresses – a voluminous white and green silk hoop with white chemisette and black mittens, old 'Nanny' (Mrs. Meighan) dressing her hair high over a cushion and powdering it, before rouge and patches completed the attire. (It seemed so daring and shocking to be using rouge!) On this occasion she and her sister did not stay at the Manor House, but at Springhill for the very first time, and it was also their first meeting with the eldest son of the house, who had just returned from India for a few months. Handsome, haughty and aloof, he refused to act, but consented to undertake the duty of prompter, and next day is remembered to have mounted a fine chestnut horse and to have galloped all over the 'Sawpit Hill.' The play was again a great success. It was followed by a dance, and when all was over the young visitors were given silver candlesticks at the foot of the broad, panelled staircase and were led along an uneven oaken floor to the Blue Room, where a bright fire was burning and where they slept out the old year in the lavender-scented four-post bed.

And that was the beginning of a New Year and of others to follow, filled with pleasant intercourse, which was to continue for many a long day.

The next few years must be very briefly reviewed. They were lean years for the Conynghams after the lands of the Drapers' Company had been sold under the Ashbourne Act and the Agency had ceased. Financial difficulties abounded, though a crash was happily averted, largely owing to the wise management of Colonel James Clark (husband of the eldest daughter of the house) who was acting as agent and receiver. The family went for a while to economize in England. Springhill was shut up and much timber sold.

During this crisis Sir William was loyally helped by his sons and daughters, his heir even writing from India to sanction the breaking of the entail. He had gone back to the East, where he lived on his Army pay and refused monetary help from home.

Three soldier sons were now serving in India, George was a housemaster at Fettes College with Barbara, his wife, Laura at Cambridge with her newly-married husband, James Duff, and Edward and his wife in the tea plantations of Ceylon.

It was in the last year of the nineteenth century that the eldest son – William Arbuthnot – married Mina Lowry of Rockdale, Co. Tyrone. Her father, Colonel Lowry, had not long before died very suddenly. He was an idolized father – the very pivot of his family, and a man of great integrity and personality, taking a leading part in Irish affairs, once having been termed by the *Freeman's Journal* 'the brain-carrier of the Tory party in Ireland.' In the next year but one after his death the following notice appeared in the newspapers:

> On the 9th of August at the parish church Desertcreight, Dungannon, Ireland, a marriage was celebrated between Major Lenox-Conyngham, eldest son of Sir William Lenox-Conyngham K.C.B., of Springhill Moneymore, and Miss Mina Lowry, younger daughter of the late Colonel Lowry V.L., of Rockdale, Co. Tyrone. The officiating clergymen were The Rev. John Richey M.A., Rector of

Mina Lenox-Conyngham

the parish, the Rev. R. Ussher Greer M.A., Rector of St. Michael's, Belfast, and the Revd. Canon Twigg M.A., Vicar of Swords, Co. Dublin. The bride, who was given away by her brother, Major Bushe, Royal Artillery, was dressed in white satin draped with Limerick lace and wore a veil of the same beautiful fabric: Her bouquet was composed entirely of white heather. The bridesmaids, Miss Alice Lenox-Conyngham, sister of the bridegroom, and Miss Evelyn Lowry, cousin of the bride, were dressed in white *Mousseline-de-soie* trimmed with lace and wore white hats arranged with chiffon and plumes. They carried bouquets of sweet pea and displayed the bridegroom's gifts in the form of gold hunting brooches. Mr. James T. Lowry, Royal Inniskilling Fusiliers, acted as best man. Mrs. T. MacGregor Greer, sister of the bride, lent her residence – Tullylagan – for a small reception of relations, and the bride and bridegroom travelled to Galway in the afternoon to spend the first portion of their honeymoon at Lough Cutra Castle lent by Lord Gough for the occasion. The bride went away in a simple toilette of white, clear muslin and a large black picture hat.

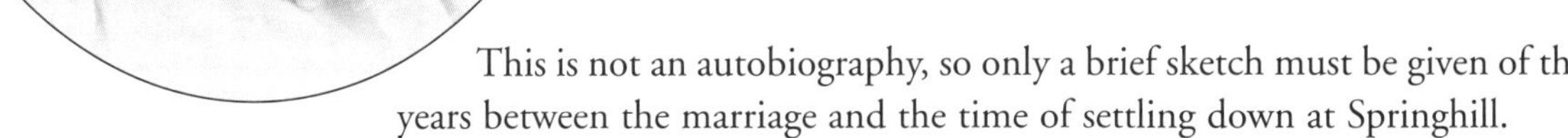

This is not an autobiography, so only a brief sketch must be given of the years between the marriage and the time of settling down at Springhill. Shortly after the wedding the bridegroom left Aldershot for South Africa, where the Boer War was in progress. From her window his wife watched him march by with his men to the station, the air vibrating with the sound of that arrogant song, 'Soldiers of the Queen' and also with Kipling's 'Absent Minded Beggar,' so popular at that period:

Duke's son, cook's son, son of a belted earl –
Forty thousand fighting men
Going to Table Bay.
Each of them doing his country's work,
And what's to become of the girl?
Pass the hat for your credit's sake
And pay, pay, pay.

Some hours later on that bleak day she stood amid hail showers on Tilbury Dock and watched the 'Braemar Castle' steaming slowly down the river, crowded with men singing and shouting 'Rule Britannia.'

It was during the following anxious year that the grand old Queen of those soldiers passed away – Victoria, whose name was truly indicative of an unconquered nation. Soon after that event the war ended and Major William returned home, and after a brief service at Aldershot, retired, and came to live in Ulster.

Mina's sister Dorinda Greer

Early in the twentieth century a girl – Diana – and then two boys – William

Left:
Mina with baby Diana and below
Desmond with William
Bottom:
Diana and William

and Desmond – were born to carry on the Springhill family – the boys each coming into the world at Portrush in a house near Ramore Head, where part of each year was spent – a house with only a stretch of the Atlantic between it and Iceland.

The summers were usually passed at Springhill or at Lissan, where the James Staples' were then living, and where at one time three perambulators might be found under the trees by the Lough Fea Avenue. A year or two later, two curly-headed boys, in blue linen suits with cut-away coats, played with their little brunette sister at Springhill among the bluebells near the Beech Walk, the world being for them full of joy and happy anticipation.

By this time their grandfather, Sir William, was an invalid, paralysed and condemned to a wheel-chair, often attended by his steward, Andy Davidson the elder (who amused the old man by his ready wit) and his long white beard and powerful frame can be remembered by his elder grandson, then only three years old. His fourth son – Arthur – was now an invalid. He had returned with his wife and child from South Africa and had rebuilt the burnt shell of the Manor House in Moneymore, where he lived, to be near his parents, whom he visited daily in his pony-chair.

Arthur's illness was a long one and full of pain; but in the intervals of ease his natural high spirits and sense of humour led him to laugh at fate. Until one day in October, 1905, when yellow leaves were fluttering down from the trees, the end came one evening with tragic suddenness.

To the family party at Springhill, which included Bill and Mina and Jack and his wife, came a message that Mr. Arthur had been taken ill while driving on the Coagh road, below 'Thompson's Brow.' But when the pony-chair reached the Manor House its occupant had passed away – on the very day after a musical afternoon at his house when he had called for the song 'Clouds will be sunshine to-morrow.' His death was a great shock to his parents and to all who loved him, and caused the first break in this large and united family. Alas another bereavement was soon to follow.

The following year, 1906, was that of the Golden Wedding – fiftieth anniversary of Sir William and Lady Lenox-Conyngham's marriage – and it was celebrated in the midst of a peaceful family gathering, the eldest son and his wife and small daughter, Diana, coming over from Lissan for the occasion and a memorial tree

William Lowry L-C with his nursemaid, *c.* 1905

William Arbuthnot L-C (in the bathchair) with Mina and Marcus Louis Stewart Clements (their son-in-law) at his home, Ashfield Lodge, Cootehill, Co. Cavan.

being planted on the lawn. But a few months later on 4th December, 1906, Sir William's long and happy life ended. He died at Springhill aged eighty-two, in his downstairs bedroom after a night of unconsciousness, during which his children kept their sad vigil around him, and he was buried in the churchyard at Moneymore.

Sir William in the gun-room with Andy Davidson Snr. Panelling covered the hand-blocked wallpaper.

Lady L-C in the drawing room at Springhill

XII

Colonel William Arbuthnot Lenox-Conyngham

HE FOUGHT IN TWO WARS
1857–1938

Colonel William Arbuthnot Lenox-Conyngham

IT WAS IN MAY, 1907, that Sir William's eldest son and his family took up their abode in the old home. They had vainly tried to persuade Lady Lenox-Conyngham to continue to live at Springhill, but she wished them to come there and preferred to take a house in Dublin with her two unmarried daughters.

Always the kindest and most loving mother-in-law, her letters of welcome and affection are treasured by her successor, who had the difficult task of trying to take the place of one who was the benefactress of the whole district. Just to shew her as an ideal mother-in-law the following trivial incident must be given. In settling down at Springhill, her son's wife had made as few changes as possible, but had slightly altered the arrangement of some of the rooms, bringing some lovely antique chairs and tables from the nurseries and servants' rooms to grace the large drawingroom. When her husband's mother was about to pay her first visit, Mina was troubled by misgivings as to whether these changes would be painful to the dear old lady. On arrival, Lady Lenox-Conyngham looked critically around. The daughter-in-law's heart beat loud with apprehension! 'Ah!' said her mother-in-law, 'I see you have made that alteration!' (more heart beats!) Then with a little smile and bow, she continued: 'It is what I had always *longed* to do, and now *you* have accomplished it!'

During Sir William's illness and the hard times which had preceded it, the Springhill house had fallen into disrepair, and a great deal of renovation was needed – bathrooms were added, new drains made and rooms refloored and repapered, and this necessitated much outlay of money. Shortly before the death of Sir William the property had been sold to Government under the Wyndham Act, and a good deal of income was lost through insecure investments, but though great economy was needed, those early days from 1907–1913 were happy, and the three lively children were a constant joy and interest. Their mother was fortunate in having – only ten miles away, at Tullylagan – her elder sister, Dorinda Greer, a wise and devoted mentor, and also her step-sister, Fanny Bushe, who lived with the Greers and devoted herself to numerous charities, doing useful work for Missions, Y.W.C.A., and Temperance.

It was during this time that another curious psychic occurrence took place at Springhill. The three children used to sleep in cots in the night-nursery (the 'Red Bed' being one of these) and their nurse, Miss Foster, occupied a 'Four-poster' in the same room. One day their mother was asked by Miss Foster if she had been anxious about the trio during the previous night, because, just before dawn, she had come up to look at them.

'Tell me exactly what happened,' said the mother.

'In the small hours of the morning,' replied Miss Foster, 'I was lying awake, when the door opened and you came in and went to each cot in turn, bending over each child. Just as I was about to strike a light to see more clearly, your hurried out of the room. I could not see your face, but of course it must have been you.'

Mina and Diana *c.* 1907

But the mother knew that she herself had not been the visitor, though she kept her own counsel, for fear of alarming the nurse. The same occurrence happened again a few weeks later, and Mina wondered whether the nocturnal visitor had been a bygone mother – perhaps Olivia – coming back in thought to nights more than a hundred years before, when her children lay ill of the smallpox, and bringing with her thought a picture of herself.

Much could be written about the childhood of these latest children of Springhill – the developing of their characters, and their quaint, childish sayings: but the writer must forbear and perhaps only mention briefly that she noticed as ruling characteristics in each, from eldest to youngest, principle, affection, and proud reserve.

After the peaceful years between 1907 and 1912, clouds began to gather once more on the political horizon. Ulster had for many years been tormented by the dread of Home Rule for Ireland, fearing that if that became law, the loyalists would be outnumbered and oppressed by the disloyal element in the South, whose deep-rooted hostility to England had never been assuaged by the latter day policy of appeasement. The Anti-Home-Rule feeling had been smouldering for years, and she who was now mistress at Springhill, having been brought up in a warmly loyalist atmosphere, had tried, as a girl, to depict the Northern point of view in the following verses, which she termed

THE CRY OF ULSTER

England, my mother, wilt thou now forsake me?
Wilt thou cast off thy loyal, trusting child
To thy fierce foes and mine, the victim make me
That rebel hatred may be reconciled?
Was ever in the history of a nation
Such base betrayal, so unearned a fate!
Oh listen to my anguished protestation,
Oh pause and pity ere it be too late!

Is it because I have not been to thee
A child of promise? Let my peaceful homes,
My towns that send their trade o'er land and sea
Deny the charge! and from their thousand looms
In ceaseless thunder be the answer spoken;
My faith is firm, my sons are loyal men
Who never yet their solemn trust have broken,
And for thy talent I have gained thee ten!

Dost thou not mark the self-reliant bearing
Of men who fear not in just cause to die?
A rugged, earnest race of dauntless daring,
Hard to arouse, yet hard to pacify.
Doubt not they will avenge my desecration,
E'en now is stern resolve in every face.
Oh fear to rouse their burning indignation,
Fear to make foemen of a kindred race!

England, my mother, in the after ages
The children of thy swift declining day
Will blush to read, inscribed in History's pages,
The record no remorse can wipe away.
Then mid the remnants of thy shattered glory
And wreck of realms snatch'd from thy sceptre's thrall
The Great Betrayal and its shameful story
Will seem the first sad step of England's fall.

ULSTER'S SOLEMN LEAGUE AND COVENANT

Being convinced in our consciences that Home Rule would be disastrous to the material well-being of Ulster as well as to the whole of Ireland, subversive of our civil and religious freedom, destructive of our citizenship and perilous to the unity of the Empire.

We whose names are underwritten, men of Ulster, loyal subjects of His Majesty King George V, humbly relying on the God whom our fathers in days of stress and trial confidently trusted.

Do hereby pledge ourselves in solemn Covenant throughout this our time of threatened calamity to stand by one another in defending for ourselves and for our children our cherished possession of equal Citizenship in the United Kingdom and in using all means which may be found necessary to defeat the present conspiracy to set up a Home Rule Parliament in Ireland.

And in the event of such a Parliament being forced upon us, we further solemnly and mutually pledge ourselves to refuse to recognize its authority

In sure confidence that God will defend the right we here subscribe our names:

And further we individually declare that we have not already signed this Covenant.

God Save the King.

With this dreaded possibility in the forefront of its mind, loyal Ulster was naturally, much alarmed when, in 1912, the British Government seemed about to fling her as a sop to appease the Cerberus of her antagonists. Feeling ran high, and a champion for Ulster and the Union arose in the person of Sir Edward Carson.

This clever, forceful and high-minded lawyer – a Southerner by birth – was convinced that a grievous wrong and blunder was about to be committed by the English Government under its premier, Mr. Asquith. He organized active resistance, giving up for the time being his important practice at the Bar in a spirit of self-sacrificing chivalry, and with no axe of his own to grind.

Recent history has sternly criticized this man in the light of after events, but it must be remembered that at that time no one could have foreseen what was coming. It has been said that in the Emerald Isle the inevitable never happens and the impossible always takes place, and whether the Ulster Movement was right or wrong, wise or unwise, it seemed at that time to be a valiant stand against oppression and injustice.

The Gentlemen of Ulster rallied round Sir Edward Carson, and history repeated itself by their raising, as of old, amateur Volunteer regiments to guard their Province from molestation.

Springhill's owner, having been for so long under military discipline in the Army, was at first disinclined to take part in this movement, and indeed was never quite a whole-hearted adherent, but he was finally drawn in and raised the South Derry Regiment of two battalions, aided by two former brother-officers, Major Norbury and Major Nunn, and a Naval Commander named Hughes.

His wife meanwhile busied herself enthusiastically in forming a Nursing Corps and in arranging for eleven Hospital Centres in S. Derry, with complete store of nurses, furniture and supplies, ready to mobilize within twenty-four hours. In this work she received valuable aid from two English ladies, now known as Dame Katharine Furse and Dame Rachel Crowdy, who stayed at Springhill as helpers and advisers, and promised immediate help from London of extra nurses, doctors and medical requirements in the event of Civil War. The word 'Embarrassment' was chosen as the code telegram which would have produced this speedy and substantial assistance.

Mrs. Furse and Miss Crowdy were charming visitors, full of humour and interested in poetry – Miss Crowdy is remembered to have repeated Kipling's 'If,' which was then new to Mina and her twelve-year-old girl, Diana. After they left, Mrs. Furse sent a post-card picture of Charles Furse's 'Diana of the Uplands' to the little girl, with the words; 'What do you think of *this* Diana?' and then they recognized that their handsome friend had stood for the picture, which her husband had painted of the girl in a large hat holding two leashed greyhounds.

In later years Dame Katharine Furse was head of the English Red Cross and Dame R. Crowdy one of the pillars of the League of Nations at Geneva.

1914 was a strenuous and stirring year at Springhill and left the writer with many vivid memories.

Let her depict some of these. She finds herself in retrospect on a hill-top near the demesne at night, signalling messages with a lamp to distant locations … Now she stands in the motor-yard watching the Volunteers drilling in the light of carbide gas produced by Stroud, the keen little English chauffeur. … Then she recalls the anxious time when the gun-running was in process – her husband and his band of helpers and cars away all night to receive, bring back and distribute the newly landed rifles. What fears haunted her during her long vigil in the gun-room, preparing food for the adventurers on their return! Then, in the early morning, the men, who with their cars awaited the weapons in the lower yard, became dangerously noisy, and she remembers stepping forth – still in evening dress – into the cool air of a May dawn to silence the roysterers.

These and other thrilling memories are still fresh in her mind.

Two days copied from the writer's 1914 Diary will give an idea of these times.

> *March 20th.* In the middle of last night 3 despatch riders on motor cycles came into the Court and awoke us with important U.V.F. despatches from Belfast. Bill summoned to Craigavon to meet the leader. Exciting day. Bill went off soon after breakfast and I with him as far as Moneymore. He drove all round the various Company Centres to warn them. I received various enquiries – Mr. Hogarth twice, young Clark of Ardtara,[152] A. Greer. Andrew arranged the yard bell to ring from the house and I arranged a place of hiding, in case they should want to take Bill. Intense excitement all over the country. An immediate rising expected. Arrest warrants said to be out for the leaders. Ulster to be flooded with British troops. The Desertlyn men said to be devoted to Springhill. Bill at Craigavon to meet Sir E. Carson and sat close to him at lunch. About twenty there to confer and to learn the orders.

> *Friday, April 24th.* Orders came by despatch riders in the morning for Bill to mobilize his men to-night. He and Mr. Hughes off all day going the rounds. Prepared the Guard-room for the Ballindrum men and tea, etc., for them. All the counties mobilized. I was told why by Bill, but of course kept the secret. He and Mr. H. were out all night till 4. I sat up till 12 and then slept in my clothes. All the world heard afterwards that 40,000 rifles had been landed at Larne, met by 70 motor lorries, and distributed at once.

Mina in evening dress

The occasion of Sir Edward Carson's visit to Springhill must be described in detail.

A few days before the event occurred, the Conynghams were suddenly surprised by seeing a long procession of vehicles coming up the front avenue. It almost looked like a funeral train, but was found to be a procession of sixteen carts, belonging to loyal tenants, who had without notice gone all the way to Lough Neagh's shore to procure the finest gravel, wherewith to cover the avenues of Springhill, so that 'S'Redward' should drive over the best surface which their loyalty could provide for his chariot-wheels!

This incident found its way into English newspapers and probably revealed that Springhill's avenues had not previously been in good order!

Then, on April 15th, the great day arrived. Preparations were complete – the Court festooned with flags, and all windows illuminated. Sir Edward's previously arrived valet, Lee, had laid out on his master's dressing-table the sedatives necessary to give oblivion to the Leader, whose responsibility lay on him so heavily that sleep had to be courted. The family and house-party were standing at the hall-door to welcome the visitors, and the lawn was thronged with observers.

Presently a sound of wheels and horses' hooves was heard, and up the straight avenue galloped a band of local outriders, who ranged themselves on each side of the Court, as the car approached and its occupants entered the house.

Sir Edward Carson was accompanied by the Commandant of the Volunteers – Sir George Richardson, and by Captain[153] and Mrs. James Craig.

A large dinner-party had been arranged, and one of the historic damask table-cloths, portraying the Siege of Derry, laid on the table, a small wreath of laurels in front of Sir Edward's place at table, and little cardboard sentries served as name-cards, with the words; 'I am guarding a place for – '

Meanwhile *real* armed sentries protected the house, and a guard of twenty men sat up all night in the western side-building and consumed twenty-one loaves of bread in the course of their vigil.

During the dinner, Sir Edward spoke of his former opponent, Colonel Lowry, whom he had once defeated at the parliamentary election for Trinity College, Dublin, and said that he had always treasured a letter written to him from the defeated Colonel praising the first speech he had made in the House of Commons and showing a rare magnanimity. A portrait which he had seen in his bedroom had reminded him of this incident. He also laughed over a remark made to him by his old aunt. 'I see your name occasionally mentioned in the newspapers,' said she, 'and am glad to hear that you are now considered to be quite a promising young man.' (His age was sixty).

Just then the three Springhill children came in to dessert and sat by their mother, Desmond still in the cream satin suit, which he had worn that day as page at his cousin's wedding.

'Well! do you belong to my army?' said Sir Edward to the trio. They gravely replied that they did.

A pleasant, quiet evening followed, Jack's wife – Violet – played '*La Fileuse*' on the piano, and there was much interesting conversation, some of it contributed to by the writer's interesting and beautiful sister, Dorinda, who with great talent and strong personality was taking a leading part in the Ulster movement. Her eloquence was inspiring, and she regarded Ulster's struggle against oppression from the highest viewpoint.

Next day the review of the South Derry Ulster Volunteers was at Garvagh – a central position. Captain Stronge,[154] the Second in Command, was present, and a large luncheon was given to the Company. The drive to Garvagh was planned so as to avoid the disloyal and dangerous village of Swatragh; and, sitting in the car next to the idol of the Province, Mina noticed hundreds of Sir Edward's adherents lining the roads and emitting deafening cheers, their recipient commenting on the peculiarly shrill sound of Ulster cheers, as the crowds squealed out their homage.

Led by their Colonel, the Volunteers acquitted themselves well, and at the luncheon Sir Edward told the writer of his deep admiration for Captain James Craig, whose strong, steadfast character and temperance principles he greatly respected. The three Springhill children had come to look on, and thoroughly enjoyed the treat, as described later in a funny letter, which the elder boy wrote to his absent governess, Miss Powell. It began:

> Dear Bovo
>
> Last night at dessert Mother said I was not to have any more chocolate, but Sir Edward Carson said I could, so I took one. Captain Craig is very nice, he called Johnny (his pet name for Desmond) a cad and said his hair was like toe (sic) &c. &c.

Desmond and William *c.* 1912

In life how incongruously do trivialities like these mingle with serious issues! One cannot think that any of those who were preparing for Civil War ever really expected that it would materialize, or that they could even attempt to picture to themselves the horror and disaster of what might have ensued in their home-land. Still less did they see the dark thunder-clouds which were gathering in the Eastern sky. And yet Sir Edward is remembered to have shewn a prophetic spirit. When strolling down the Beech Walk, he suddenly said; as in a trance; 'I see terrible times ahead – bitter fighting, rivers of blood!' And Mina incredulously deemed this an over-statement which could not apply to Civil War, for it was not thought at that time that Ulster would really be coerced into submission to Home Rule. The Curragh incident had just occurred, when Sir Hubert Gough and other notable officers had threatened to resign their Commissions if ordered to march against Ulster, and the premier, Mr. Asquith, had been required by Sir Hubert to sign a guarantee that such an order would never be given to him.

So the loyal rebels of Ulster went on with their preparations and shewed a strange paradox to the world.

And then one day the thunderbolt fell. On August the 4th, 1914, the newspapers announced that England had declared war against Germany.

It seemed unimaginable!

How did the outbreak of the Great War affect the Ulster situation? There was no more thought of Civil War; all fervour was now directed to the task of helping 'England, our mother.' And how well Northern Ireland was prepared to do so!

She had thousands of trained and armed soldiers ready for the field, hundreds of trained nurses and medical supplies ready to send to the front, and she burned to offer all that she had to the far greater cause which had arisen.

And yet for three whole weeks Ulster's leader gave no sign! He remained in England, and no orders to join up came to the eager troops which he had caused to be trained. Some individuals rushed off to join English regiments. A few self-centred provincials could not see beyond their own door-steps and wished to keep Ulster's army in their province, lest they should be attacked by their compatriots of the south. But the bulk of the Volunteers were chafing for orders from their leader to join the fray.

And then at last Sir Edward came over from England and held meetings in all parts of the province, making stirring speeches, the text of which was; 'It is your duty to go, and I know you will go.'

One of these meetings was at Coleraine, and attended by the Colonel and others of the South Derry Regiment, who listened gladly to the enthusiastic summons. Later in the day, when the party were having tea at the house of Mr. Barry, the M.P., the narrator asked Sir Edward in confidence why he had kept Ulster waiting for so long, and he told her that he had found it hard to persuade Lord Kitchener to authorise an 'Ulster Division,' which he himself wished for, because he knew that the men would join more willingly and fight better in a Home Corps. Probably he also felt reluctant that the Volunteers should be dispersed and scattered in other divisions, for post-war emergencies might one day arise. He also told her, with bitter contempt, that some of the Belfast '*un*worthies' had discouraged the idea of the Volunteers going abroad; 'At this moment,' he said, 'I have letters in my pocket which urge that not a man should leave Ulster' !

And so it was that the splendid Ulster Division was formed, and though at first it was estimated that it would consist of about twelve thousand men, many more came forward. They were commanded by Sir Charles Powell, and later by Sir Oliver Nugent, who took them to France, where they gave a good account of themselves, their valour at Thiepval having been already mentioned in this history.

At the outbreak of the war the master of Springhill had at once offered his services, requesting that the War Office would place him with one of the Service Battalions of his old Regiment – the Worcestershire, and this despite of being no longer on the Reserve after twelve years of retirement.

Meanwhile he undertook Remount work in Northern Ireland. It was on the 22nd of September that the Major's wish was granted. A letter from the War Office told him to join the 8th Service Battalion of the Worcestershire Regiment at Tidworth in Hampshire.

His wife was recovering from a heavy cold and laid up in her own room when the news came. 'How soon must we start?' she asked. 'To-morrow,' was the reply. 'But think of all the winding up of the Volunteer work, the dismissal of the household staff and all the packing?' However, difficulties had to be overcome,

and the departure took place on the next day but one, when the family left home and crossed to England, calling in Belfast en route for some necessary Army equipment. The elder boy, William, was not of the party, as he had recently gone to a preparatory school – Arnold House – in N. Wales, where his mother visited him on the way to Woolwich, his father going straight to Tidworth.

Woolwich was a busy centre indeed, the Command being held by General Bushe, Mina's half-brother. Troops were incessantly marching to the tune of 'It's a Long Way to Tipperary'; large open air services were held on Sundays in Artillery Place, each attended by five or six thousand troops; Zeppelins were hovering in the skies at night and dropping bombs, their havoc being swiftly filled up ere morning with as much secrecy as possible.

Tidworth was also a scene of intense activity, and visited as often as possible from 48 Brunswick Gardens, Campden Hill – a house lived in by Major Conyngham's family for many months, his wife going home at times to see that all went well at Springhill which was in the charge of Andrew Davidson the Second, the faithful steward, who had been born at Springhill, and, succeeding his father, had spent nearly all his life in the old place.

It was on the 18th of July, 1915, that the sixth William Conyngham of Springhill went to the front to take part in what was at that time the greatest war in Earth's history.

He started from Tidworth, his wife once again, as in 1900, watching him march off with his men to the tune of 'Soldiers of the King' (it was 'King' this time instead of 'Queen'). At the railway station she saw the Regiment off, not realizing how many of the brother officers would return no more.

Her husband was no longer young, and the doctors declined to pass him for foreign service, but he contrived to have their opinion overruled, kept strong and well in the front trenches, and though in frequent danger, he came safely home in the end.

Two of his brothers, Jack and Hubert, were also fighting in France, the former, who was Sir William's third son, going out in Command of his Regiment, the 6th Connaught Rangers.

Seldom has a C.O. been more beloved by his men, and seldom has a soldier died a more valiant death. When the attack on Guillemont was launched, John Lenox-Conyngham went 'over the top' with his men to encourage them and to share their dangers, falling at once to end his life thus gloriously. One of his officers – the celebrated writer, Stephen Gwynn – has described the incident in one of his books and also gives a vivid description of his Colonel. This account, which first appeared in the *Daily Mail* newspaper, must be given here:

A COLONEL OF THE IRISH BRIGADE.

On the day when the word to advance was given, our Battalion of the Connaught Rangers was where they had earned the right to be, in the foremost line; and the man who gave the word was the man who had made them what they were – worthy inheritors of a famous name. First out of the trench and waving them on, Colonel John Lenox-Conyngham saw them launched and he saw no more; a bullet took him in the forehead. I do not know what finer thing could have been desired for him. His work was accomplished. The battalion he had trained led the rush which swept through Guillemont that day, capturing the redoubtable stronghold of the quarries.

He was never in doubt as to how they would acquit themselves. To us officers he said things in private which would sound a little arrogant if I quoted them, and yet they have been made good. Even from the last day that I was with him in the Regiment, somewhere at the end of May, 1916, there comes up to me the sound of his voice as he inspected the Companies just out of the trenches. I was apologising for some lack of smartness. 'Yes of course,' he said, 'turn them out again when they have had dinner. But after all, don't the men look splendid after eighteen days of it?' The men – the men – it was always the men with him; it had to be with us also. That was at the root of the process by which a first rate professional soldier taught willing amateurs how to train troops. It was more difficult in our case, because three or four of us junior officers were within a few years of his own time of life – he was fifty-four – and would in ordinary circumstances have met him on entire equality. I was nearest to him in age, yet I was never in my life so much in awe of any man; I never valued praise so much from any, and was never so unresentful under reproof. Reproof was never spared if there was negligence; but no professional was ever more tolerant of the amateur or more appreciated his difficulties. 'I am asking men with six months' experience to take complete charge of a company when in the regular army they would not have been allowed to handle it for ten minutes on parade.' That in effect he said to me over and over again. Want of knowledge or want of skill were readily excused but want of thoroughness, neglect of orders, above all lack of consideration for the men, met with no mercy, and he had the talent for chastisement. Nothing could be less like the peppery Colonel of tradition than his icy dignity. Of course there could be explosions with him, but their rarity made them appalling. Once I remember we were practising a ceremonial parade past him, when suddenly he set his horse to the gallop and rode straight at one of the advancing companies, almost trampling down a man whom his eye had detected chewing tobacco and spitting. Words came then in a torrent of passion, but in a moment he was back to normal. ' We have to begin the whole thing again,' he said, 'and all for one man. The rest were very good.' But this was wholly exceptional, rebuke meant little more than contact with that grave and menacing presence. Once a defaulter, who came out white and shaking from the orderly room, was questioned: 'An' what did he say to you?' The lad stammered, hesitated and then found words: 'Oh Jasus ! when he looks at you from behind thim glasses!' That was all. The punishment was far less than the manner of inflicting it. Yet with the men he never used sarcasm; that weapon was kept for us. Almost my first experience of our Company was returning from a very unsuccessful night operation, cold and dripping, to be confronted by the announcement that we must see the men provided with cocoa before we shewed ourselves in the mess. While we stood in a rather grumbling group outside the mess-room door, a voice charged with contempt reached us through the darkness; 'I should have thought the cook-house was the proper place to see if the cocoa was being got ready' – and away we went with our tails between our legs. But my heart rejoiced for I was just out of the ranks and I knew this was the way things ought to be done and were not always done. I do not remember any collective reprimand or disapproval; but I remember many days in France when the company commanders were brought together because some compliment had been paid to him and he could not be content till, with a frank generosity, he had passed it on to his officers. 'It is you who have done it,' he said. He was right too. We did the work, and no men were ever less interfered with; but we did it as we had been taught to do it and because we were kept up to it at every point. There was another side of him that came out, though sparingly, amid the comradeship of our mess – a rare quality of charm. I found it myself in his occasional talk of men and things – above all of Ireland. I have known no better Irishman than this son of an Ulster house, whose kindred were deep in the Ulster Covenant.

I left the Regiment with his full sympathy and assent to try to help in some settlement at home; and when that settlement failed, no one, I think, regretted it more than he. But the mess in general and the subalterns in particular valued most those convivial moments over a card-table which shewed us glimpses of an infectious gaiety that belonged to less responsible days.

Of all the mourners at his burial there can have been none so deep in grief as the veterans of the old army, for none else knew him so well. When they came out to us in drafts from home there was none of them he did not know and welcome. 'Yes, sir, I saw the Colonel,' said one of these old warriors to me when he joined my Company, 'and glad I was to see him, for I'm twenty years in the Army and I know there is few like him.' More than once after that I saw little conferences between this sort of Mulvaney and my Commanding Officer, and from one the Colonel came over to me smiling: 'I'm pleased with myself,' he said, 'C. has just said to me 'I'm beginning to like this battalion of yours better.

For his outward appearance, if words can give the impression of something extraordinarily tall, thin and upright, yet without stiffness and with an easy poise, that was he. Always *point-device*, he seemed to have been born in uniform. Horseback became him, but I remember him best on foot, and for his most characteristic movement I recall the grave dignity of his salute, as he rendered it to some General-Officer. For the Regiment what had most vitality was his voice: it carried like a trumpet and had beauty as well as power. I should not be surprised if, through the din of that fierce hour, the battalion heard him all down the assembly trench, when he raised it for the last time to launch the charge on Guillemont.

Jack Lenox-Conyngham's grave at Carnoy was marked by two wooden crosses. These were brought to Ireland and are now in the Cathedral at Armagh.[155] Above them are inscribed the words:

'O Death where is thy sting?'

On the wall beside this tablet hangs a framed copy of Philip Gibbs' description of the Irishmen at Guillemont. It runs:

> The charge of the Irish troops through Guillemont was one of the astonishing feats of the war. They stormed the first, second and third German lines, sweeping all resistance away. They were men uplifted out of themselves – 'Fey' as the Scots would call it. The whole attack from first to last was a model of efficiency and courage – all the qualities that go to the making of victory were there … making a terrific weapon driven by a high spirit. The Artillery was in perfect unison with the Infantry, the most difficult thing in War. It is impossible to overpraise the men, who were wonderful in courage and discipline.
>
> So Guillemont was taken and held, not only by great gun fire but by men inspired by some spirit beyond their ordinary courage. And one day these troops will carry the name upon their colours, so that the world may remember.
>
> PHILIP GIBBS 'The Battle of the Somme'
>
> 6th Connaught Rangers
> 7th Lancers
> 6th Royal Irish
> 8th Munsters
>
> The attack was led by the 6th Connaught Rangers, commanded by Colonel J.S.M. Lenox-Conyngham.

At Springhill, at the time of this happening, Mina heard in the night a strange sound of wailing and lamenting such as she had never heard before and could not put down to any natural cause, nor was she dreading any family catastrophe. Afterwards she heard of her brother-in-law's death. When the news reached Ireland, her sister, Dorinda, sent a letter of deep sympathy and wrote as follows; 'For Jack it is indeed well. I am sure he would have wished to die like that, leading the men of his own old regiment – that splendid high-souled man. One knows he is satisfied now. One feels it is all so glorious for Jack. You know the lines;

> Because of you we will be glad and gay,
> Remembering you we will be brave and strong,
> And hail the advent of each dangerous day,
> And greet the last adventure with a song.
> And as you proudly gave your jewelled gift,
> We'll give our lesser offering with a smile,
> Nor falter on that path where all too swift
> You led the way and leapt the golden stile.
> Whether new paths, new heights to climb you find,
> Or gallop through th' unfooted asphodel,
> We know you know we shall not lag behind –

Laura, Lady Lenox-Conyngham

Nor pause to waste one moment on a tear –
And you will speed us onward with a cheer
And wave beyond the stars that all is well.[156]

Thus fell the first of Sir William's soldier sons, all four of them Colonels, though at the time of his death Jack was about to become a Brigadier.

It was in the summer of the following year that the great loss occurred of the beloved mother of this large and united family. On July 1st, 1917, Laura, Lady Lenox-Conyngham, passed away at 5 Northbrook Road, her house in Dublin.

Moneymore Assembly Rooms showing the War Memorial which includes Jack (died1916), and Hubert Lenox-Conyngham (died 1918).

After eleven years of widowhood the long life ended, during which she had been an ideal wife and mother, and most of which had been passed at Springhill, where she had been revered and loved by all who came under her gracious influence. The large bedroom next to the gun-room, which she occupied for fifty years seems to be imbued with a feeling of goodness and peace.

Her eldest son recorded her death in the Family Bible and used these words:

> Lady L.C. Lenox-Conyngham died in Dublin, 1st July, 1917, aged 87. Kindest and most unselfish and thoughtful of mothers – Last of her generation, a link with the past. Her influence will long be felt. She was buried in Moneymore Church-yard.

Lady Lenox-Conyngham never courted society nor cared much for entertaining, though her dignified, old-world charm must have attracted all acquaintances. Her heart was bound up in her family and home, where she was ever helping the poor of the district and her deep piety caused her to give generously to the affairs of the Church.

Not long after her death her two companion daughters – Charlotte and Alice – went to live in a house which their brother Edward had bought on returning from successful years in Ceylon, but which he was unable to occupy at that time. Anaverna[157] was built in the 18th century by Baron McClelland who has already been mentioned in these pages. It stands on a mountain slope within sight of the sea, and its gardens and romantic wood, threaded by a brawling stream, are of great beauty.

It was eight months after the mother's death that yet another link in the family chain was broken. John Lenox-Conyngham was not the only one of Springhill's soldier sons to give his life for his country. In 1918, the youngest brother – Hubert – died very suddenly. He had been invalided home after receiving the D.S.O. for services in France, and after a time in hospital seemed well enough to take up the Western Command of Veterinary Services with headquarters at Chester. But soon after his arrival he passed away one night in his sleep, leaving his young wife and two baby children desolate – his gay and gallant life so suddenly at an end. This happened some months before the Armistice was signed on November 11th, 1918.

The news of the Armistice came as an inexpressible relief. The writer recorded the event in her diary, writing at Sea Park, on the shore of Belfast Lough – stating that the news had been heard through the telephone, that her sister had assembled everyone in the house for prayers of thanksgiving, flags had been hung out on the tower, and fireworks had been seen on the opposite shore, the moon meanwhile shining brightly on the Lough.

The ending of the 'Great War' seemed almost too good to be true – a great joy to those whose relations had been spared, but anguish of regret to those who had lost their dear ones during the last months of the conflict. And alas how hollow were the cherished hopes that the struggle had been 'a war to end war' and to restore peace and happiness to this faulty world!

* * * * * * *

With the cessation of hostilities a new era had begun. To Springhill it meant the return of its master, and the prospect of the family taking up life again in the old home. During the previous years of foreboding, the future had seemed uncertain, and in leaving the dear old place the song 'Farewell to Loch Aber – Loch Aber no more' had often rung in the mind's ear of its mistress. But now all was well, though the master's return was delayed by his having to be in Dublin for some months, occupied in demobilizing work, his wife and little daughter and her governess living for most of the time at Springhill.

It was in the November of 1919 that an exciting episode occurred. In spite of the 'Peace,' those times were turbulent in Ireland, for lawless republican forces were active there, and in the North raids for arms were frequent.

Mina had been warned by the Police of what might easily happen. She kept a revolver at her bedside, and at dead of night had caused the large store of arms to be hidden in some of the house's secret nooks – behind panelling, between double ceilings and in hidden cupboards. A clever maid from Dublin had proved to be an agent of the I.R.A. and had been found at night admitting strange men to spy out the hiding-places. But she and her accomplices had been dismissed, and an abode had been found in Dublin for the winter, the party at Springhill moving south, and the house shut up and visited daily by Andrew Davidson, the steward.

However, soon after the departure, the dreaded visitation happened. Mina had come home from Dublin for two nights having promised to preside at a bazaar at Coagh. She did not occupy her own bedroom in the lower part of the house, but had had a room prepared for her in the top story. A former housemaid had been engaged to wait on her, but as the maid was ill, a young untrained sister had come instead.

The night was cold and a bright fire burned in the bedroom's jackdaw-haunted chimney. After some hours of sleep, Mina was suddenly awakened at four o'clock by the sound of heavy footsteps downstairs and of doors banging. 'The raiders of course!' was her first thought, but she decided to stay where she was and not to beard the intruders, lest they should force her to disclose the hiding-places of the arms. After what seemed a long time, the sounds died away, and she fell asleep again, to find out next morning that the scare had been caused by the inexperienced maid, who had risen in the moonlight, long before her time, and had gone down to light the kitchen range, losing her way and stumping about the house, banging doors as she went!

What a foolish mistake! but in reality it was a case of 'coming events casting shadows.'

Mina attended the bazaar, and on driving home in the dusk, espied about twenty men standing in one of the shrubberies, pointing at and apparently noticing her. But she slept soundly after a busy day and left early next morning for Dublin. On the next night the raid actually took place, and she fancied that it might have been delayed out of consideration for her.

Here are extracts from the newspaper account:

> During Saturday night a raid, obviously for arms was made upon Springhill, Moneymore, the residence of Lt. Colonel William Lenox-Conyngham, but no weapons were found except two old swords which were carried off. The fact was that for some time past there had been reason for expecting that a raid might be attempted, and consequently every precaution had been taken so that the raiders were baulked of the hoped for treasure.
>
> Springhill is about half a mile from Moneymore and has been the family seat of the Lenox-Conynghams for generations. It is a grand old building, situated in a very lonely spot and is surrounded by trees. No other houses are near except the two gate lodges. The occupants of these heard no noises during the night. No one was living in Springhill at the time of the raid, Mrs. Lenox-Conyngham and family having gone some weeks previously to join Colonel Lenox-Conyngham, who is engaged in military duty in Dublin. Mrs. Lenox-Conyngham had returned to the district to preside at the opening of a bazaar in Coagh. She stayed at Springhill on Wednesday and Thursday nights and left again on Friday morning by the early train. The family intended returning to take up residence at Springhill in the Spring.
>
> The raiders appear to have entered a building beside the residence, known as the Laundry, effecting an entrance through the window which they smashed. The search was apparently thorough and taken part in by a good many persons. The inside of the house presented a sorry spectacle every apartment having been completely ransacked. Every box, drawer, press or other receptacle was burst open and the contents lie scattered about the floors. A room from which a quantity of ammunition had been timely removed came in for special attention … but of course without success. … The 'visitors' apparently left by the hall-door, which was left ajar. The police had been keeping an eye on the premises

The Adam fireplace in the gun-room

> and were round the place on Friday night. The discovery was made on Sunday morning by Mr. Andrew Davidson, caretaker at Springhill. He at once informed the police who were soon on the scene. Fresh motor car tracks are plainly visible leading to and from the door, but whether these tracks were made by the motor which conveyed Mrs. Lenox-Conyngham to the train on Friday morning or by a motor conveying the raiders is a matter of doubt.

In the gun-room at Springhill a relic of the raid still remains – the mark of a hob-nailed boot on the panelling. When Mina came from Dublin she found amongst other wreckage the jam-cupboard had been ransacked and a six-pound tin of dry biscuits gobbled up, though a bottle of jam-covering whiskey was untouched. Raiders were forbidden to take drink, and these men were evidently well disciplined. Thus was Springhill raided for arms a second time, the first occasion having been when gouty old George Conyngham's firelocks were carried off in the year 1745.

After some months in Dublin, during which Colonel Lenox-Conyngham received the O.B.E. from the hands of Lord French, and William, the elder boy, was confirmed by Archbishop d'Arcy, the family returned to Springhill in April, after an absence of five years and a half. They felt the same joy as the bygone

William and Ann Conyngham must have known on coming back to the same home in 1690 after the raising of the Siege of Derry. But in the former case it was to wander no more, whereas for the present day family the ensuing years were broken by two long times of absence – a sojourn of nine months in London and a trip to South Africa many months later. The time in London was spent at a spacious flat at Albert Court (close to the Albert Hall) which belonged to a favourite cousin, Stewart Arbuthnot, who had gone to live in South Africa.

Mina, on the occasion of Diana's presentation at Court

At this time the younger William entered Magdalene College, Cambridge, and Desmond was living at his Aunt Dorinda's home – Sea Park, Greenisland, and going daily to Belfast, where he had been given an opening in the Linen business. This caused him to leave Wellington College at the age of sixteen, to his mother's regret, for he showed much promise at school.

The months spent in London by Diana and her parents were pleasant and gay. The young Diana 'came out,' was 'presented,' and enjoyed some balls and parties. What a happy lull it was before the anxious time which was to come after returning home in the July of that year!

The disturbed state of Ireland was intensified after the Treaty of 1921, when self-government was given to both of the sundered halves of the country. Hordes of gun-men came from the south into Ulster to sow discord there, and perilous times were experienced at Springhill as in other parts of the country. Many houses were entered and burned by members of a disloyal Secret Society which worked stealthily and pitilessly. Of these houses, Shane's Castle and Antrim Castle were the most prominent. The Conynghams had been invited to luncheon at Shane's on the very day of the burning, and just before the fire at Antrim Castle they were visited by an American friend, who had been allowed to store all her valuable furniture there, and was staying with Lord and Lady Massereene just before returning to the United States. She considered that her valuables were quite safe. All were destroyed! This lady was the only one to quit the doomed castle by the blazing staircase and had her feet badly burnt. Another guest, Miss Grace d'Arcy, the Primate's daughter, was more fortunate, as she let herself safely down from her window ledge.

At this time many policemen were murdered: three were shot near Ballyronan – four miles from Springhill: and the barbarous reprisals which followed may well have been planned by the same secret forces which had caused the initial outrages, their aim being to widen the breach between the opposing parties and to make Ireland impossible to govern.

During such perilous days Springhill could not be expected to remain in safety. The local police gave repeated warnings, and for many months a guard of ten 'A' special police kept guard around the house at night, the occupants never

Group on the front steps with Mina (seated), Diana (behind her with hair band) and William (third from left).

knowing whether heavy footsteps in the Court were those of raiders or of guards. Silver was buried and many valuables sent out of the dwelling, which was prepared for attack, its master and mistress keeping a Verey pistol near them at night, in readiness to fire an alarm, and for the same purpose a yard bell was suspended from a beam in one of the bedrooms.

This ominous safeguarding was thought to be upsetting to the young Diana, in spite of her courageous spirit, so without telling her the reason, she was sent unsuspectingly on a visit to a cousin – Miss F. Arbuthnot, who lived in London, at 69 Eaton Square. But this turned out to be 'out of the frying pan into the fire'! The day after the girl's arrival, when out walking close to her cousin's abode, she saw a big crowd assembled outside a house in Eaton Place. Sir Henry Wilson had just been done to death on his doorstep by members of the same Secret Society which was active in Ireland.

Those were terrible times: but in the end Springhill escaped molestation, and a year after these alarms, its owner and his wife and daughter sailed for South Africa to pay a three months' visit to the same intimate cousins whose London flat they had occupied two years before – Stewart Arbuthnot and his gifted wife Ada. What a contrast to their Irish experiences was the sojourn at Wynberg – near Capetown, amid lovely peaceful scenery, hot sunshine and gorgeous flowers. They explored the peninsula, made many pleasant and most hospitable acquaintances (amongst these the Molteno family, who remain lasting friends), and several times met General Smuts and were asked by him and his clever wife to Groote Schuur, the unique house which Rhodes had built. General Smuts made a deep impression, for no one could fail to be struck by his outstanding personality – simple, sincere and penetrating. It was interesting to talk with him and to hear him speak of his ideals for South Africa and his wish that none should be too rich and none too poor.

Many other invitations were accepted, bathing at Muizenberg was enjoyed and also a succession of balls and parties, two of these being on English battleships then anchored at Capetown; the 'Hood' and the 'Repulse,' which are now, alas, lying at the bottom of the sea, having been sunk by enemy action in the disastrous war which broke out in 1939.

At Capetown, amid such charming surroundings, three months rolled swiftly by, and then the Conynghams started for home, being 'seen off' on board the 'Suevic' by many kind friends, who brought fruit and bouquets, after the warm-hearted South African custom. Indeed on one such well attended occasion, a Dutchman, whose English was defective, was heard to exclaim 'This is a very popular departure!'

William Lowry Lenox-Conyngham, 1926

The reunion with William and Desmond was a happy one, and on reaching home the travellers realized that no matter how keenly they had admired the charms of Groote Constantia, Vergelegen and Morgenstir, the attraction of Springhill was to them far greater, and they verified the truth of the song 'there's no place like home.'

Springhill is indeed delectable in early spring, its woods paved with the gold and silver of celandines and wood anemones, purple beeches beginning to blush with foliage, and daffodils and primroses spangling the grass. Guests came and went, there were fetes and garden-parties, dancing, and sometimes gatherings of the 'Mothers' Union.' Visits to England were enjoyed and thus the happy days sped along.

But there were two saddening episodes in the decade, 1920–30. The first was in 1926, when William – the elder son – went to Kenya under Sir Hubert Gough's auspices, to learn farming, and soon had such a succession of malaria attacks that the doctors ordered him home. He would have developed black-water fever had it not been for the kind care of a Major and Mrs. Slater, who found him and nursed him through the worst attack.

After his return it was arranged that he should live at home and help his father to manage the estate.

The second grief in this decade was the death of Mina's step-sister Fanny Bushe, who was often at Springhill. Her useful life had been one of unselfish work for good causes, and the words on her tombstone: 'Always abounding in the work of the Lord' are a fitting memorial. As years pass on, inevitable losses and changes are bound to occur, and deep regret was felt at Springhill when Mina's old home – Rockdale – passed from the Lowry family. It was only eleven miles away and often visited while her uncle owned it. But he grew tired of country life and preferred to live at Bournemouth, so he sold the old family home.[158]

Other changes had also come. Tullylagan had been abandoned by Mina's sister, Dorinda, and her family for Sea Park, the Greer home near Carrickfergus: dear friends, Mrs. Gledstanes of Fardross, and Mrs. Auchinleck of Crevenagh, had passed away, and a valued neighbour, Lady Muriel Close of Drum Manor,

The drawing room

died in 1928. Lissan was seldom visited after the deaths of James Staples and his wife: and kind old friends, the Richeys of Tullyhogue Rectory, had gone. So most of the chief links with Tyrone, were no more, though there were good friends still remaining at Termon, Drumcairne, Parkanaur and a few other places. County Derry offered more society and companionship than Tyrone, for Milly Clark – the delightful sister and aunt – lived with her family at Largantogher: the Alexander cousins – Arthur and Emilia – were at Portglenone, and there was warm friendship with the McCauslands of Drenagh, whose son, Conolly, was a close associate of the elder son of Springhill. In 1930 came the saddest loss of all, when the sudden death took place of Dorinda Greer, Mina's beloved and closely united sister. Her loss left a grievous blank. She had been frequently at Springhill, which she loved, was like a second mother to the young people there, and her inspiring influence and lively wit had been felt wherever she went.

A descriptive memorial notice of Dorinda, written by a neighbour, was published shortly after her death and must be quoted here:

Dorinda Greer

> Upon the parish of Desertcreat and all the surrounding neighbourhood the shadow of a great grief has fallen, in the unexpected death of Mrs. MacGregor Greer, who passed away after a very brief illness, on Feb. 16th.
>
> To say that Mrs. Greer was beloved by all is to fall far short of the mark; she

was adored and revered. Most of her life had been spent in Co. Tyrone, first at Rockdale, the home of her father Colonel J.C. Lowry, and afterwards at Tullylagan, the former home of her mother. Of late she lived in Co. Antrim, but her heart was always at Tullylagan, and to that loved spot she had hoped to return. In the churchyard there rests all that was mortal of her, beside the grave of her parents.

Her gifts were many. Endowed with personal beauty of a rare and exquisite type, yet it was the beauty of soul which shone forth, and impressed the beholder, making him feel himself on holy ground. Eminently qualified as she was to move in society where beauty, intelligence and social charm are in demand, she rather chose her friends among those to whom life had given little. The lonely, the handicapped in any way, to these she stretched out the hands of friendship, on these she lavished herself and all she had. On the rare occasions on which she spoke in public ... her fire and earnestness were an inspiration to her hearers. Of all charitable and church work she was an active supporter ... and in her the poor had an unfailing friend. ...

One of God's saints, her pure exalted spirit has passed beyond the veil into the Better Land, which seemed always so near to her, to await the words: 'Come ye blessed children of my Father, inherit the Kingdom prepared for you.

Desmond and the tree girl with a friend in fancy dress

The year before this sad event, Desmond Lenox-Conyngham received an opening in the Ceylon Tea Plantations from his Uncle Edward. He was making a success there, but met again and married a girl whom he had previously known in London society. Cecilia Cockburn-Hood became his wife, but disliked living in the East and was the cause of his returning to London, soon after his parents had come back from a tour in Malta and Italy.

Shadow and sunshine succeed each other in this life, which has been called 'striped,' and in 1932 a joyful occurrence took place at Springhill, Diana – the only daughter of the house – became engaged to Colonel Marcus Clements, of Ashfield, Co. Cavan, whom she had known for some years. He was a distant cousin, great-grandson of The Hon. Elizabeth Stewart of Killymoon, one of the three Molesworth sisters who had leapt from their mother's burning house in the London tragedy of 1764, which has already been described in these pages. Diana descends from the elder of these sisters, The Honble. Henrietta Staples, from whom she has inherited many traits of character, so this marriage was to unite two branches of the family.

The newspaper announcement of the engagement runs thus:

> Lieut. Colonel M.L.S. Clements, late of the King's Royal Rifle Corps, whose engagement to Miss Diana Lenox-Conyngham has just been announced, is grand-nephew to Colonel William Stewart of Killymoon. The latter in his will bequeathed the extensive estates – including Cookstown – to his nephew Colonel Henry Theophilus Clements (father of the bridegroom designate). The Clements family have long been identified with the Cootehill district, where they were extensive landowners. The founder of the family came over with Cromwell's army, in 1646, and settled at Rathkenny, Co. Cavan, but later the manor of Ashfield – the residence of Colonel Clements – was leased.
>
> Several members of the family sat in the Irish Parliament, holding office as Vice Treasurers, while Colonel Clements' grandfather sat at Westminster as member for Cavan and Leitrim. In the fifth generation from the founder, the eldest son was created in 1783 Earl of Leitrim.
>
> The Conyngham family is even longer settled in Ireland. The founder, William Conyngham, who came from Ayrshire and got the townland of Ballindrum from the Salter's Company, and built the residence occupied by them, known as Springhill – just outside Moneymore. The estate from there to Ballinderry is Church lands (like so much of the Killymoon estate) but the six townlands on the Tyrone side round Coagh are freehold, purchased in 1663 from the Countess of Suffolk, who inherited the Castlestewart estate. The prefix 'Lenox' dates from 1745, when Clotworthy Lenox, grandson of one of the defenders of Derry at the siege, married Anne Conyngham, to whom the estates were left by her father, and took the name of Lenox-Conyngham.

Diana's wedding took place in April, daffodils lining the bridal path in the church nave and making golden patches on the lawn at Springhill. A cheery company of relations and friends were present, and on the previous day a large reception was held of old acquaintances, gentle and simple, from a wide area,

Diana's wedding in 1928 to Lt. Col. Marcus L.S. Clements. From left: Violet Clements, S.U. (Jim) Lucas Clements, Helen Arbuthnot, the groom and bride, Laura Lenox-Conyngham (later Mrs. Robert Alexander) and Kitty Clements.
Front row: Ruth Alexander, Robin Chichester-Clark, Daphne Alexander and Elizabeth Lucas Clements.

The pram of Mina's granddaughter Catharine Clements, summer 1937, at the rear of Springhill.

but chiefly from Moneymore and Rockdale districts.

But alas, a shadow was beginning to loom on the horizon – the suddenly failing health of the bride's father. A slight stroke had befallen him, and during the following six years he gradually lost ground – bearing his infirmity with patient fortitude, until in April, 1938, he passed away to the inexpressible grief of his family.

William Arbuthnot Lenox-Conyngham

XIII

Present Day

WILLIAM LOWRY LENOX-CONYNGHAM 1903–1957

THE SEVENTH William Conyngham of Springhill, and its tenth owner, inherited the property in 1938, on the death of his father, whom he had been helping for some years to run the place. Country life and farming appealed to this young man. After leaving Cambridge he had practised farm work for a while in Kenya, where he contracted malaria. But his heart was at Springhill, and as he was also interested in county affairs, the lines seemed to have fallen to him in pleasant places. How little the future can be foreseen! In the very next year of his succession another war against Germany broke out, and that the most devastating war in history.

William Lowry Lenox-Conyngham

William, of course, joined the Army at once and left Ireland with an Anti-Aircraft Regiment for an absence of some years. He served in East England, but to his great chagrin was not sent abroad because of gastric trouble, which finally caused him to be invalided from the Army. Just before leaving Ireland, in 1940, he had been appointed H.M. Lieutenant of County Derry, in succession to Sir Charles Stronge, and, on his return and recovery, commanded the Home Guard in the County.

William Lowry Lenox-Conyngham (front left) as HML for Co. Londonderry attending the proclamation of George VI at Coleraine Courthouse

As for his younger brother, Desmond, he had already impulsively gone out to help Finland in her war against Russia, which began in 1939, hoping to gain valuable military experience. But soon after he reached Finland, Germany annexed most of Scandinavia: and as Russia naturally forbade the Volunteers to return through her territory, Desmond and his comrades were interned near Helsinki, thus caught in a trap. Desmond was not daunted, and five times he tried to escape, each time being captured and imprisoned. His adventures were thrilling. Here is an extract from a letter in which he describes one of his attempted escapes:

> … My only method was to go to Petsamo by lorry and try to get past the four military controls on the road. I went to Tornio, where I met the drivers of three Swedish lorries who were going to Petsamo. Although none of them could speak English, I managed to make them understand, and they agreed to take me. We started off at 4 p.m. and got through Rovaniemi all right. We stopped for a meal about 40 miles N. of Rovaniemi (we had taken food and drink with us). The Swedes all got very drunk and soon after restarting we had a smash, and the lorry I was in broke its back axle. It took 8 hours to repair it, and as the Swedes were drunk the whole way, we were lucky to get to Petsamo after 46 hours on the road. The soldiers who stopped us at the controls took me for a Swede and we got through all right. The Arctic Highway is very narrow and in bad repair – runs through a very wild country and you see plenty of reindeer. The Lapland Border is about half way. There is a constant stream of lorries, both Swedish and Finnish, and the two nationalities hate each other. As neither will give way, there are constant accidents and the road is strewn with wrecked lorries. I've never had such an exciting drive. It would have been bad enough if the driver had been sober. The only good thing was that it did not get dark. The sun never sets there in Summer. Petsamo before the war was a small fishing village on the West side of a narrow fiord. As it is now the only port for Sweden and Finland, they are frantically building roads, wharves, etc. There are about 6,000 workmen there, all the bad hats in Finland, Communists, etc. who are

> sent up there by the police. It is quite the most desolate place I've ever seen – bitterly cold and raining all the time. I had a very rough time there, as I had to lie low because of the plain clothes police. I met another Englishman there and we decided to stow away on a boat sailing for U.S.A. The boat was due to sail on Monday, and on Sunday night we concealed ourselves in the rope locker, which was reached by a small trap-door in the deck. The only food we could get was a small piece of black bread, and we each had a bottle of water. There was about three feet clearance between the top of the ropes on which we were lying and the deck. Much to our annoyance, the boat did not start on Monday, as we expected, nor on Tuesday, nor on Wednesday. On Thursday morning, when we were both in rather a bad way, a sailor came to fetch a rope and found us. We were sent ashore, but fortunately did not fall into the hands of the Police. I was told that the boat was definitely sailing in 3 hours time, and I managed to get on to it again, but was caught after an hour. I was rather shaky after 3½ days without food and fell into the sea when going down the rope ladder. The Harbour-master – a Swede – took pity on me and allowed me to sleep on the floor of the Coastguards' Hut and provided me with two meals per day. As I had no money, he got me a job working as a navvy on excavation work. It was very hard work and my companions were fearful ruffians, but quite friendly. The worst part was the cold at night, as I had no blankets, and the food – maccaroni with lumps of salt pork in it at mid day, and porridge without milk at 6 p.m. ... I went on to several boats, and although the sailors were friendly they dared not take me, as the Germans search the boats at Kirkenes and threaten to sink any ship carrying Englishmen. After 18 days at Petsamo, I was arrested and sent South under escort. I am quite an expert on gaols, having been in three in Finland and one in Sweden.

Desmond

Desmond finally tried to escape from Sweden in one of the Norwegian ships, which made a dash from Gottenberg for England in the early spring of 1942. It was attacked by a German armed trawler and sunk, the Captain being killed at Desmond's side. Soon afterwards he found himself in a German prison-camp near Bremen, where he suffered hardship and privation for over three years before freedom came.

While these two sons of Springhill were absent from their home, the house was requisitioned by Government as an Officers' Headquarters and the grounds and the many outbuildings filled with soldiers. Ugly Nissen huts sprang up in the Tower Hill and elsewhere, and the laundry became 'Serjeants' Mess' and the Harness Room 'Orderly Room.' Bugle sounds filled the air, and drilling took place in the Court. The cloud of a stupendous war had over-shadowed even this remote dwelling.

Thinking to check damage to the place, the writer decided to reserve a corner of the house as a pied-à-terre for herself, and she lived in the east wing for many months, trying to help the soldiers by arranging a lending library, clothes-mending parties, etc. The knitting depot met at the Manor House and was supervised by her active sisters-in-law.

The military occupation added a new and incongruous page to the history of Springhill. The first regiment to arrive was the Berkshire Yeomanry, an exemplary corps – commanded by Colonel H. Crosland. Later experience shewed how fortunate was Springhill in being sent this regiment, which comprised men of so high a type as its Colonel, the 2nd in Command, Sir James King, Captain David Ormsby-Gore, Captain Birchall and others. The Berkshires were followed by the 119th Regiment Royal Artillery, and then came the Americans.

Diana with Tuppence in the Slaughterhouse Yard

Who would ever have imagined that those old-fashioned rooms would ever resound with American voices! The U.S.A. soldiers – mostly from Cleveland, Ohio – were everywhere in evidence, playing Baseball in the Court, carving their names on the trees and carrying off many 'souvenirs' – one of them being the large old hall-door key. Sentries kept guard day and night on the steps. They were hospitable too, and the châtelaine was often invited to dine at mess (in her own dining-room) by about twenty-two U.S.A. officers, and repasted on green corn, chicken, peanut butter, poached egg, pickles and jam all on the same plate, followed by the excellent and inevitable ice-cream.

On several occasions religious services were held in the Court, the troops facing the house, a chaplain standing on the hall-door steps, where a piano was placed to accompany such hymns as 'Through all the changing scenes of life.' An occasional Roman Catholic service also took place, a priest in gorgeous vestments officiating, the men kneeling in rows on the gravel.

Last of all the occupying troops came the Negro Americans, but these only used the Tower Hill Camp, and their stalwart frames and black faces were strange to behold and hard to detect in the dusk on the roads and paths.

The house was derequisitioned in December, 1944, and begins to resume its former appearance. At the time of writing, German prisoners are to be seen in the Tower Hill, employed by Government in tidying the Camp and cutting up the big trees, which the soldiers had barked and killed. They seem cheerful, and sing in chorus as they march to and from their work.

Soon there will be little trace left of Springhill's military occupation, though life may not again run in the old accustomed channels. The old order changes, as along the river of life we glide, and the era of Communistic destruction and of the atomic bomb is looming.

What is coming to Springhill who can say? Time's ever-rolling stream has borne so many of her sons away. And yet the impress of joys and sorrows, hopes and anxieties endures, and above all deep love of home seems to linger still around the old place, bringing us back to the days of long ago.

So now farewell to this ancient house. What is the secret of its spell? It is difficult to say; but we like to remember the evening sunlight slanting through tall trees where jackdaws chatter, and making flickering patterns on walls hung with portraits, from which many a former occupant looks mysteriously down. A strange peace pervades these quiet rooms and one feels that the leading characteristic of Springhill is that of an old home, dearly loved, and stored with relics and memories of bygone days.

Mina, in her nineties, with Diana and her great grandson Charles Clements on the steps at Springhill

Notes

1 The whole County was then called the County of Coleraine, but the name was changed to 'Londonderry' after the London Companies obtained the lands.

2 Sir Toby Caulfeild was head of a garrison of 150 men at Charlemont Fort. This fort was built by Charles Blount, Lord Mountjoy in 1602 and named *Charlemont* after himself. The Caulfeilds afterwards adopted this name as their title.

3 'Mere' at that time, meant pure, i.e., those both whose parents were Irish. It had not its present disparaging meaning.

4 Sir Hugh Clotworthy settled in Co. Antrim 1603. Married Mary, daughter of Roger Langford of Muckamore. Their daughter, Mary, sister of 1st Viscount Masserene, married Henry Upton, who was born 1591 and settled at Castle Upton. She was the mother of Col. Arthur Upton, M.P.

5 This Colonel William Conyngham had been one of Cromwell's Commissioners for Co. Armagh and had held land in Co. Armagh (Drumcrow) and house property in the town of Armagh. In 1661 he owned a house there and 20 acres of land and several tenements, paving £6 0s. 0*d*. rent for the former and £4 0s. 0*d*. for the latter house. One was in Furtagh Street (now Scotch Street) and the other in Market Street. In 1676, his widow lived in a house on the North side of the town with a garden and 'little parke' called 'Garreturne' and 20 acres on the S. side with one tenement and garden plott, and Ballarath and Umgola in the Liberties.

6 If this account of Mr. Conyngham (often spelt Cunningham in past days) refers to the Springhill family, it is difficult to identify the person mentioned: for 'William Conyngham the elder' died in 1666 and his son in 1721. Possibly the words 'only son' are incorrect, and the tale refers to one of the latter's brothers.

7 See Hill's *Plantation of Ulster*.

8 In the reign of Charles II a document, still at Springhill, was drawn up on 24th October, 1672, by James, Earl of Suffolk, Henry Howard and Mary, his wife, daughter and heir of Lord Castlestewart, and William Cunningham (son and heir of William Cunningham of Mullinahoe, Co. Tyrone, deceased), Lease for ever of townland of Mullaghnahoe, Co. Tyrone. Consideration, £20. Rent, 14s. 4*d*. p.a. Confirmation of Lease held by William Cunningham, deceased, title deeds having been lost or destroyed in recent rebellion (as were those of Ballydrum) William Coningham is also mentioned as 'of Coagh, Co. Tyrone' and 'of Ardmagh.'

9 Ballydrum is the townland in which Springhill is situated.

10 *Fighters of Derry* by The Right Hon. William Young.

11 These lines are from a contemporary poem, 'Londonderriados.'

12 Ancestor of the Harveys of Malin Hall, Inishowen.

13 This Gun is shown, standing upright, in the photograph of the Gun Room.

14 Son of William Conyngham's sister Anne (?) who had married David Butle, son of Randal Butle of Glenarm and probably grandson of The Revd. David Butle, minister of Ballymena, who came from Scotland, 1627.

15 These names continue at Springhill.

16 'Turf' or peat.

17 'Dr.' is a contraction for 'Dear,' and 'Beckse' a diminutive of Rebecca.

18 The Primate of that day was generally the Chief Lord Justice and possessed great temporal power.

19 Now called 'Drenagh.'

20 Abraham Hamilton is mentioned as 'of Bellaghy.'

21 In 1745, the year of his marriage, Clotworthy Lenox Esqre's Commission shews that he was appointed Captain of a Company in the room of his father, John Lenox Esqre., deceased, in the Regiment of Foot commanded by our very good Lord Marcus Viscount Tyrone in the Militia of the County of Londonderry. (Signed) Chesterfield. W. Bristow.

22 A very full calendar of the papers appeared in the *Co. Louth Archaeological Journal*, vol. VII. pp. 124–153.

23 Ireland's several Provinces are in these papers always termed 'Nations.'

24 Probably transportation, for Dr. Michael MacDonough died in Lisbon in 1746.

25 Her brother, Clotworthy Upton.

26 Stone who became Primate in 1747 was an ardent politician. It was not till after his death that calumnies were uttered against him and those were probably unfounded. Archbishop d'Arcy writes thus in his *Adventures of a Bishop*: 'The writer has seen private letters of Stone's which reveal a very warm heart and generous kindness in saving a young man from the results of his indiscretions, which make all such (slanderous) statements impossible of belief. It is also to be recorded that Stone made most

gallant efforts to lighten the very unfair and oppressive disabilities which then were imposed on Roman Catholics.'

27 Cousin.

28 His home was at Summerhill in Co. Meath and he built Langford Lodge in Co. Antrim, on the shore of Lough Neagh.

29 Robert Lenox—Governor of Bencoolin in Sumatra, a brother of John Lenox and Uncle of Clotworthy Lenox.

30 Capt. John Conyngham's Commission signed by King George the Second appoints him to be Captain in the Fourth Regiment of Foot or Royal Fusiliers commanded by Lord Robert Bertie. It ends 'given at our Court at Kensington the Fifteenth day of October, 1759. By His Majesty's Command, Holderness.'

31 Governor of Bencoolin.

32 William Stewart, M.P., of Killymoon, b. 1710, died 1797.

33 There were two successive Matthew Georges—father and son—who in turn acted as agents or land stewards to the Conynghams for a long period of years.

34 Rector of Desertcreat. m. Ann Sinclair of Holyhill, Co. Tyrone, b. 1707, d. 1787. Built Pomeroy and Rockdale.

35 These hang in the dining-room at Springhill.

36 Rector of Desertlyn (Moneymore).

37 Thomas Staples was married to Grace Houston on May 15th, 1735, by Mr. Close, T.C.D., M.A., Rector of Donaghenry Parish 1721 to 1742.

38 The black marble chimney-piece in the present drawing-room.

39 See page 39

40 Henry Richardson was a brother of Hester, who in 1747 married the Revd. James Lowry, who built Pomeroy, Rockdale and Somerset. She was ancestress of Mrs W.A. Lenox-Conyngham. The father of Henry and Hester was John Richardson of Richhill Castle, and their sister was Mary, Viscountess Gosford. In the old family Bible of the Richardsons, dated 1680, the following entries appear: 'My son Henry was born Tuesday ye 2nd of June, 1719...'
'My daughter Hester was born in Richhill House on Monday morning half an hour past two ye 11th of Oct. 1715, She was christened ye last day of ye month. Her godfathers were Oliver St. John Esqre. and Colonel George McCartney, her godmothers were Mrs Wheeley and Miss Thompson.' Hester was buried in the Lowry vault in Desertcreat churchyard and on the tablet to her memory she was thus alluded to: 'Hester, best of wives and loveliest of women, farewell.'

41 Afterwards The Right Hon. John Staples of Lissan, M.P. for Limavady, son of the Rev. Thomas Staples, Rector of Derryloran (Cookstown) and Grace Houston.

42 The present Lord Herbert has written the life of this peer and of his wife and son: *Henry, Elizabeth and George*, published in the nineteen thirties.

43 Miss Catherine Hunter, daughter of Thomas Orby Hunter, Esq., at this time, 1762, one of the Lords of the Admiralty. Miss Hunter afterwards married Capt. Alured Clarke who died September, 1832, aged 87. (Field Marshal Sir Alured Clarke, G.C.B.) Horace Walpole described Miss Hunter as 'a handsome girl with a fine person, but silly and in no degree as lovely as His (Ld. Pembroke's) own wife who has the face of a Madonna.' Lady Pembroke had been Lady Elizabeth Spence, younger sister of George, Duke of Marlborough. This great beauty did not die till April 30th, 1831, aged 93. *Letters* (H. Walpole) 'Lord Pembroke and his nymph (Miss Hunter) were brought back by a privateer, who had obligations to her father, but the father desired no such recovery, and they are again gone in quest of adventure. The Earl was so kind as to ask his wife to accompany them, and she, who is *all* gentleness and tenderness, was with difficulty withheld as acting as mad a part from goodness, as he had done from guilt and folly.'

44 In *Lloyd's Evening Post* April 23–25, 1770 among the advertisements is a small paragraph: This day is published price 2*s*. Julia to Polio; or Miss Hxx to Lord Pxx upon his leaving her Abroad. This shews that interest in the scandal continued for many years.

45 James Fortescue was M.P. for Dundalk, son of Thomas Fortescue M.P. of Clermont Park and Elizabeth Hamilton of Tollymore Park, Co. Down. James was born in 1725 and married Mary Henrietta, daughter of Thomas Orby Hunter Esq., of Crowland, Lancs., the aunt of Kitty Hunter. He died in 1782 and his eldest brother, W. Henry, became the 1st Earl Clermont.

46 It is surmised that William brought with him from Holland the two portraits by Cornelius Jansson which are at Springhill. These were found rolled up in the attics.

47 Elizabeth, daughter of Chichester Fortescue of Dromiskin, Co. Louth, who married in 1763, the Marquis of Lothian.

48 The Staples family lived at Lissan, about four miles from Springhill, and were twice connected in marriage with the Conynghams. The baronetcy dates from 1628. In the eighteenth century the family held a leading position in Co. Tyrone, wealthy, brilliant and much respected. The Right Hon. John Staples was the owner of Lissan during the latter half of

the century and was a comrade of William Conyngham in the Wars in Germany. His portrait, by Batoni, is in the dining-room at Castletown the Conolly house in Co. Kildare, and a duplicate is at Springhill.

49 'William Conyngham Esqe.' had been appointed a Deputy Governor of the County of Londonderry in May, 1765—two months after his father's death. His Commission as Deputy Governor is signed by Jn. Ponsonby and W. Roseingrave.

50 The following is a letter from the well-known Squire Conolly, written from Castletown, October 1st, 1767:

'Dr. Sir,

Pursuant to your commands, I waited on the Speaker and he has promised to have you immediately appointed Colonel of the Regiment of Militia that your father formerly commanded, and Mr. Dawson lately. I am sorry I did not succeed in my 1st application in your favour, but I hope that now you are sure of it as *you* really have the best right to it. I am Dr. Sir, your most humble servt.

Thos. Conolly,'

Some letters exist written to William Conyngham from his many warm friends at this epoch of his life. One of these is from Arthur Acheson, who became 2nd Viscount Gosford, son of Archibald, Ld. Gosford and Mary Richardson of Richhill, Co. Armagh (sister of Mrs. Lowry). Another letter, from Bath, is from Samuel Campbell who mentions The Governor, and Sister Donnellan and 'Cousin Rowley.' Query, was this Samuel Campbell descended from the cousin mentioned in Good Will Conyngham's Will of 1720 'George, son of my cousin Col. Josias Campbell of Dublin'?

51 She had two brothers Dr. Arthur Saunders and John Saunders Esq.

52 In his will he leaves legacies to his doctor and apothecary at Bath, to his housekeeper, Eliza Lodge, to Matthew George, the Springhill agent, and his share (a 3rd of the townlands of Ballydawley and Crosspatrick) to Clotworthy Rowley, part of his property to his brother David, and all his goods, pictures, plate, linen, china and implements and household furniture, money and securities to his brother and executor William Conyngham. The Will is witnessed by Thos. Knox, W. Black and N. Gordon.

53 The marriage took place on August 31st, 1775.

54 The Revd. James Hamilton was Rector of Maghera, Co. Derry. He was possibly J. Hamilton's brother and grandson of James Hamilton of Ballynagarvey. Mrs. Jean Hamilton had a jointure of £300 a year from the Castlefin property, which had belonged, to her first husband. Her four daughters inherited this property.

55 George's weak-minded brother, Clotworthy.

56 Probably wife of Francis Price, of Hollymount, Co. Down. Ancestor of the Blackwood-Prices of Saintfield, who married Charity Forde, of Seaforde, Co. Down, and died 1794.

57 'Quadrills'—an old game played by four with forty cards. It resembles 'ombre.'

58 It must be remembered that he was agent for the Hamiltons' property at Castlefin.

59 A postscript adds, 'I heard Lord Erne was married last Saturday to Miss Hervey at Mr. Jones' in the Co. of Leitrim and are to visit Derry this week.'

60 Still at Springhill.

61 The Right Hon. John Staples, P.C., was for years M.P. for Newtown Limavady. He has been previously mentioned. He married 1st in 1764 Harriet Conolly of Castletown Co. Kildare and secondly the Hon Henrietta Molesworth.

62 The little medicine chest which he carried with him throughout the campaign is preserved at Springhill.

63 William Conyngham in a letter from Springhill to his nephew George in September, 1774, writes:

'Dear George, as I expect Lord Templetown here between the 15th and 20th of this month, I should be glad if you could come here for a day, as I should like to make you known to him. You make nothing of riding here from Derry in a day. I hope you are doing something to the purpose at Castlefin and will have some money ready for us. I suppose the Mayor made a noble Fuss with Mr. Conolly and Ly: Louisa.'

64 Lord Castlestewart carried out this good intention, in 1781, when he married Sarah, daughter of Judge Lill. His 2nd son married, in 1814, Sophia Lenox-Conyngham.

65 The Lord Clanbrassil here mentioned was a bridegroom himself at this time. In the previous year he had a written to his friend Conyngham to announce the completion of his courtship with Miss Grace Foley.

66 This Lord Clanbrassil, James Hamilton, was the second and last Earl of the second creation. He died without issue in 1798; his sister had married Robert, 1st Earl of Roden. The first creation also, to a James Hamilton, son of Viscount Clandeboye in 1647, became extinct by the death of his grandson in infancy.

67 Wife of the Rector.

68 In an old letter which survives at Ashfield Lodge, Mrs, Stewart wrote from England to her husband hoping that 'Nash would not exceed his estimate for the house of a hundred thousand.'

69 Killymoon was left to Marcus Clements' father

who was son of Louisa Stewart and Henry John Clements, M.P. for Co. Leitrim and the only nephew of Colonel William Stewart. The last of the family at Killymoon. Mr. Clements sold the demesne.

70 The very chair and table used by Dean Swift were still in the summer-house till the year 1803, when Mrs. Robert Knox (née Lindesay) brought them to her house in Co. Kilkenny after the sale of Loughry. Her daughter presented them to the Deanery of St. Patrick's in Dublin.

71 'The Hon. Mr. Hewitt was at this time Rector of Derryloran (Cookstown), He succeeded to the Lifford peerage in 1786 and was father of the Hon. John Pratt Hewitt, who for years was Rector of Desertlyn (Moneymore).

72 Mrs. Stafford was George's sister, Rebecca. The Staffords had a daughter who became Mrs Mauleverer—and was mother to the old Miss Mauleverer who in old age lived in Armagh and collected teapots.

73 William Conyngham was member for the borough of Dundalk in Grattan's Parliament. A letter from R. Lindesay to him (undated) of the time deals with affairs in Dundalk and to one. Reed, whose conduct had been 'villanous.' Lindesay offered legal help free of charge A postscript states 'I hope the Insolvent Bill passed.' When in Dublin William Conyngham's address was 22 College Green. 'I get my letters there,' he writes, 'some hours sooner than elsewhere.'

74 A pastel portrait, by Hugh Hamilton, of Lord Buckinghamshire hangs at Springhill, shewing a clever cynical face. He was connected with the Conynghams through the Staples family, having married Caroline Conolly of Castletown, sister of the first wife of The Right Hon. John Staples, P.C., M.P., whose daughter. Charlotte, married William Lenox-Conyngham in 1819.

75 He commanded the Coagh Volunteers in the year 1779.

76 David Conyngham's house at Belfast.

77 He was 57 years of age.

78 Dr. Halyday was a well known Belfast doctor—a great friend of the Volunteer Lord Charlemont who used to stay with him during his visits to Belfast on Volunteer business.

79 Her husband having refused a peerage she became Lady Langford in her own right. She was a niece of the Anne Upton who married 'Good Will' Conyngham in 1680.

80 This letter was found at Ashfield Lodge, Cootehill, among old papers in a cabinet which had been brought there when Killymoon was sold, This cabinet also contained the valuable Molesworth MSS.

81 Still at Springhill.

82 Still at Springhill.

83 This meeting resolved that only the King, Lords and Commons of Ireland had legal power to bind Ireland—and declared for the free right of private judgement in matters of Religion, and approved the relaxation of penal laws against the Roman Catholics.

84 Hervey, Lord Bristol.

85 Of Killymoon, Co. Tyrone.

86 The above mentioned particulars were found in old papers now at Ashfield Lodge, Co. Cavan, the home of Col. Stewart's great-grandson.

87 There are also instances of R.Cs. being admitted to Volunteer Companies in Co. Armagh and County Down.

88 Each of the Hamilton sisters possessed a diamond cluster ring, and three of these rings are in the keeping of descendants—Jane's remains at Springhill and for several generations has been given to the wife of the eldest son and heir. It contains a large diamond surrounded by smaller stones and is so small that it is worn on the little finger of an owner less diminutive than little 'Jenny.'

89 One of the Colthursts of Blarney Castle, Co. Cork.

90 This episode is mentioned in Stephen Gwynn's *Life of Grattan* thus: 'On November 16th a mob of the 'working manufacturers' crowded the approaches to Parliament claiming for a 6 Months Money Bill and then rushed to the Attorney General's private dwelling, which they entered by force. Except some window breaking no harm was done. All parties in Parliament condemned the violence.'

91 Rector of Cavan.

92 John Boscawen Savage, afterwards K.C.B. He succeeded his cousin. Henry Savage at Rock Savage (Ballygalget).

93 The child of William Lenox and Jane (Savage) was William John Lenox. who went to sea as a youth, as a volunteer in the same ship as his Uncle, John Boscawen Savage. He was appointed to the India Office in 1805, was made Assistant Clerk to the Public Department, 1822, was placed in charge of the Department 1828 and died about 1830. It was said of him by his distinguished Uncle, Sir John, during a naval engagement: 'Billy is below, nursing the cat.'

94 Lord Buckinghamshire's second wife was Caroline Conolly, sister of the Right Hon. Thomas Conolly.

95 Robert Stewart soon afterwards became engaged to Lady Emily Hobart.

96 Pastel portraits, by Hugh Hamilton, of Thos. Conolly and his wife, Lady Louisa, are at Springhill.

97 In Co. Fermanagh, now called Necarne.

98 Her sister, Mrs. Colthurst.
99 Ancestor of the Earl of Ranfurly.
100 W. Orr was afterwards executed.
101 General Lake was instrumental in inflicting cruel reprisals on the rebels of 1798.
102 First cousin to Gervase Parker Bushe (the brother-in-law of Henry Grattan) who was great-grandfather of the present Brig. General Francis Bushe and of Sir Grattan Bushe, Governor of Barbadoes.
103 Lord Cornwallis became Lord Lieutenant of Ireland in 1798.
104 William Pitt.
105 Son of the Right Hon. John Staples by his first wife.
106 Grace Staples, daughter of the Right Hon. John Staples, married Marquis of Ormonde.
107 John Staples' daughter, Charlotte afterwards married George Conyngham's elder son.
108 Colonel Portlock's life has been written. He published *A Geological Report on Londonderry, Tyrone and parts of Fermanagh.*
109 Possibly of Ards in Co. Donegal.
110 While the new house at Killymoon was being built, at a cost of £100,000, on the old site, Colonel and Mrs. Stewart lived in the white-washed house with bay windows now incorporated in the street of Gortalowry, Cookstown.
111 George's elder son 'Wims.'
112 The Lenox Crest.
113 The Conyngham Crest.
114 This cedar, behind the house, fell in 1859 and layered itself.
115 A certificate exists:— Willm. L. Conyngham Esqre. from the Honble. Society of Lincoln's Inn. that William Lenox-Conyngham of the University of Glasgow Esq. eldest son of George Lenox-Conyngham of Springhill in the Co. of Londonderry, Kingdom of Ireland, was admitted into the Hon. Society of this Inn on 24th day of Jan. 1814. Hath kept eight terms Commons in the Dining Hall of this Society ... & paid all Duties due ... and that his deportment therein hath been proper. ...
signed by Chas. Thomson, Treasurer.
witness, D. Logan, sub-Treasurer.
116 The eldest girl Henrietta, as already mentioned, married The Right Hon. John Staples, M.P., of Lissan, Co. Tyrone, as his second wife. The second, Elizabeth, married Colonel James Stewart, M.P., of Killymoon, Co. Tyrone, and the youngest, Louisa, married, firstly Lord Ponsonby, and secondly Lord Fitzwilliam. One of her sons. Sir William Ponsonby, fell in 1815 at Waterloo and another son, Richard, became Dean of St. Patrick's and Bishop of Derry.
117 Née Ellinor Fitzgerald. The surname of the Lord Blessinton of this period was Stewart. This branch died out and was revived two generations later in favour of the Gardiners. Lady E. Blessington's pastel portrait is at Springhill—and The Earl of Blessington's library remained later at Springhill, having evidently been bequeathed to the adopted daughter.
118 Among these were Lady Sarah Napier (née Lady Sarah Lenox) and Col. Napier, her second husband. Col. Napier's letters to the Right Hon. John Staples have already been given.
119 Harriet Rebecca who married, in 1854, Marcus Gage of Streevehill, Co. Derry.
120 L.O. stands for Lord Ormonde.
121 Two of Colonel and Mrs. Stewart's four children were Mary, who died unmarried—and William who was the last Stewart at Killymoon. A friend of the Prince Regent, he built the wall round the demesne, gambled away his fortune and died a bachelor, leaving Killymoon to his nephew, Henry Clements of Ashfield, the only son of his sister, Louisa.
122 Afterwards Rector of Kildress (Drumshambo), Co. Tyrone.
123 In Sir William Lenox-Conyngham's account book for 1835 are the entries:
Entrance fee to Mr. Parley's College, Dungannon, on sending my dear son William there .. £5 5 0
Aug. 17. The Revd. Mr. Darley for one half-year's schooling of my dear son William .. £37 13 7
William on going to school .. £1 10 0
To the Housekeeper, Dungannon School .. 10 0
124 Mauleverer.
125 We may wonder what became of the wretched 'Edwards' and must hope that none of his descendants will ever turn up to molest the family at Springhill.
126 The home of William's Uncle and Aunt, Sir James and Lady Galbraith.
127 Charlotte's sister, Grace, Marchioness of Ormonde.
128 Christopher Nicholson of Balrath who had married Anne Lenox-Conyngham, William's step-sister.
129 Son of Sophia and Godfrey Stuart of Lisdhu.
130 Henry John and Louisa Clements of Ashfield, Co. Cavan.
131 Major Kennedy.
132 The old Springhill nurse.
133 His brother John, then aged ten years.
134 Catherine, wife of Sir Thomas Staples of Lissan, who was Mrs. Lenox-Conyngham's brother.
135 The Rev. John Staples, a younger brother, and Rector of Lissan parish.
136 Afterwards Lady Clermont, of Ravensdale, Co. Louth.
137 This lady was afterwards the mother of George Stanhope, who became Lord Chesterfield.

138 Charlotte Lenox-Conyngham's step-sister, nee Harriett Staples whose portrait is at Springhill, married Richard, 2nd Earl of Clancarty, May 1796. He was afterwards Ambassador at the Hague.
139 The residence of former Bishops of Meath.
140 Mrs. and Miss Kennedy.
141 Of Ashfield, Co. Cavan, who had married Louisa Stewart of Killymoon—Charlotte Lenox-Conyngham's first cousin.
142 She had been one of the Hewitts of Moneymore Rectory.
143 Mrs. Sinclair of Holy Hill, Strabane.
144 Mrs. Conyngham's age at that time was 55.
145 On the very night of Mrs. Conyngham's death, her son William, who was with his Regiment in the West Indies, had a dream in which he stood by his mother's bedside and saw her lying there surrounded by her mourning family.
146 Afterwards Countess of Castlestewart.
147 Lady Elizabeth Butler, daughter of her Aunt Grace.
148 Blown down in September, 1945.
149 They were not brother and sister, as stated erroneously in Lord Halifax's Ghost Book.
150 Probably her daughter, Lady Riverston, mother of the Lady Betty Cobbe, who later was said to be in possession of the pocket book in which the ghost had written.
151 Sister of Sir Edmund Turton, MP and grand-daughter of Lord Miltown.
152 Son of Mr H.J. Clark who throughout was a prominent supporter of the U.V.F. movement. The above mentioned 'young Clark' was in later years father of two gallant young guardsmen, the younger of whom – Blake – sacrificed his own life to save a brother officer.
153 Afterwards Lord Craigavon
154 Afterwards Sir Charles Stronge
155 These crosses were first erected at Carnoy on the Somme by the officers and men of the 6th Connaught Rangers in the 16th Irish Division over the grave of their Commanding Officer Lt. Col. John Lenox-Conyngham, who, after a life time of service with the Regiment, at the age of fifty-four, on Sept. 3rd 1916, fell leading his battalion to the capture of Guillemont.
156 Sonnet by Maurice Baring in memory of Julian Grenfell who died for his country in the war of 1914–18.
157 At Ravensdale, Co. Louth.
158 The entail had been broken just before his son's death.

Mina with daughter Diana and son William
c. 1906

Index